HORIZONS IN COMPUTER SCIENCE RESEARCH

VOLUME 11

HORIZONS IN COMPUTER SCIENCE

Additional books in this series can be found on Nova's website
under the Series tab.

Additional e-books in this series can be found on Nova's website
under the e-books tab.

HORIZONS IN COMPUTER SCIENCE RESEARCH

VOLUME 11

THOMAS S. CLARY

EDITOR

nova publishers

New York

NOTICE TO THE READER

Library of Congress Cataloging-in-Publication Data

ISBN: 978-1-63482-499-6
ISSN: 2159-2012

Published by Nova Science Publishers, Inc. † New York

CONTENTS

PREFACE

This book presents original results on the leading edge of computer science research. Each article has been carefully selected in an attempt to present substantial research results across a broad spectrum. Topics discussed include weighted fusion of shape descriptor for robust shape classification; metaheuristics for curve and surface reconstruction; stream-based parallel computing methodology and development environment for high performance many core accelerators; h-infinity recursive wiener fixed-interval smoother based on innovation approach in linear discrete-time stochastic systems; and virtual supercomputers as the basis of scientific computing.

Shape classification in computer vision is a vibrant field of study with wide ranging applications involving object classification, motion tracking, image segmentation, and image retrieval. In Chapter 1 we propose an ensemble of approaches harnessing the power of many shape descriptors (inner distance shape context, shape context, height functions, etc.) that are transformed into a matrix from which a set of texture descriptors are extracted and compared using the Jeffrey distance. The experimental results confirm that our new ensemble of texture descriptors clearly improve previous texture-based ensembles for shape classification.

Our ensemble is validated and compared with the state-of-the-art on several benchmark datasets, representing different shape classification tasks (MPEG7 CE-Shape-1, Kimia silhouettes, Tari dataset, a leaf dataset, and an animal shape dataset). The parameters of each method used in our ensemble and the weights of the weighted fusion by sum rule are kept the same across each of these datasets, thereby demonstrating that our proposed ensemble is a general-purpose shape classification system.

Moreover, the texture descriptors based approach is also coupled with the Bag of Contour Fragments method permitting a boost of the performance obtained by the standard approach.

The MATLAB code of our proposed system will be available online at https://www.dei.unipd.it/node/2357.

The accurate reconstruction of curves and surfaces is a major problem in many theoretical and applied fields, ranging from approximation theory for numerical analysis and statistics to computer-aided design and manufacturing (CAD/CAM), virtual reality, medical imaging, and many others. Most of currently-used methodologies in the field are based on the application of traditional mathematical optimization techniques. However, such methods are still pretty limited and cannot be successfully applied to this problem in all its generality. As a consequence, researchers have turned their attention to artificial intelligence and other modern optimization techniques, such as metaheuristics. By metaheuristics we refer to a set of very diverse computational methods for optimization aimed to obtain the optimum by successive iterations of a given population of candidate solutions that evolve according to some kind of quality metric (the fitness function). In Chapter 2, we provide the reader with a gentle, comprehensive overview on the field of curve/surface reconstruction by using metaheuristic techniques. The chapter will describe the main methodologies applied so far to tackle this issue, along with the analysis of their major advantages and limitations. The chapter also shows some examples of the application of this exciting technology to some practical problems of interest in industrial and applied settings. We also outline some hints about the most recent trends in the field along with some exciting future lines of research. Finally, an updated bibliography on the field is also provided.

The latest supercomputers incorporate a high number of compute units under the form of manycore accelerators. Such accelerators, like GPUs, have integrated processors where a massively high number of threads, in the order of thousands, execute concurrently. Compared to single-CPU throughput performance, they offer higher levels of parallelism. Therefore, they represent an indispensable technology in the new era of high performance supercomputing. However, the accelerator is equipped via the peripheral bus of the host CPU, which inevitably creates communication overheads when exchanging programs and data between the CPU and the accelerator. Also, we need to develop both programs to run on these processors that have distinct architectures. To make it simpler for the programmer to use the accelerator and exploit its potential throughput performance, Chapter 3 describes the Caravela platform. Caravela provides a simple programming interface that overcomes the difficulty of developing and running parallel kernels not only on single but also on multiple manycore accelerators. This chapter describes parallel programming techniques and methods applied to a variety of research test case scenarios.

Chapter 4 designs the H-infinity recursive Wiener fixed-interval smoother and filter, based on the innovation approach, in linear discrete-time stochastic systems. The estimators require the information of the observation matrix, the system matrix for the state variable, related with the signal, the variance of the state variable and the variance of the white observation noise. It is assumed that the signal is observed with additive white noise.

A numerical simulation example is shown to demonstrate the estimation characteristics of the proposed H-infinity fixed-interval smoother and filter.

Nowadays supercomputer centers strive to provide their computational resources as services, however, present infrastructure is not particularly suited for such a use. First of all, there are standard application programming interfaces to launch computational jobs via command line or a web service, which work well for a program but turn out to be too complex for scientists: they want applications to be delivered to them from a remote server and prefer to interact with them via graphical interface. Second, there are certain applications which are dependent on older versions of operating systems and libraries and it is either non-practical to install those old systems on a cluster or there exists some conflict between these dependencies. Virtualization technologies can solve this problem, but they are not too popular in scientific computing due to overheads introduced by them. Finally, it is difficult to automatically estimate optimal resource pool size for a particular task, thus it often gets done manually by a user. If the large resource pool is requested for a minor task, the efficiency degrades. Moreover, cluster schedulers depend on estimated wall time to execute the jobs and since it cannot be reliably predicted by a human or a machine their efficiency suffers as well.

Applications delivery, efficient operating system virtualization and dynamic application resource pool size defining constitute the two problems of scientific computing: complex application interfaces and inefficient use of resources available - and virtual supercomputer is the way to solve them. The research shows that there are ways to make virtualization technologies efficient for scientific computing: the use of lightweight application containers and dynamic creation of these containers for a particular job are both fast and transparent for a user. There are universal ways to deliver application output to a front-end using execution of a job on a cluster and presenting its results in a graphical form. Finally, an application framework can be developed to decompose parallel application into small independent parts with easily predictable execution time, to simplify scheduling via existing algorithms.

The aim of Chapter 5 is to promote the key idea of a virtual supercomputer: to harness all available HPC resources and provide users with convenient access to them. Such a challenge can be effectively faced using contemporary virtualization technologies. They can materialize the long-term dream of having a supercomputer at your own desk.

In: Horizons in Computer Science Research. Volume 11 ISBN: 978-1-63482-499-6
Editor: Thomas S. Clary, pp. 1-31 © 2015 Nova Science Publishers, Inc.

Chapter 1

WEIGHTED FUSION OF SHAPE DESCRIPTOR FOR ROBUST SHAPE CLASSIFICATION

Loris Nanni[1,], Alessandra Lumini[3] and Sheryl Brahnam[2]*
[1]Department of Information Engineering, Padova, Italy
[2]DISI, University of Bologna, Cesena, Italy
[3]Computer Information Systems, Missouri State University, Springfield, MO, US

Abstract

Shape classification in computer vision is a vibrant field of study with wide ranging applications involving object classification, motion tracking, image segmentation, and image retrieval. In this work we propose an ensemble of approaches harnessing the power of many shape descriptors (inner distance shape context, shape context, height functions, etc.) that are transformed into a matrix from which a set of texture descriptors are extracted and compared using the Jeffrey distance. The experimental results confirm that our new ensemble of texture descriptors clearly improve previous texture-based ensembles for shape classification.

Our ensemble is validated and compared with the state-of-the-art on several benchmark datasets, representing different shape classification tasks (MPEG7 CE-Shape-1, Kimia silhouettes, Tari dataset, a leaf dataset, and an animal shape dataset). The parameters of each method used in our ensemble and the weights of the weighted fusion by sum rule are kept the same across each of these datasets, thereby demonstrating that our proposed ensemble is a general-purpose shape classification system.

Moreover, the texture descriptors based approach is also coupled with the Bag of Contour Fragments method permitting a boost of the performance obtained by the standard approach.

The MATLAB code of our proposed system will be available online at https://www.dei.unipd.it/node/2357.

---

* E-mail address: loris.nanni@unipd.it

Keywords: shape classification, ensemble, weighted sum rule, Jeffrey distance, texture descriptors

1. Introduction

The number of images on the internet is growing exponentially, thanks to the proliferation of image capturing devices and of cameras on the market today. As a result, large amounts of data continuously need to be classified and searched by users on a daily basis and often in real-time. Image retrieval has thus become a fundamental problem in computer vision and plays an indispensable role in many applications, ranging from content-based image retrieval to object detection, action tracking and recognition, and medical imaging.

While human beings are capable of classifying different objects quickly and very reliably, even in cluttered environments, automated classification and retrieval of relevant objects in digitized images and videos remains a difficult task in computer vision. The main problems encountered in developing robust machine retrieval and matching systems are related to the large intra-class variance among images of objects belonging to the same class and the presence of changes in lighting, scale, rotation, and other transformations which complicate the recognition process.

In the computer vision literature, there are mainly two classes of methods for image retrieval: key-word-based methods and content-based methods. Keyword methods are simpler and easier to use, but they suffer from subjective variance since people often employ different keywords to index the same image. Keyword methods are also impractical since manually labeling digital images is a time-consuming and cost prohibitive task. For these reasons and more, there is great interest in the design of accurate automated image retrieval systems based on features that are intrinsic aspects of images, such as texture, color, and shape. The main critical issues that need to be addressed when designing content-based image retrieval systems include developing strategies for selecting appropriate features, as well as for selecting the best image representations, similarity metrics, and classification methods. Arguably the most widely studied image feature, and the one considered the most suited for many applications, is shape [1], which is the focus of this paper. Specifically, we are interested in examining the selection of an accurate shape representation and in the definition of an efficient and robust similarity measure.

In the past few years shape matching has been an area of intense investigation, and many important shape matching strategies have been proposed. Some examples include Fourier analysis, moments analysis, and distance measures (see [1] for a survey). The approach taken by each of these methods depends on whether shape is defined in terms of contour or region. Contour-based methods can be classified into global and local methods, depending on the feature extraction process. In global contour-based approaches, a shape is usually represented by a feature vector extracted from the entire contour, while in local shape approaches a shape is typically represented by a set of local descriptors capturing only local shape information.

A standard global shape approach is the Curvature Scale Space (CSS) [2], which locates the zero-crossings of the contour curvature function at different scales as a feature that is used for shape matching. Another global method is the Polygonal Multi-resolution and Elastic Matching (PMEM) algorithm [3], which extracts three primitives of each contour segment at different scales and uses the Sum of Absolute Differences (SAD) to measure the similarity.

An approach based on the histogram is the Contour Points Distribution Histogram (CPDH) [4], which represents a shape by the spatial distribution of contour points in the polar coordinate system. Two novel global shape representations are proposed in [5], which capture the angular information among contour points: the final descriptor is based on the multiscale integration of such features, namely angular patterns (AP) and binary angular patterns (BAP), which are both invariant to scale and rotation.

In local shape approaches, a shape is typically represented by a set of local descriptors. Shape similarities are then derived from two layers of comparison: the low-level similarities between local descriptors and the comparison of high-level similarities on top of the lower similarities. A classic example in this category is shape context (SC) [6], where parts of objects are represented by simplified polygons and a two dimensional histogram representation that captures the Euclidean distance and the angle of the polygons. SC has the properties of being invariant to translation, rotation, and scale. Hence, it performs well on rigid objects but is susceptible to articulations. An evolution of SC that is designed to overcome this weakness is the Inner Distance shape context method (ID) [7], where part structures of shapes are defined using the inner-distance (i.e., the length of the shortest path connecting the two points) and the inner angle rather than the Euclidean distance and angle. Dynamic programming is used for shape matching. A hierarchical approach is proposed in [8], called Hierarchical Procrustes Matching (HPM), that captures shape information across different hierarchies. The height function (HF) is a novel method proposed in [9], where the contour of each object is represented by a fixed number of sample points, each of which is defined by its distance to other sample points on its tangent line. Dynamic programming is used for matching these descriptors. Recently, a new shape representation inspired by the classical Bag of Words (BoW) model is proposed in [10]. Called the Bag of Contour Fragments (BCF). This method decomposes a shape into contour fragments each of which is individually described using a shape descriptor (e.g., SC) that is encoded into shape codes. A compact shape representation is then built by pooling the shape codes in the shape, and shape classification is performed with an efficient linear SVM classifier. A similar approach is presented in [11], where a classification framework for binary shapes with scale, rotation, and strong viewpoint variations is presented. This approach is also based on a BoW model, where the spectral magnitude of a log-polar transform is used as a local feature and where contextual information is included by extracting bi-grams from the spatial co-occurrence matrix. Local shape descriptors usually outperform global ones in terms of shape matching accuracy; however, they have the disadvantage of requiring higher computation time.

Similarity measures pose a number of problems. A major problem revolves around the inability of many similarity methods to take into account the intrinsic properties of shapes [12], as well as the relative significance of the variations in these properties. This problem has been explored in [13-16]. These studies have shown, for instance, that shapes belonging to the same class can exhibit large differences because of nonrigid transformations and distortions. This is not a problem with statistical definitions of shape such as those proposed in [17] and [18]. However, these statistical methods assume that the correspondences are known.

Most approaches extract descriptors only from the object's contour and are unable to handle cases where indentations in the boundaries are present, areas that the human visual system has evolved to ignore (the so-called Gestalt effect). Techniques based on human perception have been developed that are able to deal with these cases. Two perceptually motivated morphological strategies (PMMS) have recently been proposed in [19] that rely on two human perception behaviors that relate to shape retrieval. PMMS can also be applied to popular shape matching methods, such as ID and the Locally Constrained Diffusion Process (LCDP). PMMS have been shown to enhance performance: for instance, the retrieval rate in [19] on the MPEG-7 dataset is 98.56% (using learned affinities). Some other descriptors that model internal shapes, without explicitly modelling human perception, include the Medial Axis Transform (MAT), skeletons [20], and skeletal contexts [21]. A novel way of extracting shape descriptors that capture the object's shape in its entirety is proposed in [22]. This method is a variant of the SC descriptor, which captures the shape properties in their entirety, but is also able to handle indentations in boundaries.

More recently, methods have been developed that consider the relevance of shape differences by capturing the essence of a shape class, see e.g., [12]. Using this approach, an improvement in retrieval performance is achieved when other similar shapes are allowed to influence the pair-wise scores. For a given similarity measure, a new similarity measure is learned within the context of a set of shapes using graph transduction.

Some of the best state-of-the-art performances have been obtained by methods that use the similarity learning approach based on shape similarities (see, e.g., [23-27]). For example, a method called co-transduction [25] fuses similarity and distance measures via a semisupervised learning framework. Combining two shape similarities, this method obtained 97.72% accuracy in the MPEG-7 dataset, with the bull's-eye measure, and 99.06% when combining three shape similarities. In [26] a graph diffusion process on the tensor product graph (TPG) is shown to be equivalent to a novel iterative algorithm on the original graph that is guaranteed to converge. New edge weights can be obtained after convergence that can be interpreted as new learned affinities. This approach succeeded in obtaining an accuracy close to 100% on the MPEG7. A generic formulation of the diffusion process is proposed in [28] that describes an iterative updating of the pairwise similarity matrix $A \in \Re^{N \times N}$ into a novel, diffused version A' which is used for retrieval. The diffusion processes consists of three main steps: initialization, definition of the transition matrix, and definition of the diffusion process. The initialization and definition steps interpret the matrix A as a graph $G = (V, E)$ consisting of N nodes and $N \times N$ edges that link the nodes to each other. The initial edge weights are given similarity values. The diffusion step spreads the similarity values through the entire graph, based on the edge weights. One way to interpret this process is as a random walk on the graph, where a "transition matrix" defines the probabilities for walking from one node to a neighboring node.

Recent results on the MPEG7 dataset provide a clear sense of the progress that has been made by the new generation of shape retrieval methods. The best result using the MPEG7 database a decade ago was ~ 80%. Aside from the results presented above, several pairwise matching algorithms have reported performance (bull's eye testing protocol) close to 90% [29], and some context-based algorithms have recorded performance between 97% and 99.9% [25, 26]. Of interest is the fact that each of these approaches start from an affinity matrix obtained by a pairwise matching algorithm. Thus, they could be viewed as post-processing methods that could be combined with any pairwise matching algorithm.

In this paper, we improve the performance of state-of-art pairwise matching algorithms using an ensemble of methods combined by weighted sum rule[1]. Our fusion approach applies a method where the resulting shape descriptors are transformed into a matrix from which a set of texture descriptors are extracted. The Jeffrey distance is then used to compare the different

---

[1] Notice that before each fusion the scores of each method are normalized to mean 0 and standard deviation 1.

texture descriptors. Our rationale for using texture descriptors is based on the experiments reported in [30] and [31].

The novelties introduced in this work include the following:

- Better performing ensembles of texture descriptors are used for describing matrix shape descriptors;
- Texture descriptors are also combined with the BCF approach permitting a considerable boost of the performance;
- New variants of the BAP shape descriptors are proposed;
- An ensemble based on different approaches using the weighted sum rule is proposed for shape retrieval/classification (where the same weights are used in the all the tested datasets to avoid overfitting) that obtains state-of-the-art performance in all the tested datasets.

To show the generality of our proposed system, we validate our approach on several well-known benchmarks: the MPEG7 CE-Shape-1, the Tari dataset, Kimia, a Leaf Database, and an animal shape dataset. The MATLAB code of our proposed system is available online at https://www.dei.unipd.it/node/2357.

The remainder of this paper is organized as follows. In section 2 we describe the base approaches (the shape matchers and texture descriptors) used in our system, and in section 3 we present our weighted ensemble. In section 4, we describe the datasets used in our experiments along with the experimental results. We conclude in section 5 by summarizing the significance of our work and by highlighting some future directions of exploration.

2. Base Methods

The purpose of this section is to introduce the different shape descriptors and other base methods examined in this chapter and used in our proposed ensembles. It should be noted here that the output of the various shape descriptors are transformed into a matrix, after which they are represented by different texture descriptors.

2.1. Shape Descriptors

2.1.1. Inner Distance Shape Context (ID)

Inner distance is the length of the shortest path between landmark points within a shape silhouette [7]. It can be formally defined as follows. Given a connected and closed shape O in $\Re^2$ and two boundary points $x,y \in O$, the inner-distance $d(x,y;O)$ between x and y is the shortest path connecting x to y within O.

In the case where more than one path exists that is so defined, one is selected randomly.

Here is the pseudo code for computing the inner-distance:

1. BUILD A GRAPH by taking a pair of sample points, p_1 and p_2:
   a) Treat each point as a node in a graph;

b) If the line segment between p_1 and p_2 falls within the boundary of the object, then add the edge to the graph with a weight equal to the Euclidean distance.

2. APPLY SHORTEST PATH ALGORITHM TO THE GRAPH (e.g., using those reported in [32]);

The inner distance does not consider whether a line segment crosses the shape boundary, unlike the Euclidean distance, rather it captures the structure of parts by considering interior shape boundaries. Although the inner-distance is sensitive to the structure of the parts within a shape, it is insensitive to the articulation of the parts (see [7]). The MATLAB code for the inner distance is available at http://www.ist.temple.edu/~hbling/code_data.htm.

The inner distance is similar to the shock-graph skeleton technique [13, 14, 33] in that the inner-distance is computed by measuring the distance between two landmark points that are first approximated as the closest points on the shape boundary, or skeleton. Unlike most skeleton techniques, however, the inner-distance discards the structure once these lengths are measured, thereby producing a measure that is more robust to boundary disturbances and more flexible for building shape descriptors.

Once the inner distance is obtained, a histogram is extracted for each point describing the contour, where the x-axis denotes the orientation bins and the y-axis denotes the log distance bins. This matrix is transformed into a vector, these vectors (one for each point) are concatenated for building a matrix from which the texture descriptors are extracted.

2.1.2. Shape Context (SC)

SC is proposed in [34] and describes the relative spatial distance and orientation (distribution) of landmark points around feature points. Formally SC is defined as follows. Given n sample points $x_1, x_2, \ldots, x_n$ on a given shape, SC at point x_i is a histogram h_i of the relative coordinates of the remaining n-1 points:

$$h_i = \#\{x_j : j \neq i, x_j - x_i \in bin(k)\} \tag{1}$$

where the bins divide the log-polar space uniformly, and the distance between two SC histograms is defined using the Chi Square statistic.

Although Thin-Plate-Splines (TPS) are used in [34] for shape comparison, we replace TPS in our experiments with dynamic programming (DP) [25] as this method enhances SC performance.

When the texture descriptor are used for describing a shape, the different histograms h_i are concatenated for building a matrix from which the texture descriptors are extracted.

2.1.3. Height Functions (HF)

HF is proposed in [9] and is a descriptor that represents each contour of each object by a fixed number of sample points. This is accomplished by applying a height function to each sample that is defined based on the distances of the other sample points to its tangent line.

Formally, HF is defined as follows. Let $X = \{x_i\}$ (i= 1, 2, ... , N) denote the sequence of equidistant sample points along the outer contour of a given shape, and let the sampling point i follow the contour in an ordered counter-clockwise direction. For each sample point, x_i, a reference axis is determined using the tangent line l_i, which inherits its orientation through the contour orientation. The distance between the jth (j = 1, 2, ..., N) sample point x_j and the tangent line l_i is defined as the height value $h_{i,j}$. Depending on whether the jth sample point x_j is to the left, to the right, or located on axis l_i, the height value $h_{i,j}$ is either positive, negative, or zero, respectively. Being positive or negative provides a precise representation of the relative location of x_j to the axis l_i because both the distance and the side that x_j lies on is represented by the sign. Height values are calculated for every sample point, and the shape descriptor of point x_j with respect to shape X becomes the ordered sequence of height values:

$$H_i = \left(h_i^1, h_i^2, ..., h_i^N,\right)^T = \left(h_{i,i}, h_{i,i+1}, ..., h_{i,N}, h_{i,N}, h_{i,1}, ... h_{i,i-1}\right)^T \tag{2}$$

where $h_{i,j}$ (j = 1, ... ,N) denotes the height value of the jth sample point x_j according to the reference axis l_i of the point x_i.

HF has the properties that it is insensitive to noise and occlusion and is invariant to a number of geometric transformations such as translation, rotation, and scaling. However, because it contains the relative location of every sample point to the reference axis, HF can be overly sensitive to local boundary deformations. A smoothing function is able to overcome this problem (see [9] for details). In our experiments with HF, texture descriptors are extracted from the height representation matrix.

2.1.4. Shapelet (SH)

SH is proposed in [35] and is a sparse representation of a two-dimensional planar shape that is based on the composition of warping functions and localized termed formlets, which can be composed to produce complex shapes while preserving topology. Formally, SH is defined as follows. Given an image represented in the complex space $\mathbb{C}$, a formlet can be defined as a diffeomorphism of the complex plane localized in scale and space. Such a deformation can be obtained by centering f around a point $\zeta \in \mathbb{C}$ and allowing it to deform the place within a ($\sigma \in \mathcal{R}^+$)–region of ζ. Formlet composition can thus be defined as the problem of determining the resulting deformed shape $\Gamma^K(t)$ given an embryonic shape $\Gamma^0(t)$ (e.g., an ellipse) and a sequence of K formlets $\{f_1 ... f_k\}$.

Pseudo code for SH is as follows:

INITIALIZE: define $A(\Gamma_0 + z_0)$ to be a best matching ellipse approximating Γ^{obs}:

For k=1, ...,K do

OPTIMAL FORMLET: compute maximal error reducing transformation:

$$f_k = \text{argmin}\zeta \left(\Gamma^{obs}, f(\Gamma^{k-1})\right), f \in D \tag{3}$$

UPDATE APPROXIMATION: apply optimal formlet:

$$\Gamma^k = f_K(\Gamma^{k-1}) \tag{4}$$

Equation 3 presents a difficult non-convex optimization problem since the formlet parameter space has many local minima. Thus, the search for an optimal formlet requires sampling from a dictionary over location ζ and scale σ (see [35] for more details).

2.1.5. Curvature (CU)

CU, proposed in [36], takes a set of edge point samples and a set of circular masks with varying radii as its input and counts the number of samples falling in each mask when the mask is centered on edge points that represent some contour. This count serves as the basis for a measure of curvature.

Formally, CU is defined as follows. Given a set of edge points X_i and a set of S circular masks $M_s(X_i), s = 1, \dots, S$ with radius r_s centered on each edge point, $V(X_i, s)$, the number of edge points falling within the mask $M_s(X_i)$ can be described as

$$V(X_i, s) = \frac{\sum x_{j \in M_s(X_i)} B(X_j)}{|M_s(X_i)|}, \qquad (5)$$

where $|M_s(X_i)|$ denotes the cardinality of $M_s(X_i)$ and $B(X_j)$ is the binary mask B centered on the edge point corresponding to X_j.

The values of $V(X_i, s)$ are in the range $[0,1]$, where 0 indicates an extremely convex shape, 1 indicates an extremely concave shape, and 0.5 indicates a straight line. These values are quantized in a histogram of N bins of equal size, from which a set of curvature features are extracted (see [36] for details). We use the following parameters in our experiments: number of bins=64, minimum radius=2, and maximum radius=30. Also from the histograms extracted from curvature texture descriptors are obtained, here we use the set based on Local Phase Quantization (LPQ), Histogram Of Gradients (HOG) and wavelet (WA) as proposed in [31]. In the following with CUtxt we named the ensemble given by the following weighted sum rule: *2×CU* (standard approach without considering the texture descriptors) + *LPQ(CU)* (LPQ extracted from the matrix obtained by CU) + *HOG(CU)* + *WAVE(CU)* (see [31] for details). As in the others tests also for these texture descriptors the matching is performed with Jeffery distance. Obviously, as in all other fusions, the scores of each method are normalized to mean 0 and standard deviation 1 before the sum rule.

2.1.6. Fast Radial Symmetry Transform (SY)

SY is proposed in [37] and employs local radial symmetry to highlight points of interest. SY is a feature detection technique that maps the original image to the transformed image according to its contribution to the radial symmetry of the gradients. When SY is applied to an image, the magnitudes of the symmetric regions are increased and the magnitudes of the asymmetric regions are decreased. We use this transform to extract a histogram of symmetry descriptors.

SY is calculated at one or more radii $n \in N$, where N is the set of radii of the radially symmetric features detected. At radius n this transform measures the contribution to the radial symmetry of the gradients at distance n from each point, and two images, a magnitude projection image M_n and an orientation projection image O_n, is formed by examining the gradient g at each point p in the image. A corresponding positively affected pixel p_{+ve} and a negatively affected pixel p_{-ve} are then determined. The positively affected pixel p_{+ve} is defined as the pixel that the gradient vector $g(p)$ is pointing to, n distance away from p. The negatively affected pixel p_{-ve} is the pixel the gradient vector $g(p)$ is pointing away from, n distance away from p.

Given the above and initializing M_n and O_n to zero for each pair of affected pixels, the corresponding p_{+ve} in M_n is incremented by $\|g(p)\|$ and the corresponding p_{+ve} in O_n is incremented by 1. Likewise, the corresponding p_{-ve} in M_n and O_n is decremented by the same value that was used to increment p_{+ve}.

The radial symmetry contribution at radius n is defined as the convolution

$$S_n = F_n * A_n, \tag{6}$$

where

$$F_n(p) = \frac{M_n(p)}{k_n}\left(\frac{|\tilde{O}_n(p)|}{k_n}\right)^{\alpha}, \tag{7}$$

and

$$\tilde{O}_n(p) = \begin{cases} O_n(p) \ if \ O_n(p) < k_n \\ \quad k_n \ otherwise. \end{cases} \tag{8}$$

A_n is a two-dimensional Gaussian, α is the radial strictness parameter, and k_n is a scaling factor that normalizes M_n and O_n across different radii. The full transform is the average of the symmetry contribution over all the radii considered.

For a given image, the SY is calculated to extract the feature vector. The histogram is then calculated using the following intervals [0:0.1:5 5:0.5:20].

2.1.7. Weighted Spectral Distance for Measuring Shape Dissimilarity (WE)

WE, proposed in [38], is a method for measuring shape dissimilarity between objects and uses the sequence of eigenvalues of the Laplace operator. Given two closed bounded domains with piecewise smooth boundaries, $\Omega_\lambda, \Omega_\xi \subset \mathcal{R}^d$, WE can be defined as

$$\rho(\Omega_\lambda, \Omega_\xi) \triangleq \left[\sum_{n=1}^{\infty}\left(\frac{|\lambda_n - \xi_n|}{\lambda_n \xi_n}\right)\right]^{1/p}, \tag{9}$$

with $p \in \mathcal{R}$ and $p > d/2$.

WE possesses some useful properties. It is multi-scale, pseudometric, defined over the entire sequence of eigenvalues with a guarantee of convergence, invariant to global scale differences, and accurately approximated with a finite set of eigenvalues. Moreover, it can be mapped to the [0,1) interval.

2.1.8. Geodesic (GEO)

GEO, proposed in [39], provides a set of algorithms for efficiently computing geodesic paths between two surfaces that can be used for deforming, comparing, and matching surfaces. Representations and metrics are selected in such a way that the resulting geodesics between curves are invariant to reparameterization transformations such as rotation, translation, and uniform scaling. A Reismannian framework is proposed where the problems of registration (parametrization) and shape analysis (distance based comparisons) are jointly, rather than sequentially, solved. The geodesic computation is essentially a path-straightening technique that iteratively straightens paths between two surfaces until geodesics are obtained. In other words, given two surfaces f_1 and f_2 in a space $\mathcal{F}$ of surfaces that have been normalized by centering, rescaling, rotation, and reparameterization (see [39] for normalization details), the idea is to connect f_1 and f_2 by any initial path (e.g., using a straight line under the L^2 metric) and then strengthen it iteratively (based on the gradient of a path energy that is approximated using a large set of basis elements in the perturbation space) until it becomes a geodesic.

2.1.9. Bag of Contour Fragments (BCF)

This method is based on Bag of Contour Fragments (BCF), proposed in [10]. Inspired by the Bag or Words technique, BCF takes a shape and decomposes it into contour fragments after which each fragment is described using a shape descriptor (SC in [10]). A compact shape representation is built by pooling the shape codes that make up the shape.

Given a shape S, the BCF shape representation $f(S)$ is computed and used for classification as follows:

- Decompose a shape contour into meaningful fragments using Discrete Contour Evolution (DCE) [41]. Let $S(t) = (x(t), y(t))$ be the outer contour of a shape S parameterized by $t \in [0,1]$. DCE is applied to obtain a simplified polygon with vertices $\vec{u} = (u_1, u_2, \ldots, u_T)$, where T is the number of vertices not previously known but which can be computed automatically given some threshold τ;

- Compute the contour fragments set $C(S)$, i.e., the segments between every pair of critical points (u_i, u_j), for S. Let c_{ij} denote the contour fragment between u_i and u_j:
$$C(S) = \{c_{ij} = (u_i, u_j), i \neq j, i, j \in [1, \ldots, T].$$

- Describe each contour fragment c_{ij} using a shape context $x_{ij} \in \mathcal{R}^{d \times 1}$, where d is the dimension of the feature vector of c_{ij}. The value for x_{ij} is determined by sampling five reference points on c_{ij} equidistantly from u_i and u_j and then by computing five shape context histograms based on each of the reference points. The shape descriptors for c_{ij} is the concatenation of the five shape context histograms.

- Encode the contour features x_{ij} by mapping the feature vectors of the contour fragments into a new space $\mathcal{B}$ spanned by some shape codebook B and represented in the new space $\mathcal{B}$ by shape codes w_{ij}. A k-means algorithm is run on a randomly selected training set of shape features for clustering, and the clustering centers are then used as the shape codebook $B = [b_1, b_2, \ldots, b_M] \in \mathcal{R}^{d \times 1}$, where each column is a clustering center, and the M clustering centers can be considered approximately as M prototypes describing the entire shape space. The shape codes w_{ij} are computed by Local-constraint linear coding (LLC), which uses k-nearest neighbors in B as the local bases for x_{ij} to form a local coordinate system (see [42] for details).

To describe a given segment, we use SC, as defined in [10], as well as HF. Moreover, we combine the idea of BCF with our idea to describe each SC/HF descriptor using texture descriptors.

2.1.10. Contour Descriptors (CD)

CD is a set of novel contour descriptors (called Contour Points Distribution Histogram) proposed in [4] for 2D shape matching that conforms to human visual perception but that that only fits shapes with a single closed contour. CD is based on the distribution of points on the contour of an object under polar coordinates and is invariant to scale and translation and partially invariant to rotation in the matching process through circular shifting and a mirror matching scheme.

Generating CD descriptors is a two-step process:

1. Contour points are extracted.
   a) Extract contour points using the standard Canny operator to produce a set of P points on the contour: $P = \{(x_1, y_1), (x_2, y_2), ..., (x_n, y_n)\}, (x_i, y_i) \in \mathcal{R}^2$, where n denotes the number of points on the contour;
   b) Sample N points in P as described in [34] to produce $\tilde{P}$, a reduce set of points describing the contour;

2. Extract CD descriptors from the Contour Points Distribution Histogram:
   c) Build a minimum circumscribed circle by denoting the object centroid (x_c, y_c) as the center;
   d) Set the centroid as the origin and translate $\tilde{P}$ into polar coordinates: $\tilde{P} = \{(r_1, \rho_1), (r_2, \rho_2), ..., (r_n, \rho_n)\}, (r_i, \rho_i) \in \mathcal{R}^2$, where $r_i = ((x_i - x_c)^2 + (y_i - y_c)^2)^{1/2}$ is the distance between the points (x_i, y_i) and (x_c, y_c), and $\theta_i = \arctan\left(\frac{y_i - y_c}{(x_i, y_i)}\right)$ is the angle between ρ_1 and the x-axis;
   e) Obtain a minimally described circle C with center (x_c, y_c) and radius ρ_{max}, where $\rho_{max} = \max\{\rho_i\}, i = \{1, 2, ..., N\}$.
   f) Divide the area of C into $u \times v$ bins, with u bins for ρ_{max} and v bins for θ.
   g) Count the number of points in each bin to construct the Contour Points Distribution Histogram of the shape image. Each bin can be described as a triple $H_i = (\rho_i, \theta_i, n_i)$, where ρ_i denotes the radius of the concentric circles, θ_i denotes the angle space, n_i denotes the number of points located in the bin r_i, and the entire collection of bins is the Contour Points Distribution Histogram.

In our experiments we extract texture descriptors directly from the Contour Points Distribution Histogram.

2.1.11. Angular Patterns (ANG)

ANG is an integrated multiscale global shape descriptor proposed in [5] that is computationally efficient. ANG integrates two angular features: Angular Patterns (AP) and

Binary Angular Patterns (BAP), both of which are intrinsically invariant to scale and rotation. Integrating the different scales of AP and BAP is accomplished by applying the z-score normalization for the distance matrices computed at each scale. The normalized distance matrices are then summed together to create a new distance matrix for shape retrieval. Sequential Forward Selection selects a set of scales that effectively capture discriminative information.

Given n uniformly sampled points on a shape contour with one point labelled Q and letting A and B be two points on the contour of equal distance s from Q, with s ranging from 1 to floor $(n-1/2)$ and A lying before and B after Q, the anticlockwise angle θ_s (ranging from 0 to 2π) between vectors QA_s and QB_s can be used to describe the geometric properties of point Q. In other words, given a shape with n points on a shape contour along with a specific value s, then n angles can be drawn that capture the geometric properties of the shape at scale s. This representation of a shape is the angular pattern (AP). A total of floor$((n-1)/2)$ APs can be extracted from a contour at different scales and used to generate a histogram H as follows:

1. Given a contour with n points and a value for s, extract n angular features:

$$AP_s = \{AP_s(i), i = 1,2,\dots,n\};$$

2. Uniformly divide $[0, 2\pi]$ into K bins;
3. Construct $h = \{h(k), k = 1,2,\dots,K\}$ with each bin as:

$$h(k) = card\left\{a \middle| a \in AP_s, k - \frac{1}{K} \cdot 2\pi < a \le \frac{k}{K} \cdot 2\pi\right\}, k = [1,2,\dots,K].$$

The χ^2 distance measure is used to compare two AP histograms H_{s_1} and H_{s_2} as follows:

$$D(H_{s_1}, H_{s_2}) \equiv \frac{1}{2}\sum_{1 \le k < K} \frac{[h_{s_1}(k) - h_{s_2}(k)]^2}{h_{s_1}(k) - h_{s_2}(k)}, \tag{10}$$

where $h_{s_1}(k)$ and $h_{s_2}(k)$ are the k-th bin of the corresponding histograms and K is the number of bins. A total of floor$((n-1)/2)$ AP histograms can be constructed by varying the scale s. It should be noted that AP by definition does not capture relations between adjacent angular features.

The binary version of AP uses the idea of Local Binary Patterns (LBP), where the intensities of pixels within a neighborhood are compared with the intensities of the pixel in the center of the neighborhood. A pixel is coded with 1 if its intensity is larger than the intensity of the central pixel, and 0 otherwise. Given a point Q along with its equal distance point pairs (A,B) and (C,D), a segment with five points can be constructed and three angular features $(\theta_Q, \theta_A, and\ \theta_B)$ can be calculated. Comparing θ_A and θ_B, a code if 1 is given if either θ_A or θ_B is larger than θ_Q, 0 otherwise. In this way a two-bit binary pattern is generated. BAP can be constructed using more than two bits to form a BAPmP pattern, which is obtained when m angular features of the neighborhood points are compared with the angular feature of the central point, respectively, to obtain an m-bit pattern.

BAP can also be extended to multiscale. If the pattern is constructed with Q, A_s, B_s, C_s, and D_s as defined above, then the computed two-bit binary pattern captures another scale of angular relations. The BAPmP pattern multiscale representation can be constructed as follows:

1. AP features are extracted from a given central point whose distances from the central point are $t \times s$, where t is a positive integer that varies from 1 to $m/2$;
2. These AP features are compared with the AP feature (with scale s) of the central point to form the m-bit binary pattern. In this way, m-bit binary patterns of all points on the contour can be extracted from the scale s (see [5] for more details).

In this work we extract three sets of features for each shape:

*   Set1: ANG extracted using a histogram where the bins are 0:10:360 (i.e., the first bin counts the element with degree angle between 0° and 9°);
*   Set2: BAP with eight neighbors;
*   Set3: BAP with four neighbors.

In our experiments, we used the multiscale version, with the scale = 1:45. Since no feature selection is performed, our approach does not need a training set. Moreover, we extract these features both from the contour of the shape and from the skeleton of the binary shape image.

2.2. Textural Descriptors

2.2.1. Local Phase Quantization (LPQ)

The LQP operator proposed in [43] is based on the blur invariance property of the Fourier phase spectrum and is used in this work (based on the results of [44]) as a texture descriptor. Standard shape matchers are based on a distance that does not consider the correlation among the different elements in the descriptors that are being compared. By using descriptors based on local neighborhoods, as in LPQ, the correlation among the elements of the matrix that belong to a given neighborhood can be compared [43].

In this work, LPQ is set to radius 5 and 3. The Gaussian derivative quadrature filter pair for local frequency estimation is also used. A difference distance is calculated for each radius and then summed. The MATLAB LPQ code used in this work is available at http://www.cse.oulu.fi/CMV/Downloads/LPQMatlab.

2.2.2. Histogram of Gradients (HOG)

HOG descriptors proposed in [45] contain the local statistics of the orientations of the image around a key point. Basically, HOG calculates intensity gradients from pixel to pixel and selects a corresponding histogram bin for each pixel based on the gradient direction.

HOG descriptors are obtained as follows:

1. A region of interest is divided into a grid;

2. The orientation and magnitude of each pixel in each cell of the grid is calculated by dividing the absolute orientations over n equally sized bins in the 0°- 180° or 0°- 360° range, depending on whether the gradient is signed or unsigned;

3. Each pixel contributes the magnitude of its orientation to the corresponding histogram bin, which results in one n-bin histogram for each cell.

4. Since the HOG descriptors are not scale and rotation invariant, the entire descriptor needs to be normalized.

A grid of size 5 x 6 and 9 bins representing the absolute values (0-180) is used in this work, and normalization is performed using the L2-sqrt normalization scheme. HOG is calculated directly to the input image to obtain a vector descriptor. It is also calculated as a texture descriptor for each matrix descriptor obtained by the methods described above.

2.2.3. Binarized Statistical Image Features

The *Bsif* [61] descriptor assigns an n-bit label to each pixel of a given image. It does this by exploiting a set of n linear filters. Given a neighborhood of l x l pixels and a set of n linear filters of the same size, a n-bit label is assigned to the central pixel of the neighborhood by binarizing $s = Wx$, where x is the l^2 x 1 vector notation of the l x l neighborhood, and W is a n x l^2 matrix representing the stack of the vector notations of the filters. Specifically, the i-th digit of s is a function of the i-th linear filter w_i, and s_i is expressed as:

$$s_i = w_i^T x, \tag{11}$$

In this way, each bit of the *Bsif* code can be obtained as:

$$b_i = \begin{cases} 1, if \ s_i > 0 \\ 0, if \ s_i \leq 0 \end{cases} \tag{12}$$

The set of filters w_i is estimated by maximizing (using independent component analysis) the statistical independence of the filter responses s_i of a set of patches from natural images.

The stand-alone version of *Bsif* is improved here by combining (sum rule) different *Bsif* generated by varying the filter *size*= {3, 5, 7, 9, 11}. The resulting ensemble is labeled *eBSIF* in the experimental section. Before the fusion the scores of the single *Bsif* are normalized to mean 0 and standard deviation 1.

2.2.4. Multiscale Histograms of Principal Oriented Gradients

A variant of the HOG descriptor, MHPOG, proposed in [46], addresses the inability of HOG to consider the lack of stability in the computed gradients, which are sensitive to image blur, noise, and low resolution.

2.2.5. Rotation Invariant Co-Occurrence LBP (RLBP)

RLBP, proposed in [47], is a novel LBP operator that introduces a rotation equivalence class to the co-occurrence among adjacent LBPs (CoALBP). CoALBP extends LBP by looking at the co-occurrence among LBPs in order to extract information related to the more global structures of the input image.

Let I be an image intensity and $\mathbf{r} = (x, y)$ be a position vector in I, the CoALBP (the LBP pair) can be written as follows:

$$P(\mathbf{r}, \Delta\mathbf{r}) = (LBP(\mathbf{r}), LBP(\mathbf{r} + \Delta\mathbf{r})), \tag{13}$$

where $\Delta\mathbf{r} = (r\cos\theta, r\sin\theta)$ is a displacement vector between an LBP pair. The value of r is an interval between an LBP pair, and $\theta = 0, \frac{\pi}{4}, \frac{\pi}{2}, \frac{3\pi}{4}$.

Here we concatenate the histograms obtained with the following parameters (scale of LBP radius, interval of LBP pair): (1, 2); (2, 4); (4, 8).

2.2.6. Wavelet Preprocessing (WAV)

The WAV transform is used in many computer vision problems related to the detection and recognition of objects of interest. To be used for 2D decomposition [48], WAV requires a 2D scaling function, $\varphi(x, y)$ and three 2D wavelets functions, $\psi^i(x, y)$, where i represents the three possible intensity variations along horizontal, vertical, and diagonal edges $i = \{H, V, D\}$.

We use the Daubechies [49] wavelet family (Wa) with four vanishing moments in our experiment, and WAV is utilized as a preprocessing step before texture descriptors are extracted. The texture descriptors are extracted from the approximation image (CA) and the horizontal details image (CH).

2.3. Dissimilarity Measures

Many similarity measures from computational geometry, statistics, and information theory have been defined and utilized in shape classification and image retrieval. A systematic investigation into the applicability and performance of different similarity measures in image retrieval is performed [50], resulting in the conclusion that the Jeffrey Divergence is one of the best recommended measures for content-based image retrieval. Following this guideline, all texture descriptors are compared in this work using the Jeffrey divergence.

The Jeffrey Divergence is an information-theoretic measure derived from Shannon's entropy theory. It treats objects as probabilistic distributions, so is not applicable to features with negative values.

Formally, the Jeffrey Divergence can be defined as follows. Given two object $A, B \in \Re^N$, their Jeffrey Divergence is:

$$JD(A, B) = \sum_{i=1}^{n} \left(a_i \log \frac{2a_i}{a_i + b_i} + b_i \log \frac{2b_i}{a_i + b_i} \right) \tag{14}$$

As can be seen in the above equation, Jeffrey divergence is numerically stable and symmetric.

MATLAB code is available at:

http://www.mathworks.com/matlabcentral/fileexchange/15935-computing-pairwise-distances-and-metrics.

3. Description of Our Approach

Below is a simple pseudocode description of our proposed algorithm, which is schematized in figure 1:

1.   CONVERT Image into a binary image;
2.   EXTRACT CONTOUR;

Every image in a given dataset is cropped and resized to the same dimension. A surrounding frame of pixels belonging to the background[2] is affixed to avoid problems with the contour extraction). To handle mirrored and rotated shapes, we extract the contour not only from the original image (OR) but also from the flipped left/right image (LR), using the MATLAB function fliplr.m. Each of these images, the original and the flipped, is then rotated between 22.5° and 337.5° (step 22.5°) and another contour is extracted, thereby producing a total of 32 extracted contours. The creation of rotated images is not performed in some methods (Curvature and Symmetry) since they are rotation invariant. In addition, since WE is partially rotation invariant, each image using WE is rotated only between 22.5° and 67.5° (step 22.5°).

1.   CALCULATE DESCRIPTORS;

For each contour extracted in the STEP1, we calculate the shape descriptors discussed in section 2:

1.1. Standard descriptors: i.e., standard application of shape matchers;
1.2. Matrix descriptors from which extract texture features.

2.   DESCRIBE MATRIX WITH TEXTURE DESCRIPTORS;

The matrixes extracted in step 3.2 are described by several texture descriptors. The matrix is divided into $K1 \times K2$ subwindows without overlap, and the texture descriptor is calculated separately on each of the $K1 \times K2$ subwindows. We use $K1=K2=4$, except $K1=K2=2$ for HF and $K1=K2=1$ for CD.

3.   BCF

A codebook is trained by clustering some features locally extracted as in steps 2.1 and 2.2 (using SC and HF), and each shape is labeled according to codebook assignation as described in [10]:

3.1. Training: performed only one time to generate a codebook;
3.2. Codebook assignation: each shape is assigned to a codebook according to a minimum distance criterion;

---

[2]   Let IMG be the processed image and 0 the value of the background pixels, then: IMG(:,1)=0;IMG(1,:)=0;IMG(:,size(IMG,2))=0;IMG(size(IMG,1),:)=0;

4.   MATCH;

Given two shapes, i and j, each is compared to the other (a different descriptor is extracted from each of the images created in STEP1), with the lower distance used as the match value between the two shapes. To reduce computation time, we consider only the original contour for the first shape i; for the second shape j, all contours extracted from each of the images created in STEP1 are considered;

5.   NORMALIZE & FUSE;

Before fusion, the distances obtained by each method are normalized to mean 0 and standard deviation 1. We combine the resulting distances using the weighted sum rule (see section 4) with the same settings applied in all tests.

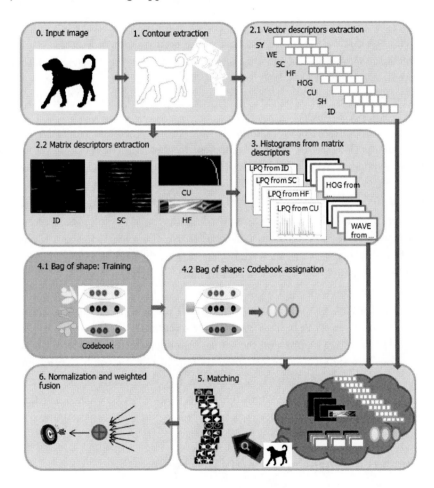

Figure 1. Proposed approach.

4. Experimental Results

4.1. Datasets

To verify our approach and to build a general shape matcher, the following large benchmark datasets are used: *MPEG7 CE-Shape-1*[51], *Kimiasilhouettes* [13], *Tari dataset* [52], *Smithsonian Isolated Leaf Database* [53], *Animal Shape dataset* [54].

The *MPEG7 CE-Shape-1* (MPEG7) [51] is one of the most widely used shape benchmarks. This dataset has 1400 silhouette images from 70 classes with 20 shapes each. The recognition rate is measured using what is called the Bullseye test, where each image in the dataset is matched with all others; the top 40 most similar candidates are counted. The retrieval rate is the ratio of correct hits in the top 40 to the maximum possible number of hits (20×1400).

The *Tari dataset* (TARI) [52] contains 1000 silhouette images from 50 classes (20 images in each class). The Bullseye test is used as the performance indicator.

The *Kimia silhouettes* (KIMIA) [13, 55] is composed of two databases of silhouettes. We use the second database [13] which contains 99 images from 9 classes. Results are summarized based on the Bullseye test, which in this paper considers the top 10 most similar candidates for each query image.

The *Smithsonian Isolated Leaf Database* (LEAF) [53] comes from the Smithsonian project and contains 343 leaves from 93 species. In the LEAF experiments, the retrieval performance is evaluated using the accuracy among the top 5 classes, if the correct class is among the five retrieved classes.

The *Animal shape dataset* (ANIMAL) [54] is a collection of 20 classes×100 shapes. The 20 classes represents the following creatures: Bird, Butterfly, Cat, Cow, Deer, Dolphin, Duck, Elephant, Crocodile, Fish, Flying Bird, Chicken, Horse, Leopard, Monkey, Mouse, Spider, Tortoise, Rabbit, and Dog. All shapes were obtained from the segmentation of real images. In the ANIMAL experiments, the retrieval performance is evaluated using the classification accuracy. The standard testing protocol for ANIMAL dataset consists in repeating the experiments 10 times and averaging results using half the images as the training set and the other half as the testing set (with both sets randomly selected).

Across all databases we maintained the same parameters for each approach since our aim is not focused on optimizing the performance of our system for each dataset but rather to show that our generalized method works well across all datasets without ad hoc tuning. In all databases, settings are set to the following: ID/SC ($n_d = 8$; $n_\theta = 12$; $n = 100$), HF ($k=5$; $M=19$), Curvature (see section 2.1.5), Symmetry (vector of radius 5 at which to compute transform).

4.2. Experiments on Shape and Matrix Descriptors

The first experiment provides a baseline of comparisons between the different stand-alone shape descriptors (extracted in step 2.1): SY, WE, HOG, SH, ID, SC, HF, CUtxt, and ANG. The performance of the ANG descriptor includes some new variants proposed here for extracting the original descriptor in [5] and are denoted as follows (see section 2.1.11 for set descriptions):

- ANG(1): the Set1 of [31] extracted from the contour image;
- ANG(F): a weighed sum rule fusion of four angular descriptors extracted both from the contour (as in [31]) and the skeleton (tested here): 15×Set1(contour) + Set2(contour) + Set3(contour) + Set1(skeleton) + Set2(skeleton) + Set3(skeleton)

In table 1 the classification performance achieved on the five datasets is reported. Note that the performance indicators vary among tables as specified by the specific datasets (described in 4.1).

Table 1. Performance comparison among vector descriptors in different databases

		Dataset				
		MPEG7	KIMIA	TARI	LEAF	ANIMAL
Shape descriptors	SH	63.5	70.0	72.5	55.1	35.3
	HOG	78.2	81.2	77.2	69.2	62.5
	SY	37.6	51.3	46.9	39.7	28.8
	CUtxt	55.0	82.3	52.8	78.2	32.9
	ID	85.0	95.1	95.1	87.2	82.8
	SC	86.2	96.7	93.7	86.5	81.5
	HF	89.2	97.1	94.2	87.2	81.2
	GEO	79.9	94.2	88.2	81.4	68.4
	ANG(1)	78.5	84.2	85.5	76.3	61.5
	ANG(F)	78.9	83.6	86.7	82.7	63.4

The aim of the second experiment is to select the best stand-alone or ensemble of texture descriptors to represent each matrix shape descriptor. For each dataset a different table is produced (tables 2-6) reporting the classification performance achieved extracting different texture descriptors or their combination. In each table the performance of five stand-alone texture descriptors and several fusion methods related to the following matrix descriptors are reported: ID, SC, HF, edge image (EI)[3], skeleton image (SI)[4] and contour descriptors (CD), respectively. The stand-alone descriptors are HPOG, LPQ, HOG, RIC, BSIF, while the fusion approaches are the following:

- eBSIF, ensemble of BSIF obtained as described in section 2.2.3;
- FUS, weighted sum rule among the texture descriptors. FUS is different in each matrix descriptor since performance of the different texture descriptors varies depending on the matrix from which they were extracted. Nonetheless, the same weights (given a matrix descriptor) are used in all the five datasets. The weighted sum rules are:

---

[3] single(edge(Image));
[4] single(bwmorph(IMMAGINE,'skel',inf));

ID: $5\times$LPQ+$3\times$eBSIF[5]+$3\times$HPOG+$3\times$HOG+$3\times$RIC;

SC: $5\times$LPQ+$3\times$eBSIF+$3\times$HPOG+$3\times$HOG+$3\times$RIC;

HF: $5\times$LPQ+eBSIF+$3\times$HOG;

EI, SI: $5\times$LPQ+eBSIF+$3\times$HOG+$3\times$RIC;

CD: $3\times$LPQ+$3\times$eBSIF+$3\times$HOG.

- FUSw, weighted sum rule among the texture descriptors extracted after wavelet postprocessing: the sum rule is: $4\times$FUS (extracted from the original image) + FUS (extracted from the CA image) + FUS (extracted from the CH image).
- FUSm, weighted sum rule among the texture descriptors extracted after preprocessing the input image by the method proposed in [41], which consists in the application of the closing morphological operator[6], the sum rule is: $5\times$FUS (on the original image) + FUS (on the image after the closing operator).
- FUSmw, the combination of the two previous processing techniques; the sum rule is: $5\times$FUSw + FUSwm (as FUSw but instead of the original image the input is the preprocessed image by morphological operator[7]).
- TXTr, the best ensemble proposed in our previous paper [31] based on texture descriptors (named TXTr in the original paper). Here we report the performance reported in that paper Notice that in [31] only ID, SC and HF were used as matrix descriptors.

Table 2. Performance comparison (bullseyes) among texture descriptors in the MPEG7 database

MPEG7 (Bullseye)		Matrix Descriptors					
		ID	SC	HF	EI	SI	CD
Descriptors	HPOG	71.8	79.1	66.1	---	---	---
	LPQ	75.7	81.2	84.7	71.7	62.7	53.9
	HOG	70.4	81.3	81.5	52.4	41.5	60.6
	RIC	73.4	79.8	71.5	57.1	53.5	37.4
	BSIF	71.8	81.3	83.9	70.6	62.4	67.8
Ensembles	eBSIF	77.9	83.2	85.8	71.0	62.5	74.5
	FUS	81.6	85.4	87.1	72.4	64.4	76.6
	FUSw	82.5	86.1	87.1	71.6	64.1	76.2
	FUSm	83.3	86.7	87.9	72.0	64.6	76.8
	FUSmw	84.0	87.5	88.0	72.1	64.5	76.8
	TXTr[31]	80.4	84.6	86.0	---	---	---

[5] eBSIF is already an ensemble, so eBSIF means: (BSIF(3) + BSIF(5) + BSIF(7) + BSIF(9) + BSIF(11)); where BSIF(k) means bSIF with size filter of k

[6] We select the structuring element as a disk of radius RD, variable according to the image size (using the MATLAB Image Processing Toolbox): RD=15 except for KIMIA where RD=5.

[7] i.e., The wavelet post processing is performed on the preprocessed image

**Table 3. Performance comparison (bullseyes) among texture descriptors
in the TARI database**

TARI (Bullseye)		Matrix Descriptors					
		ID	SC	HF	EI	SI	CD
Descriptors	**HPOG**	76.3	81.5	65.5	---	---	---
	LPQ	81.2	87.0	88.9	68.8	58.4	57.5
	HOG	74.8	85.1	85.6	45.9	35.9	68.5
	RIC	79.2	85.0	75.6	49.3	46.5	39.9
	BSIF	76.6	87.4	88.4	67.1	56.2	70.0
Ensembles	**eBSIF**	83.8	88.6	90.1	67.3	56.1	76.5
	FUS	87.5	89.8	91.6	69.8	60.3	79.6
	FUSw	87.9	90.6	91.5	68.1	59.3	77.4
	FUSm	88.7	90.1	91.6	70.3	61.7	79.6
	FUSmw	88.9	90.7	91.3	68.5	60.8	79.2
	TXTr[31]	85.9	89.1	90.7	---	---	---

**Table 4. Performance comparison (bullseyes) among texture descriptors
in the KIMIA database**

KIMIA (Bullseye)		Matrix Descriptors					
		ID	SC	HF	EI	SI	CD
Descriptors	**HPOG**	73.1	79.9	66.2	---	---	---
	LPQ	78.0	85.0	90.4	81.6	72.4	63.6
	HOG	71.2	84.9	84.0	45.6	25.8	73.0
	RIC	76.4	84.2	71.3	63.5	54.3	53.3
	BSIF	69.2	82.7	90.4	77.3	69.4	69.9
Ensembles	**eBSIF**	78.2	86.7	92.5	78.4	69.9	80.0
	FUS	83.5	88.3	93.2	84.2	75.3	83.0
	FUSw	83.7	89.7	92.5	83.2	74.7	83.3
	FUSm	85.5	88.5	93.3	85.8	78.9	86.4
	FUSmw	86.2	90.5	92.7	84.1	78.0	86.3
	TXTr[31]	82.9	89.1	91.6	---	---	---

Missing values (HPOG) in the previous tables are due to the high computation time and low performance. From the results reported in tables 2-6, the following conclusion can be drawn:

- Combining different descriptors improves the performance with respect to the standalone methods. Our ensembles clearly outperform our previous *TXTr* approach.

**Table 5. Performance comparison (range5) among texture descriptors
in the LEAF database**

LEAF (Range5)		Matrix Descriptors					
		ID	SC	HF	EI	SI	CD
Descriptors	HPOG	72.5	79.5	66.0	---	---	---
	LPQ	85.9	85.9	86.5	71.2	56.4	59.0
	HOG	69.2	83.3	79.5	48.0	32.7	57.1
	RIC	81.4	87.2	75.0	49.4	48.1	48.1
	BSIF	78.9	87.2	83.3	69.9	56.4	68.0
Ensembles	eBSIF	85.9	90.4	83.3	71.2	54.5	68.6
	FUS	85.9	87.8	86.5	70.5	57.1	69.2
	FUSw	86.5	86.5	86.5	69.2	56.4	70.5
	FUSm	88.5	89.1	86.5	69.9	59.6	67.3
	FUSmw	88.5	87.2	87.8	68.6	58.3	69.2
	TXTr[31]	80.1	85.3	87.2	---	---	---

**Table 6. Performance comparison (accuracy) among texture descriptors
in the ANIMAL database**

ANIMAL (Accuracy)		Matrix Descriptors					
		ID	SC	HF	EI	SI	CD
Descriptors	HPOG	60.3	68.6	47.1	---	---	---
	LPQ	62.9	71.9	73.8	61.4	50.1	32.9
	HOG	55.6	69.2	68.2	37.0	25.8	44.0
	RIC	56.6	69.2	53.8	43.4	37.9	18.9
	BSIF	52.3	71.5	68.9	62.9	49.3	48.2
Ensembles	eBSIF	65.4	74.7	74.7	62.0	49.4	55.7
	FUS	70.4	75.7	76.9	60.4	49.9	58.4
	FUSw	71.5	76.2	77.3	58.6	50.1	59.4
	FUSm	71.1	75.4	76.6	61.4	50.4	59.6
	FUSmw	71.9	76.7	76.7	59.4	50.2	59.5
	TXTr[31]	67.5	72.6	74.5	---	---	---

The third experiment compares the performance of the single descriptors tested in this work with their weighted fusion. Differently from the fusion methods tested above, in this experiment we exploit ensembles obtained using different shape descriptors. Before each fusion the scores are normalized to mean 0 and standard deviation 1. The results reported in table 7 are related to the following ensembles:

- SDF1 [30]: is a weighted sum rule of standard descriptors (no texture) [30]: SDF1 = ID+SC+4×HF.
- SDF2 [30]: is another weighted sum rule of standard descriptors (no texture) [30]: SDF2 = 2×ID+SC+2×HF

- TXT[30]:the ensemble of texture descriptors proposed in [30].
- TXTall: the ensemble of texture descriptors tested in [31].
- MT, weighted sum rule fusion among the seven *FUS* method tested in the second experiment (tables 2-6) from the seven matrices obtained by ID, SC, HF, EI, SI, CD with the following weight configuration: {1,1,4,0,0,1} or {1,1,8,1,1,1}. If the first configuration is used, then the method is labelled MT(a) otherwise it is MT(b).
- MTw, weighted sum rule fusion among the seven FUSw method tested in the second experiment (tables 2-6) from the seven matrices obtained by ID, SC, HF, EI, SI, CD with the following weight configuration: {1,1,4,0,0,1} or {1,1,8,1,1,1}. If the first configuration is used, then the method is labelled MTw(a) otherwise it is MTw(b).
- MTmw, weighted sum rule fusion among the seven FUSmw method tested in the second experiment (tables 2-6) from the seven matrices obtained by ID, SC, HF, EI, SI, CD with the following weight configuration: {1,1,4,0,0,1} or {1,1,8,1,1,1}. If the first configuration is used, then the method is labelled MTmw(a) otherwise it is MTmw(b).
- WF1, WF2: the best ensembles proposed in [31], when coupled with morphology the methods are labelled WF1_m and WF2_m.
- OL: the best ensemble proposed in [30].
- SHTX1, proposed ensemble which combines shape and texture, it is the following sum rule: 2×CUtxt + 2×MTmw(b) + 6×SDF2
- SHTX2, proposed ensemble which combines shape and texture, it is the following sum rule: HOG + 2×CUtxt + 2×MTmw(b) + 6×SDF1.

Table 7. Performance comparison among tested methods

		Datasets					Average
		MPEG7	KIMIA	TARI	LEAF	Animal	
	ID	85.0	95.1	95.1	87.2	82.8	89.0
	SC	86.2	96.7	93.7	86.5	81.5	88.9
	HF	89.2	97.1	94.2	87.2	81.2	89.7
	SDF1	89.9	97.8	95.5	89.1	82.5	90.9
	SDF2	89.2	98.0	96.2	87.2	84.1	90.9
	TXT	85.9	90.7	90.8	86.5	76.2	86.0
	TXTall	87.3	91.3	91.9	87.2	76.3	86.8
	MT(a)	87.0	92.1	92.2	89.1	79.6	88.0
Methods	MTw(a)	88.0	91.9	93.1	88.5	79.1	88.1
	MT(b)	87.8	93.9	92.6	87.2	79.9	88.2
	MTw(b)	88.5	93.5	92.9	88.5	79.7	88.6
	MTmw(a)	88.9	93.0	92.8	87.8	79.4	88.3
	MTmw(b)	89.1	93.9	92.5	87.8	81.1	88.9
	WF1	90.9	98.0	95.9	89.7	83.0	91.5
	WF1_m	**91.6**	98.0	95.7	**91.0**	83.1	91.8
	WF2	90.2	98.0	**96.6**	89.1	**84.4**	91.6
	WF2_m	91.0	97.7	96.3	89.1	**84.4**	91.7
	OL	90.2	97.6	95.6	88.5	82.9	90.9
	SHTX1	90.4	98.3	96.5	90.4	84.3	**92.0**
	SHTX2	91.1	**98.6**	95.8	**91.0**	83.7	**92.0**

For comparison purposes the baseline ID, SC, and HF performances are also reported. Notice as well that TXT and TXTall were not tested in their original papers on the Animal dataset, but we ran tests on that dataset here using the original code for those methods.

The results reported in table 7 experimentally confirm that our new methods improve our previous texture-based ensembles (i.e., *TXT* and *TXTall*). We give a statistical confirmation of the advantage of our approach *MTw* and *MTmw* against our previous *TXTall* using the Wilcoxon Signed-Rank test [56], where the null hypothesis (no difference between the performance of *TXTall* and *MTw(a)/MTw(b)/MTmw(a)/ MTmw(b)* is rejected with a level of significance of 0.05.

In table 7 it is clear that that our best ensemble *SHTX2* performs very well across the different datasets with no ad-hoc parameter tuning. The ensemble of texture descriptors clearly outperforms previous ones; however, the complete system based on different descriptors is only slightly better that our previous one (i.e., *SHTX2* only slightly improves *WF1_m*). It is likely that a plateau has been reached; as a result, in future tests new matrix descriptors for improving the diversity among the systems that belong to the ensemble will need to be explored.

4.3. Experiments on BCF

The first experiment on BCF is aimed at comparing the original BCF approach [10] with the variants proposed in this work. Since BCF is a trained approach, the following results have been obtained on each dataset using the same testing protocol of ANIMAL (except for the LEAF dataset as it is already divided into training and testing sets): half the images form the training set and the other half the testing set, with results averaged over ten experiments (as in [10]). The performance reported in table 8 are expressed in terms of accuracy, except for the leaf dataset, where the performance is evaluated using the accuracy among the top five classes (as in the previous test on this dataset). Only results obtained on the ANIMAL/LEAF dataset are directly comparable with those reported in the previous tables, since the results on the other datasets were obtained using different testing protocols (i.e., those specified by the dataset).

The results reported in table 8 are related to different descriptors used to train the BCF approach:

- [10], performance reported in [10] using SC as shape descriptor for creating the codebook and where parameter optimization is performed *for each dataset*:
- Shape descriptors (SC, HF), performance obtained by using our SC or HF for creating codebooks. The original code shared by the authors of the [10] is used for BCF, but using the different descriptors and *without any parameter optimization* performed for each dataset (we use a set of parameters that work well in both the datasets).
- Matrix descriptors (SC, HF), matrix descriptors SC or HF are coupled to texture descriptors (as in the previous tests) for describing a shape; these features are then used for creating codebooks.
- Ensemble descriptors (based on SC or HF), with performance obtained by fusing different BCF approaches (all related to the same shape descriptors, i.e., SC or HF):

o FUS$_{sd}$ is the weighted sum rule of results obtained by sd descriptor, $sd \in \{$SC, HF$\}$:

   ▪ FUS$_{SC}$= 15×HOG+eBSIF[5];

   ▪ FUS$_{HF}$= 3×LPQ+3×eBSIF+3×HOG+3×RIC;

o FUSw$_{sd}$, $sd \in \{$SC, HF$\}$ is the weighted sum rule weighted sum rule among the texture descriptors extracted after wavelet postprocessing, i.e., 2× FUS$_{sd}$(extracted from the original image) + FUS$_{sd}$ (extracted from the wavelet CA band) + FUS$_{sd}$ (extracted from the wavelet CH image);

o FULL$_{sd}$, is the weighted sum rule between FUSw$_{sd}$and the sd descriptor ($sd \in \{$SC, HF$\}$):

   ▪ FULL$_{SC}$= FUSw$_{SC}$ + SC;

   ▪ FULL$_{HF}$ = FUSw$_{HF}$ + 0.25×HF;

The results displayed in table 8 show the usefulness of combining different descriptors extracted in different ways. Our best variants outperform, without any ad hoc dataset tuning, the original BCF approach ([10]).

An interesting behavior occurs in these tests, HF works poorly but the texture descriptor extracted from the matrix obtained from HF obtained very good results.

Table 8. Classification accuracy obtained by BCF method coupled with different descriptors (SD=shape descriptor)

BCF (accuracy)			Datasets				
			MPEG7	TARI	KIMIA	LEAF	ANIMAL
[10]		SC	97.1	-	-	-	83.4
SD		SC	96.4	98.6	100	84.0	79.6
		HF	91.9	95.0	98.0	69.2	66.4
Matrix Descriptors	SC	LPQ	93.1	96.4	100	73.1	73.5
		HOG	96.4	98.6	100	85.3	79.2
		RIC	91.0	92.4	93.9	67.3	65.0
		BSIF	94.0	95.2	98.0	71.2	69.3
		eBSIF	94.7	97.0	98.0	76.3	78.0
	HF	LPQ	96.7	97.8	100	87.8	82.6
		HOG	96.1	94.8	100	77.6	78.0
		RIC	94.4	95.6	100	83.3	71.8
		BSIF	96.7	99.0	100	87.8	83.1
		eBSIF	97.7	99.0	100	89.1	85.7
Ensembles	SC	FUS$_{SC}$	97.1	98.4	100	86.5	82.1
		FUSw$_{SC}$	97.4	98.8	100	86.5	81.8
		FULL$_{SC}$	97.3	98.8	100	88.5	82.0
	HF	FUS$_{HF}$	97.7	99.0	100	90.4	87.0
		FUSw$_{HF}$	97.7	99.4	100	90.4	87.0
		FULL$_{HF}$	97.7	99.0	100	91.0	84.7

As a final result obtained using the above testing protocol, a global fusion involving different shape descriptors is evaluated using the following:

- GF(w): the weighted sum rule among $FULL_{SC}$ + $w \times$ $FUSw_{HF}$;
- SHTX2: our final ensemble described in section 4.2 (results are different from table 7 because of the change in the testing protocol[8]);
- SHTX2 +GF(w): fusion between SHTX2 and the BCF ensemble.

It is clear that the proposed ensemble improves performance even further. We want to stress that using the proposed ensemble nearly 100% accuracy is obtained on both the MPEG and TARI datasets.

Table 9. Classification accuracy obtained by several ensemble approaches

	Accuracy	Datasets				
		MPEG7	TARI	KIMIA	LEAF	ANIMAL
Ensembles	GF(1)	98.4	99.2	100	90.4	85.9
	GF(3)	97.7	99.4	100	91.7	87.0
	SHTX2	99.1	99.0	100	91.0	83.7
	SHTX2 + GF(3)	99.6	99.6	100	92.3	87.2

4.4. Comparison with the Literature

In table 10 several state-of-the-art approaches are compared on the KIMIA dataset. According to [34], performance in KIMIA is measured counting the number of shapes of the correct class retrieved in a fixed rank position. Since the number of samples in KIMIA is 99, a value of 99 means that all shapes are correctly classified. The last column in table 10 reports the average number of correct matching in the first 10 rank positions.

From the results in table 10, it is evident that our ensemble competes very well with state-of-the-art approaches. In our opinion, further improvement of our best approach could be gained using new ad hoc texture descriptors (this hypothesis will form the starting point for future research).

Finally, in Table 11 a summary comparison on MPEG7, TARI and ANIMAL datasets is reported for several state-of-the-art approaches. The performances are compared in terms of the bull's-eye testing protocol or standard accuracy (on the ANIMAL dataset). This comparison shows the usefulness of the proposed ensemble. It is not our intention here to include the results of all papers reporting a performance on the datasets examined in this work, but only the best results published over the years. If we examine the tables in [10] and [11], it is clear that our proposed approach outperforms several other recent systems not compared in this paper. Moreover, please refer to the website http://www.dabi.temple.edu/~shape/MPEG7/results.html for a public report on systems tested using the MPEG7 database.

---

[8] Each shape of the test set is matched against each shape of the training set, the similarity of a given test shape to each class is given by the minimum distance of that shape with the training shapes of that class

Table 10. Performance comparison with the state-of-the-art approaches in the KIMIA dataset

Approach	Year	Accuracy										
		1st	2nd	3rd	4th	5th	6th	7th	8th	9th	10th	Average
SC [34]	2002	97	91	88	85	84	77	75	66	56	37	75.6
Generative Model [57]	2004	99	97	99	98	96	96	94	83	75	48	88.5
ID [58]	2007	99	99	99	98	98	97	97	98	94	79	95.8
Symbolic [59]	2008	99	99	99	98	99	98	98	95	96	94	97.5
HF [9]	2011	99	99	99	99	98	99	99	96	95	88	97.1
OL [30]	2012	99	97	97	96	96	96	96	96	94	73	94.0
WF1 [31]	2012	98	97	97	96	98	95	97	97	96	86	95.7
SC [34]	2012	99	99	99	98	98	97	98	95	95	83	96.1
Generative Model [57]	2012	99	99	99	98	98	99	98	98	92	86	96.6
ID [58]	2014	99	99	99	98	99	98	99	98	92	89	97.0
SHTX2 [here]	2015	99	99	99	98	99	98	99	98	96	91	97.6

Table 11. Performance comparison with the state-of-the-art (without considering context based algorithms) in the MPEG7, Animal and Tari datasets

Dataset	Approach	Year	Perfformance
MPEG7	SC [34]	2002	76.51%
	Generative Model [57]	2004	80.03%
	ID [58]	2007	85.40%
	ID+EMD [60]	2007	86.56%
	Symbolic [59]	2008	85.92%
	AIR [29]	2010	93.6%
	HF [9]	2011	90.35%
	[30]	2012	90.24%
	WF1_m [31]	2014	91.6%
	SHTX2 [here]	2015	91.1%
TARI	SC[34]	2002	94.17%
	ID[58]	2007	95.33%
	ASC [23]	2010	95.44%
	[30]	2012	96.06%
	WF1_m [31]	2014	95.7%
	SHTX2 [here]	2015	95.8%
ANIMAL	[10]	2014	83.4%
	WF1_m [31]	2014	83.1%
	Bi-gram [11]	2015	83.5%
	Final [11]	2015	86.0%
	GF3 [Here]	2015	87.0%
	SHTX2 + GF(3) [Here]	2015	87.2%

Notice that some methods reported in table 11 optimize the parameters of their approach separately on each dataset. Because we use always use the same set of parameters on all five of these large datasets, we are confident that our proposed approach could be used on different shape classification problems with almost no tuning.

Conclusion

In this paper we perform experiments to develop an ensemble that works well on different shape datasets without any ad hoc dataset tuning. We propose a general-purpose ensemble based on a weighted sum rule for combining standard shape matchers and approaches that are based on features extracted by texture descriptors. These new feature sets are compared using the Jeffrey distance. The experimental results confirm that our new ensemble of texture descriptors clearly improve our previous texture-based ensembles. Finally, we proposed an ensemble of different shape descriptors combined by weighted sum rule (using the same weights across all tested datasets to avoid overfitting). Our proposed methods were tested across five benchmark databases: *MPEG7 CE-Shape-1*, *Kimia*, *Tari*, *Animal shape* and the *Leaf Database*. The experimental results demonstrate that our proposed approach provides significant improvements over baseline shape matching algorithms.

The texture descriptors based approach is also coupled with the BCF method, also in this test a considerable performance improvement (respect the original method) is gained.

The Matlab code of our tests will be freely available at https://www.dei.unipd.it/node/2357.

In the future we plan to study different matrix descriptors on this problem, as well as methods for combining different distances.

References

[1]   Veltkamp, R.C. and M. Hagedoorn, State of the Art in Shape Matching. *Principles of Visual Information Retrieval*, 2001: p. 89-119.

[2]   Mokhtarian, F., S. Abbasi, and J. Kittler, Efficient and robust retrieval by shape content through curvature scale space, in Image Databases and Multi-Media Search, A.W.M. Smeulders and R. Jain, Editors. 1997, World Scientific Publishing Co. Pte. Ltd.: Singapore. p. 51-58.

[3]   Attalia, E. and P. Siy, Robust shape similarity retrieval based on contor segmentation polygonal multiresolution and elastic matching. *Pattern Recognition*, 2005. 38(12): p. 2229-2241.

[4]   Shu, X. and X.-J. Wu, A novel contor descriptor for 2D shape matching and its application to image retrieval, *Image and Vision Computing*, 2011. 29(4): p. 286-294.

[5]   Hu, R.-X., et al., Angular Pattern and Binary Angular Pattern for Shape Retrieval. *IEEE Transactions on Image Processing*, 2014. 23(3): p. 1118-1127.

[6]   Latecki, L.J. and R. Lakamper, Shape similarity measure based on correspondence of visual parts. *IEEE Transactions on Pattern Analysis and Machine Intelligence*, 2000. 22(10): p. 1185-1190.

[7]   Ling, H. and D.W. Jacobs, Shape classification using the inner-distance. *IEEE Transactions on Pattern Analysis and Machine Intelligence*, 2007. 29(2): p. 286-299.

[8]   McNeill, G. and S. Vijayakumar, Hierarchical procrustes matching for shape retrieval, in *IEEE Computer Society Conference on Computer Vision and Pattern Recognition* (CVPR). 2006: New York City. p. 885-894.

[9]   Wang, J., et al., Shape matching and classification using height functions. *Pattern Recognition Letters*, 2012. 33(2).

[10] Wang, X., et al., Bag of contour fragments for robust shape classification, *Pattern Recognition*, 2014. 47(6): p. 2116-2125.

[11] Ramesh, B., C. Xiang, and T.H. Lee, Shape classification using invariant features and contextual information in the bag-of-words model. *Pattern Recognition,* 2015. 48(3): p. 894-906.

[12] Bai, X., et al., Learning context-sensitive shape similarity by graph transduction. *IEEE Transactions on Pattern Analysis and Machine Intelligence*, 2010. 32(5): p. 861-874.

[13] Sebastian, T.B., P.N. Klein, and B.B. Kimia, Recognition of shapes by editing their shock graphs. *IEEE Transactions on Pattern Analysis and Machine Intelligence*, 2004. 26(5): p. 550-571.

[14] Siddiqi, K., et al., Shock graphs and shape matching. International *Journal of Computer Vision*, 1999. 35(1): p. 13-32.

[15] Shokoufandeh, A., et al., Indexing hierarchical structures using graph spectra. *IEEE Transactions on Pattern Analysis and Machine Intelligence,* 2005. 27(7): p. 1125-1140.

[16] Gorelick, L., et al., Shape representation and classification using the poisson equation. *IEEE Transactions on Pattern Analysis and Machine Intelligence,* 2006. 28(12): p. 1991-2005.

[17] Bookstein, F.L., Morphometric tools for landmark data: Geometry and biology. 1991: Cambridge University Press.

[18] Kendall, D., Shape manifolds, procrustean metrics and comples projective spaces. *Bulletin of London Mathematical Society*, 1984. 16: p. 81-121.

[19] Hu, R.X., et al., Perceptually motivated morphological strategies for shape retrieval. *Pattern Recognition*, 2012. 45(9): p. 3222-3230.

[20] Xie, J., P. Heng, and M. Shah, Shape matching and modeling using skeletal context. *Pattern Recognition*, 2008. 41(5): p. 1756-1767.

[21] Kontschieder, P., M. Donoser, and H. Bischof, Beyond pairwise shape similarity analysis, in *9th Asian Conference on Computer Vision*. 2010, Springer: Xi'an, China. p. 655-666.

[22] Premachandran, V. and R. Kakarala, Perceptually motivated shape context which uses shape interiors. *Pattern Recognition*, 2013. 46(8): p. 2092-2102.

[23] Ling, H., X. Yang, and L. Latecki, Balancing deformability and discriminability for shape matching, in LNCS: ECCV 2012, K. Daniilidis, P. Maragos, and N. Paragios, Editors. 2010, Springer-Verlag: Berlin, Heidelberg. p. 411-424.

[24] Temlyakov, A., et al., Two perceptually motivated strategies for shape classification, in CVPR. 2010, *IEEE: San Francisco*, CA. p. 2289-2296.

[25] Bai, X., et al., Co-transduction for shape retrieval. *IEEE Transactions on Image Processing,* 2012. 21(5): p. 2747-2757.

[26] Yang, X., L. Prasad, and L.J. Latecki, Affinity learning with diffusion on tensor product graph. *IEEE Transactions on Pattern Analysis and Machine Intelligence,* 2013. 35(1): p. 28-38.

[27] Yang, X., S. Köknar-Tezel, and L.J. Latecki, Locally constrained diffusion process on locally densified distance spaces with applications to shape retrieval, in *CVPR 2009*. 2009.

[28] Donoser, M. and H. Bischof, Diffusion processes for retrieval revisited, in Conference on Computer Vision and Pattern Recognition (CVPR). 2013: Portland, OR. p. 1320-1327.

[29] Gopalan, R., P.K. Turaga, and R. Chellappa, Articulation-invariant representation of non-planar shapes, in *ECCV* 2010. 2010. p. 286-299.

[30] Nanni, L., S. Brahnam, and A. Lumini, Local phase quantization descriptor for improving shape retrieval/classification. *PatternRecognition Letters*, 2012. 33(16): p. 2254-2260.

[31] Nanni, L., A. Lumini, and S. Brahnam, Ensemble of shape descriptors for shape retrieval and classification. *International Journal of Advanced Intelligence Paradigms*, 2014. 6(2): p. 136-156.

[32] Cormen, T.H., et al., *Introduction to algorithms*. 2 ed. 2001, Cambridge: The MIT Press.

[33] Kimia, B.B., A.R. Tannenbaum, and S.W. Zucker, Shapes, shocks, and deformations, I: The components of shape and the reaction-diffusion space. *International Journal of Computer Vision*, 1995. 15(3): p. 189-224.

[34] Belongie, S., J. Malik, and J. Puzicha, Shape matching and object recongtiion using shape contexts. *IEEE Transactions on Pattern Analysisand Machine Intelligence*, 2002. 24(24): p. 509-522.

[35] Elder, J.H., et al., On growth and formlets: Sparse multi-scale coding of planar shape. *Image and Vision Computing*, 2013. 31: p. 1-13.

[36] Dominio, F., M. Donadeo, and P. Zanuttigh, Depth gives a hand to gesture recognition. *Pattern Recognition Letters*, submitted 2013.

[37] Loy, G. and A. Zelinsky, Fast radial symmetry for detecting points of interest. *Ieee Transactions On Pattern Analysis And Machine Intelligence*, 2003. 25(8): p. 959-973.

[38] Konukoglu, E., et al., Wesd-weighted spectral distance for measuring shape dissimilarity. *CoRR,* 2012. abs/1208.5016.

[39] Kurtek, S., et al., Elastic geodesic paths in shape space of parameterized surfaces. *IEEE Transactions on Pattern Analysis and Machine Intelligence,* 2012. 34(9): p. 1717-1730.

[40] Kurtek, S., et al., A novel riemannian framework for shape analysis of 3D objects, in *IEEE Conference on Computer Vision and Pattern Recognition.* 2010. p. 1717-1730.

[41] Latecki, L.J. and R. Lakämper, Convexity rule for shape decomposition based on discrete contour evolution *Computer Vision and Image Understanding,* 1999. 73(3): p. 441-454.

[42] Wang, J., et al., Locality-constrained linear coding for image classification, in *Computer Vision and Pattern Recognition* (CVPR). 2010.

[43] Ojansivu, V. and J. Heikkila, Blur insensitive texture classification using local phase quantization, in *ICISP*. 2008. p. 236–243.

[44] Nanni, L., S. Brahnam, and A. Lumini, Matrix representation in pattern classification. *Expert Systems with Applications*, In Press.

[45] Dalal, N. and B. Triggs, Histograms of oriented gradients for human detection, in *9th European Conference on Computer Vision*. 2005: San Diego, CA.

[46] Song, F., et al., Eyes closeness detection from still images with multi-scale histograms of principal oriented gradients. *Pattern Recognition*, 2014. 47: p. 2825-2838.

[47] Nosaka, R., C.H. Suryanto, and K. Fukui, Rotation invariant co-occurrence among adjacent LBPs, in *ACCV Workshops*. 2012. p. 15-25.

[48] Mallat, S., A theory for multiresolution signal decomposition. *IEEE Transactions on Pattern Analysis and Machine Intelligence*, 1989. 11: p. 674–693.

[49] Daubechies, I., Orthonormal bases of compactly supported wavelets. *Communications on Pure Applied Mathematics*, 1988. 41: p. 909-996.

[50] Liu, H., et al., Comparing dissimilarity measures for content-based image retrieval in Information Retrieval Technology: *4th Asia Information Retrieval Sympsium, AIRS* 2008, H. Li, et al., Editors. 2008, Springer-Verlag: Harbin, China. p. 44-50.

[51] Latecki, L.J., R. Lakamper, and U. Eckhardt, Shape descriptors for non-rigid shapes with a single closed contour, in *IEEE Conference on Computer Visions and Pattern Recognition*. 2000. p. 424-429.

[52] Aslan, C., et al., Disconnected skeleton: Shape at its absolute scale. *IEEE Transactions on Pattern Analysis and Machine Intelligence*, 2008. 30(12): p. 2188-2203.

[53] Söderkvist, O., *Computer vision classification of leaves from swedish trees*. 2001, Linköping University.

[54] Bai, X., W. Liu, and Z. Tu, Integrating contour and skeleton for shape classification, in *IEEE 12th International Conference on Computer Vision Workshops (ICCV Workshops)*. 2009. p. 360-367.

[55] Sharvit, D., et al., Symmetry-based indexing of image database. *Journal of Visual Communication and Image Representation,* 1998. 9(4): p. 366-380.

[56] Demšar, J., Statistical comparisons of classifiers over multiple data sets. *Journal of Machine Learning Research*, 2006. 7 p. 1-30.

[57] Tu, Z. and A.L. Yuille, Shape matching and recognition using generative models and informative features, in *European Conference on Computer Vision* (ECCV04). 2004: Prague. p. 195-209.

[58] Ling, H. and D. Jacobs, Shape Classification Using the Inner-Distance. *IEEE Transactions on Pattern Analysis and Machine Intelligence*, 2007. 29(2): p. 286-299.

[59] Daliri, M.R. and V. Torre, Robust symbolic representation for shape recognition and retrieval. *Pattern Recognition Letters*, 2008. 41(5): p. 1782-1798.

[60] Ling, H. and K. Okada, An efficient earth mover's distance algorithm for robust histogram comparison. *IEEE Transactions on Pattern Analysis and Machine Intelligence*, 2007. 29(5): p. 840-853.

[61] Kannala J. and Rahtu E.. Bsif: binarized statistical image features. In *Proc. 21st International Conference on Pattern Recognition* (ICPR 2012), Tsukuba, Japan, pages 1363–1366, 2012. 1.

In: Horizons in Computer Science Research. Volume 11   ISBN: 978-1-63482-499-6
Editor: Thomas S. Clary, pp. 33-61

Chapter 2

METAHEURISTICS FOR CURVE AND SURFACE RECONSTRUCTION

Andrés Iglesias[1,2,*]*and Akemi Gálvez*[1,†]
[1]Department of Applied Mathematics and Computational Sciences
E.T.S.I. Caminos, Canales y Puertos, University of Cantabria
Avenida de los Castros, s/n, 39005, Santander, SPAIN
[2]Department of Information Science, Faculty of Sciences
Toho University, 2-2-1, Miyama, Funabashi, JAPAN

Abstract

The accurate reconstruction of curves and surfaces is a major problem in many theoretical and applied fields, ranging from approximation theory for numerical analysis and statistics to computer-aided design and manufacturing (CAD/CAM), virtual reality, medical imaging, and many others. Most of currently-used methodologies in the field are based on the application of traditional mathematical optimization techniques. However, such methods are still pretty limited and cannot be successfully applied to this problem in all its generality. As a consequence, researchers have turned their attention to artificial intelligence and other modern optimization techniques, such as metaheuristics. By metaheuristics we refer to a set of very diverse computational methods for optimization aimed to obtain the optimum by successive iterations of a given population of candidate solutions that evolve according to some kind of quality metric (the fitness function). In this chapter, we provide the reader with a gentle, comprehensive overview on the field of curve/surface reconstruction by using metaheuristic techniques. The chapter will describe the main methodologies applied so far to tackle this issue, along with the analysis of their major advantages and limitations. The chapter also shows some examples of the application of this exciting technology to some practical problems of interest in industrial and applied settings. We also outline some hints about the most recent trends in the field along with some exciting future lines of research. Finally, an updated bibliography on the field is also provided.

Keywords: curve reconstruction, surface reconstruction, artificial intelligence, metaheuristics, geometric modeling

AMS Subject Classification: 65D, 65K, 68T05, 68U, 68W25, 90C.

---

*E-mail address: iglesias@unican.es; Web site: http://personales.unican.es/iglesias
†E-mail address: galveza@unican.es

1. Introduction

The problem of recovering the shape of a curve or a surface, also known as curve (respectively surface) reconstruction, is one of the most difficult and challenging "unsolved" problems in geometric modeling during the last two decades. In this chapter, when we talk about the issue of curve (surface) reconstruction we refer to the following problem: given a collection of (possibly noisy) data points in 2D or 3D, how to compute a parametric curve (surface) that "follows" the shape of these data points. Depending on the nature of these data points, two different approaches can be employed for this problem: *interpolation* and *approximation*. In the former, a parametric curve or surface is constrained to pass through all input data points. This approach is typically employed for sets of data points that come from smooth shapes and that are sufficiently accurate. On the contrary, approximation does not require the fitting curve or surface to pass through all input data points, but just close to them, according to some prescribed distance criteria. The approximation scheme is particularly well suited for the cases of highly irregular sampling and when data points are not exact, but subjected to measurement errors. In real-world problems the data points are usually acquired through laser scanning and other digitizing devices and are, therefore, subjected to some measurement noise, irregular sampling, and other artifacts [119, 122]. Consequently, a good fitting of data should be generally based on approximation schemes rather than on interpolation [98, 107, 118, 142].

This curve/surface reconstruction problem has received much attention during the last few decades. One of the main reasons to explain such interest is the wide range of applicability of this problem in many theoretical and applied domains (see our discussion in Section 2 below). In fact, this issue has been considered a very hot topic in research for almost 50 years. It is also a very elusive and challenging problem. In spite of the intensive research effort carried out since the first theoretical developments in the 50s and 60s, the problem is still far from being solved in all its generality. There are two main reasons to explain this situation:

- on one hand, the problem can be formulated in many different ways, according to the specific criteria used for classification. For instance, the problem has been addressed in completely different ways depending on the input of the problem (cross-sections, clouds of points, iso-parametric curves, mixed information, etc), the geometric structures used for representation (polygonal meshes, solid primitives, parametric curves and surfaces), the mathematical approach employed (interpolation, approximation), the mathematical constraints (if any), and many other factors. In other words, there is no universal solution for this issue, as different conditions require different approaches to this problem. So instead of a *"for all"* single method, we are facing a myriad of specialized methods to deal with.

- on the other hand, most of the techniques developed so far to solve this problem have been usually based on the application of traditional mathematical optimization techniques. Although they are still very powerful and able to cope many different situations, the particular conditions of this problem (noisy data, little or no information about the problem, no continuity or differentiability of objective function ensured) limit the applicability of such techniques in this particular field. Furthermore, it has been shown during the last two decades that such methods cannot be successfully applied to solve very difficult nonlinear continuous optimization problems. In particular, they fail to solve the curve/surface reconstruction problem with free-form parametric fitting functions such as Bézier, B-splines and NURBS, by far the most common geometric entities in industrial and applied domains.

Owing to these critical limitations, the scientific community in the field have turned their attention to artificial intelligence and other modern optimization techniques, such as metaheuristics. By metaheuristics we refer to a high-level procedure or strategy designed to help a low-level search strategy or heuristic so that it can find a good solution to an optimization problem, usually under challenging conditions such as little or incomplete information about the problem to be solved or strong constraints regarding the computational resources [29, 60, 92, 111, 155, 156]. Although the field of metaheuristics is very diverse and we can find many different strategies under its umbrella, a common factor is that they do make few (or none) assumptions about the problem to be solved. This means they are very general and can be applied to many different problems with only minor modifications (if any). The counterpart for this exuberance of applications is the fact that they do not guarantee to reach a global optimum solution. Most metaheuristic methods aim to obtain the optimum by successive iterations of a given population of candidate solutions that evolve according to some kind of quality metric (the fitness function). Classical examples of this strategy are ant colony optimization (ACO), genetic algorithms (GA), particle swarm optimization (PSO), artificial bee colony (ABC), firefly algorithm (FFA), and many others [73, 91, 93, 153, 154]. In other cases, the method considers only one individual, which is modified along the iterations seeking to improve the solution. Typical examples of this single-population approach are simulated annealing, iterated local search, variable neighborhood search, and guided local search. Finally, metaheuristics can be combined with other local/global search methods or procedures to yield hybrid metaheuristics, including memetic approaches, where individual learning or local improvement search is combined with a global metaheuristics for further improvement.

There are four main reasons that explain why it is advisable to apply metaheuristic techniques to solve the curve/surface reconstruction problem:

1. *they can be used even when we have very little information about the problem.* Many alternative methods can only be applied to academic examples whose data have some kind of topological or geometric structure. This does not happen, however, in real-world reverse engineering applications, where typically little or no information about the problem is known beyond the data points.

2. *their objective function does not need to be continuous or differentiable.* In fact, metaheuristics have shown to be able to deal with optimization problems whose underlying function is non-differentiable (even non-continuous).

3. *they can be successfully applied to multimodal and multivariate nonlinear optimization problems.* Metaheuristic techniques are able to find optimal solutions to nonlinear optimization problems in high-dimensional search spaces. Curve and surface reconstruction are two of such problems. Moreover, due to the (potential) existence

of many local optima of the least-squares objective function, it is also a multimodal problem. Metaheuristic techniques are also well suited for multimodal problems.

4. *they can deal with noisy data*. This is a very important issue in many real-world applications. For instance, laser scanner systems yield an enormous amount of irregular data points. They are also known to be less accurate than their contact-based counterparts [85]. As a consequence, reconstruction methods must be robust against this measurement noise.

1.1. Aims and Structure of this Chapter

In this chapter, we provide the reader with a gentle, comprehensive overview on the field of curve/surface reconstruction by using metaheuristic techniques. The chapter will describe the main methodologies applied so far to tackle this issue, along with the analysis of their major advantages and limitations. The chapter also shows some examples of the application of this exciting technology to some practical problems of interest in industrial and applied settings. We also outline some hints about the most recent trends in the field along with some exciting future lines of research. Finally, an updated bibliography on the field with more than 150 entries is also provided.

The structure of this chapter is as follows: in Section 2 we describes some interesting applications of the reconstruction of curves and surfaces to different theoretical and applied fields. Section 3 is devoted to curve reconstruction. We start our discussion stating the problem we are dealing with in Section 3.1, then previous work in the field is described in Section 3.2, and finally the metaheuristic methods for curve reconstruction are described in Section 3.3. The same structure is kept in Section 4 for the field of surface reconstruction. Finally, Section 5 provides the reader with some emerging trends and future lines of research for curve and surface reconstruction.

2. Motivation

As stated in previous section, the curve/surface reconstruction problem is a classical problem in many different fields. In this section, we summarize some of the most relevant applications of this subject in both theoretical and applied domains. The list is by no means exhaustive, but it still provides our readers with a gentle overview about a number of interesting applications.

2.1. Theoretical Fields

Numerical and functional analysis: Curve and surface reconstruction is a key technique in approximation theory, a major topic in numerical and functional analysis [13, 35, 36, 37, 61, 72, 106, 107]. *Spline interpolation* is an issue of particular importance because it yields similar results to polynomial interpolation but does not require high degree polynomials thus avoiding the instability associated with Runge's phenomenon [131, 132]. Spline functions are also very flexible and simple enough, so they are usually preferred over canonical polynomial functions for data interpolation. Spline functions are also widely used in data approximation, as their flexibility make them an excellent tool to capture the underlying shape and structure of noisy data [6, 12, 23, 79, 80, 149].

Statistics and machine learning: Curve and surface reconstruction with splines is a major procedure in *data fitting* and *regression* [22, 24, 25, 98, 102, 104, 112], as they are more stable than other fitting functions. Besides, some splines can perform very well for these tasks even for low-degree polynomial fitting functions, particularly when piecewise functions are involved. This ability to tune the degree of the fitting functions is essential to prevent overfitting in statistical and machine learning predictive models and to minimize the number of free parameters of the model [26, 65]. Finally, it is a key ingredient for other problems such as *smoothing*, *filtering*, *nonparametric regression*, and many others [27, 79, 81, 83].

2.2. Applied Fields

Most applications of curve/surface reconstruction in industrial and applied settings are associated with a process commonly known as *reverse engineering*. While conventional engineering transforms engineering concepts and models into real parts, reverse engineering represents the other side of the process. In reverse engineering real parts are transformed backward into engineering models and concepts, typically stored in digital form. Some relevant examples include:

Medical imaging: two typical problems in medical imaging are to construct a curve (or collection of curves) from data points and to obtain the external surface of a 3D object from a set of cross-sections of that object. For instance, authors in [4, 5, 87, 103, 110, 116] address the problem of obtaining a surface model from a set of given cross-sections. The starting point is a dense cloud of data points of the surface of a volumetric object (an internal organ, for instance) acquired by means of noninvasive techniques such as computer tomography, magnetic resonance imaging, or ultrasound imaging. The primary goal in these cases is to obtain a sequence of cross-sections of the object in order to construct the surface passing through them, a process called *surface skinning*. In other cases, the input is directly a sequence of 2D cross-sections or thin layers. Then, the reconstruction method aims to generate an accurate *volumetric representation* of the surface of the object to be displayed for diagnosis and other medical purposes. Other classical input data include iso-parametric curves on the surface [63] and even mixed information, such as scattered points and contours [3, 9, 108, 136] or iso-parametric curves and data points [81, 82].

Biomedical engineering: The use of reverse engineering techniques is very common in biomedical engineering for the design and manufacturing of prosthesis of different types. Other typical problem is the generation of customized medical implants, where the basis geometric is acquired from the real model by using some digitizing devices and/or medical imaging. These orthopedic implants are designed to replace a missing joint or bone or as a supporting element of a damaged rigid body structure. In some instances, the reconstruction techniques in this field make use not only of parametric functions but also of implicit functions [103, 110, 116, 136, 138].

Automotive, aerospace and ship hull building industries: In automotive, aerospace, and ship hull building industries it is common to build prototypes in a real workshop as part of the initial design process [141, 142]. Those prototypes, usually made with materials such as foam, clay, wood, metal or plastics, help the designers to explore conceptual ideas for shape, size, proportions, and the human sense of interacting with the model. The resulting model is digitally stored through data sampling by means of technologies such as 3D laser scanning. Data points can readily be manipulated by computer and then converted into digital models, generally described in terms of mathematical curves and surfaces [65, 66, 119, 122]. Advantages of this process are obvious: digital models are easier and cheaper to modify and analyze than the physical counterparts. In addition, digital data are very well suited for efficient storage and transmission among providers and manufacturers and can still be used even when the real objects are lost or become unavailable. Classical examples include turbine blades, airplane wings, car body parts, boat parts, and many others.

Computer design and manufacturing (CAD/CAM): Surface reconstruction is also used to improve some CAD/CAM processes [23, 31, 45, 49, 67, 119, 141, 146] such as the determination of trajectories for *tool-path generation* in *computer-numerically-controlled* (CNC) operations such as *milling* and *machining* and other manufacturing-related processes (*filing*, *turning*, *grinding*, etc). Curve and surface reconstruction is also involved in variational analysis for *fairing* and *smoothing* [64, 68, 77, 89].

Rapid prototyping and rapid manufacturing: the application of curve/surface reconstruction techniques for *rapid prototyping* (the generation of scale models of physical parts from CAD data) is becoming increasingly popular during the last few years [7, 119, 122, 141]. A major reason of this popularity is the quick availability of very efficient methods for generating physical prototypes, particularly *3D printing* and *additive layer manufacturing* technology. In such technologies, successive layers of material are laid down until the entire object is created. Each of these layers can be seen as a very thin horizontal cross-section of the eventual object. Printing of such layers is performed through different methods such as selective laser sintering (SLS), fused deposition modeling (FDM), and stereolithography (SLA). 3D printing is also used for *rapid manufacturing*, where 3D printers are used to produce the actual end user products rather than merely prototypes. This is an emerging field nowadays, particularly regarding the mass customization of personal goods.

Metrology and product assessment: reverse engineering is widely used for metrology purposes (measurement of physical properties of a manufactured product). Classical technologies in this field are *coordinate-measuring machines*, *laser scanners*, *structured light digitizers*, or *industrial computer tomography scanners* [122, 141, 142]. Other uses involve the creation of digital models of manufactured goods, the assessment of competitors' products and identification of possible patent or copyright infringement. The range of applications can even go to microscopic sizes. For instance, the paper in [95] reports an interesting application of a genetic algorithm for the reconstruction of 3D surface topography in scanning electron microscopy.

Computer animation and computer-generated movies: Curve/surface reconstruction methods are an essential ingredient of modern computer animation techniques for computer-generated movies and video games. A typical example of application are the motion capture (*mo-cap*) systems where movements of real actors are recorded through sensors and the resulting information is used to animate digital characters by computer by using sophisticated computer animation techniques. In this regard, curve reconstruction is used to generate the trajectories of individual parts of the character through inverse kinematics, a process that interpolates the positions of joints at specifically selected frames (keyframes) to generate the frames in between, a process usually called *keyframing*, *inbetweening*, or *tweeing*. On the other hand, surface reconstruction is applied to generate the 3D model of the digital character. Curve reconstruction techniques are also used to generate paths for the digital characters moving in a virtual environment for computer movies and video games, and to determine trajectories for *camera walkthrough* rendering in computer animation and scientific visualization, a technique in which a predefined walkthrough animation of a scene is obtained by placing the camera on a path according to a prescribed trajectory or procedural sequence. Also, curve reconstruction techniques appear in animation approximation, a field that aims to compactly represent an animation sequence (such as mesh animations or skeletal animations) through non-uniform B-splines, taking advantage of the temporal coherence of the animation data [114].

Geometric modeling and processing: curve/surface reconstruction methods are at the core of many processes in geometric modeling and processing [2, 18, 19, 31, 78, 89]. Approaches in these fields have typically relied on polygonal meshes, for which very powerful, advanced techniques have been developed [28, 75, 76]. More recently, schemes based on solid geometry [99, 148] and mathematical curves and surfaces have also been developed [41, 46, 58, 62, 84, 117, 118, 133, 152, 157, 158, 161].

Archeology and digital heritage: A major step in this area was given by the ambitious "Digital Michelangelo" project [100]. Carried out in 1998-99 by a team of 30 faculty, staff, and students from Stanford University and the University of Washington who spent one year in Italy scanning the sculptures and architecture of Michelangelo, it represented the starting point for a number of similar projects aimed at applying shape reconstruction for the digital representation, storage, and analysis of historical and cultural artifacts. The project received a lot of attention not only from the scientific community but also from mass media, and contributed significantly to the popularization of the application of these techniques to archeology and digital heritage. The field has also benefited from the popularization and miniaturization of affordable handheld laser scanners and portable coordinate-measuring machines, which have assisted the archeologists in capturing the shape and details of engravings of historical objects and artifacts. In addition, the use of photogrammetry techniques have revealed to be very useful in capturing the geometry of historical buildings. Also, LIDAR technology is widely used to create high-resolution digital elevation models (DEMs) of archaeological sites that help archeologists to discover micro-topography hidden by vegetation and/or additional natural or artificial actions. The combination of this technology with Geographical Information Systems (GIS) have proved to be capital for the analysis, interpretation and documentation of historical heritage and its preservation for future generations [15, 16, 17].

3. Curve Reconstruction

3.1. Statement of the Problem

The problem of curve reconstruction can be stated as follows: given a collection of (possibly noisy) data points $\{\mathbf{Q}_j\}_{j=1,...,m}$, assumed to lie on an unknown curve $\mathbf{C}(t)$, obtain a parametric curve $\hat{\mathbf{C}}(t)$ that approximates $\mathbf{C}(t)$ at the given points, i.e., $\mathbf{Q}_j(= \mathbf{C}(t_j)) \approx \hat{\mathbf{C}}(t_j)$, $\forall j = 1, \ldots, m$. In other words, the curve reconstruction problem is formulated as a data fitting process so that the fitness function is given by:

$$E = \sum_{j=1}^{m} \left(\mathbf{Q}_j - \hat{\mathbf{C}}(t_j) \right)^2 \tag{1}$$

and our goal is to minimize this objective function. The usual way to proceed is to assume that the approximating function $\hat{\mathbf{C}}(t)$ can be expressed as a linear combination of basis functions:

$$\hat{\mathbf{C}}(t) = \sum_{i=0}^{n} \mathbf{C}_i \phi_i(t) \tag{2}$$

where $\{\mathbf{C}_i\}_{i=0,...,n}$ are vector coefficients usually called *poles* and functions $\{\phi_i(t)\}_{i=0,...,n}$ (usually called *blending functions*) are assumed to be linearly independent functions in the vector space of polynomial functions of degree $\leq n$, which has dimension $n + 1$. Therefore, they form a basis of such a vector space, so they are usually called basis functions. Functions $\{\phi_i(t)\}_i$ can be assumed to be valued on a finite interval $[\alpha, \beta]$, the same for all basis functions. Without loss of generality, we can assume that $[\alpha, \beta] = [0, 1]$. Note that in this chapter vectors are represented in bold.

Several functions can be chosen as basis functions. In general, they can be classified into two groups: global-support functions and local-support functions. In first case, all basis functions have their support on the whole domain $[0, 1]$. In practical terms, this means that the blending functions provide a global control of the shape of the approximating curve. Typical examples of global-support functions are the canonical polynomial basis functions $\{\phi_i(t)\} = \{t^i\}$ and the Bernstein polynomials $\{B_i^n(t)\}$ given by: $B_i^n(t) = \binom{n}{i} t^i (1-t)^{n-i}$ where $\binom{n}{i} = \frac{n!}{i! (n-i)!}$. Other examples include the Hermite polynomial basis, the trigonometric basis, the hyperbolic basis, the radial basis, and the polyharmonic basis.

On the contrary, local-support curves have their support on a subset of the whole domain, and are typically expressed as piecewise functions. Some examples of local-support functions are the piecewise linear basis, the piecewise quadratic basis, the piecewise sinusoidal basis, the piecewise Lagrange basis, the piecewise Harmut basis, the piecewise radial basis, and many others. However, because of their outstanding mathematical properties and the fact that they are the standard in several applied and industrial fields such as computer graphics, computer-aided design and manufacturing (CAD/CAM), computer-generated movies, and many others, the most classical choices for local-support basis functions are the B-spline basis functions.

3.2. Previous Work

Minimization of the fitness function E is usually a nonlinear problem since Eq. (1) generally involve basis functions that are nonlinear in their parameters. But even in the (simpler) case of global-support basis functions, another critical problem remains: how to obtain a proper parameterization of data points, i.e., to determine suitable values of the parameters t_j to be associated with data points $\mathbf{Q}_j$. In general, it can be proved that when the parameterization is given, the minimization of E becomes a standard least-squares problem. However, if no parameterization is given a priori, the problem becomes a nonlinear continuous optimization problem [23, 31, 78].

There are two key components for a good approximation of data points: a proper choice of the approximating function and a suitable parameter tuning. Due to their good mathematical properties regarding evaluation, continuity, and differentiability (among many others), the use of polynomial functions (specially splines) is a classical choice for the approximation function. In particular, free-form parametric curves such as Bézier, B-spline and NURBS, are widely applied in many industrial settings due to their great flexibility and the fact that they can represent well any smooth shape with only a few parameters, thus leading to substantial savings in terms of computer memory and storage capacity [39, 41, 46, 47, 83, 86, 98, 101, 117, 118]. Best approximation methods make commonly use of least-squares techniques [42, 98, 107, 121, 142]. In this case the goal is to obtain the control points of the optimal fitting curve in the least-squares sense.

This problem is far from being trivial; since the curve is parametric, we are also confronted with the problem of obtaining a suitable parameterization of the data points [6, 31, 44]. It is not surprising, therefore, that parameterization has been the subject of research for many years [7, 23, 120, 123]. One of the reasons for this interest is that obtaining a proper parameterization can be crucial for some specific problems. For instance, in some practical situations it is advisable to obtain a parameterization resembling the arc-length parameterization. The ultimate reason for this is that a constant step on the parametric domain automatically translates into a constant distance along an arc-length parameterized curve. In other words, for constant parameter intervals, the curve exhibits a point spacing that is as uniform as possible. As a consequence, this parameterization is very convenient for problems such as such as measuring distances on a surface [50, 126, 127, 128, 129]. Furthermore, since some industrial operations require an uniform parameterization, this property has several practical applications. For example, in computer controlled milling operations, the curve path followed by the milling machine must be parameterized such that the cutter neither speeds up nor slows down along the path [119]. This property is only guaranteed when the curve is parameterized with the arc-length parameterization. Consequently, this has been the preferred and most classical choice for curve parameterization. It is worthwhile to mention, however, that this parameterization can also be inconvenient for other problems. For instance, other alternative parameterizations can be more suitable when the distribution of data points is uneven or when the curve exhibits strong oscillations. Therefore, the determination of the best parameterization is a problem-dependent and challenging issue. Unfortunately, it is also a very hard problem. It is well-known that it leads to a difficult over-determined nonlinear optimization problem. It is also multivariate; it typically involves a large number of unknown variables for a large number of data points, a case that happens very often in real-world instances.

Research in this area started during the 50s and 60s of last century. First approaches in the field were mostly based on numerical procedures [88, 123, 131]. More recent approaches in this line use error bounds [117], curvature-based squared distance minimization [146], or dominant points [118]. A very interesting approach to this problem consists of exploiting minimization of the energy of the curve [1, 30, 109, 143, 160]. This leads to different functionals expressing the conditions of the problem, such as fairness, smoothness, mixed conditions, and others [10, 113, 135, 144]. Generally, research in this area is based on the use of nonlinear optimization techniques that minimize an energy functional (often based on the variation of curvature and other high-order geometric constraints). Then, the problem is formulated as a multivariate nonlinear optimization problem in which the desired form will be the one that satisfies various geometric constraints while minimizing (or maximizing) a measure of form quality. A variation of this formulation consists of optimizing an energy functional while simultaneously minimizing the number of free parameters of the problem and satisfying some additional constraints on the underlying model function.

Unfortunately, the optimization problems given by those energy functionals and their constraints are very difficult and cannot be generally solved by conventional mathematical optimization techniques. On the other hand, interesting research carried out during the last two decades has shown that the application of artificial intelligence techniques can achieve remarkable results regarding this parameterization problem [26, 65, 72, 79, 81, 94]. Most of these methods rely on some kind of neural networks, such as standard neural networks [65], and Kohonen's SOM (Self-Organizing Maps) nets [72, 97], or the Bernstein Basis Function (BBF) network [94]. In other cases, the neural network approach is combined with partial differential equations [6] or other approaches [84]. The generalization of these methods to functional networks is also analyzed in [26, 79, 80, 81, 83]. Although these artificial intelligence-based techniques represented a significant step forward in the field, they still fail to provide a good solution to general problem, and hence, new solutions are needed to overcome this limitation. Recent papers reported in the literature show that metaheuristic techniques (discussed in next section) are arguably the best tools developed so far to tackle this issue.

Regarding the local-support curves, an additional (and very difficult) problem is how to compute the breakpoints associated with the different intervals accounting for the support of the piecewise functions. Intensive research on this subject has been carried out during the last decades (the reader is kindly referred to [120, 141, 142] for a comprehensive review of the field). Most of these methods address this problem by using fixed values for the breakpoints [86, 117, 118, 120, 146, 152]. However, pioneering work dating back in the 60s and 70s showed that the approximation of functions by splines improves greatly if the breakpoints are treated as free variables [11, 21, 88, 131]. In general, two different approaches have been proposed to tackle this issue. The first one consists of computing the number and location of breakpoints *a priori* according to some prescribed formula [86, 117, 118, 146, 152]. The simplest way to do it is to consider equally spaced breakpoints.

Very often, this approach is not appropriate as it may lead to singular systems of equations and does not reflect the real distribution of data. A more refined procedure is given by the de Boor method, which consists of computing breakpoints such that every span between consecutive breakpoints contains at least one parametric value [20]. Other methods use more sophisticated approaches, such as dominant points [118], discrete curvature [146, 152], or support vector machines [86].

As mentioned, the approximation of functions by splines improves dramatically if the breakpoints are treated as free variables of the problem [11, 20, 21, 88, 131]. In this case, the problem becomes much more complicated, because the objective function depends on the poles and the basis functions, which are nonlinear functions of the breakpoints, leading to a very difficult continuous nonlinear minimization problem [88]. Two conventional approaches to this problem consist of starting with a certain number of breakpoints and iteratively modify such amount either by adding extra breakpoints (knot insertion) or by removing some of them (knot removal) in order to satisfy a prescribed error bound [23, 88, 106, 123]. Usually, these methods require terms or parameters (such as tolerance errors, smoothing factors, cost functions or initial guess of breakpoint locations) whose determination is often based on subjective factors [2, 23, 61, 88, 106]. Therefore, they fail to *automatically* generate a good vector for the breakpoints. Other methods yield unnecessary multiple breakpoints [123], so the smooth shape of the curve is lost or degraded. Some approaches that avoid free breakpoints to coalesce have been proposed to overcome this drawback [23, 88, 104, 112]. Obviously, they cannot be applied to fit data to functions with discontinuities and cusps, where multiple breakpoints are actually needed. A different approach is based on the idea of using curvature information extracted from input data [19, 74, 107, 121, 130]. However, these algorithms are generally restricted to smooth data points. A more recent adaptive iterative breakpoint placement method is proposed in [101]. The method performs well but it is restricted to differentiable functions. Furthermore, the method relies heavily on the determination of feature points (such as curvature extrema and inflection points), which are hard to be obtained. Finally, since noise in the curvature is more severe than noise in data themselves, all these methods are strongly affected by noise intensity. Unfortunately, all those previous methods are generally not well suited for discontinuous functions. This is, however, a very remarkable feature of some nature-inspired metaheuristic techniques. Consequently, researchers turned recently their attention towards these techniques, which are described in next section.

3.3. Metaheuristic Methods for Curve Reconstruction

The case of global-support curves by using metaheuristic techniques has been addressed in several papers. Genetic algorithms have been applied to parameter optimization for B-spline curve fitting in [96]. Other cases consisted of a combination of neural networks or functional networks, such as in [39], which describes the application of genetic algorithms and functional networks yielding pretty good results. This approach was then extended to other population-based metaheuristics, such as tabu search in [54, 55], artificial immune systems in [47] for the polynomial case and in [59] for the rational one, electromagnetism algorithm in [52], firefly algorithm in [53], and cuckoo search in [57]. See also [14] for a general overview of the problem for both global-support curves and surfaces by using genetic algorithms and particle swarm optimization. The case of single-population was also addressed in [105] through simulated annealing.

Regarding the case of local-support curves, first papers reporting the application of metaheuristic techniques to curve reconstruction appeared at the end of last century and the beginning of this one. In 1999, Yoshimoto and co-workers published a paper about the application of a discrete version of genetic algorithms to the problem of computing the knots of B-spline curves [157]. These first approaches in the field converted the original problem into a discrete combinatorial optimization problem solved by either genetic algorithms [133, 157] or artificial immune systems [140]. Obviously, these methods are affected by the discretization errors derived from the conversion process. The work in [158] overcomes this limitation by using a real-code genetic algorithm. However, none of these methods can deal accurately with features such as discontinuities and cusps. The ultimate reason is that it is almost impossible to obtain identical values by using purely stochastic approaches. In this sense, obtaining underlying functions of data exhibiting discontinuities or cusps is by far, more complicated than the optimization problem in Eq. (1). Solving it requires intensive exploitation at later stages of the optimization process in order to obtain identical values when required. A recent paper solved this problem by using particle swarm optimization [41], where the inertia weight was modified adaptively to promote exploration at initial stages and exploitation at later stages. In other words, an adequate trade-off between exploration and exploitation is required, but it must be modified adaptively over the generations. This breakpoint allocation problem was addressed for explicit curves by using a firefly algorithm in [48] and through artificial immune systems in [58]. The more challenging case of parametric curves was addressed in [49] by using a hybrid approach combining the firefly algorithm and the indirect approach, in [45] by using a hybridization of genetic algorithms and particle swarm optimization, and in [56] by using a new memetic firefly algorithm for continuous optimization that extends previous approaches in [33] (see also [32] for further details). Other interesting approach uses estimation of distribution algorithms [161], but is only applicable to closed curves and does not compute singularities or discontinuities.

4. Surface Reconstruction

4.1. Statement of the Problem

The problem of surface reconstruction can be stated as follows: *given a set of sample points X assumed to lie on an unknown surface U, construct a surface model S that approximates U.* This problem is generally addressed by means of the least-squares approximation scheme, a classical optimization technique that (given a series of measured data) attempts to find a function (the *fitness function*) which closely approximates the data. The typical approach is to assume that f has a particular functional structure which depends on some parameters that need to be calculated. In this chapter, we consider the case of f being a free-form parametric surface $\mathbf{S}(u, v)$ whose representation is given by:

$$\mathbf{S}(u, v) = \sum_{i=0}^{M} \sum_{j=0}^{N} \mathbf{C}_{i,j} \phi_i(u) \psi_j(v) \tag{3}$$

where $\phi_i(u)$ and $\psi_j(v)$ are the univariate blending functions, u and v are the surface parameters assumed to take values on the intervals $[\alpha_l, \beta_l]$, for $l = u, v$ respectively, and the coefficients $\mathbf{C}_{i,j}$ are the surface poles. Given a set of 3D data points $\{\mathbf{Q}_k\}_{k=1,\ldots,n_k}$, we can compute, for each of the cartesian components, (x_k, y_k, z_k) of $\mathbf{Q}_k$, the minimization of the sum of squared errors referred to the data points:

$$Err_\mu = \sum_{k=1}^{n_k} \left(\mu_k - \sum_{i=0}^{M} \sum_{j=0}^{N} C_{ij}^\mu \phi_i(u_k)\psi_j(v_k) \right)^2 \quad ; \quad \mu = x, y, z \quad (4)$$

Coefficients $\mathbf{C}_{ij} = (C_{ij}^x, C_{ij}^y, C_{ij}^z)$, $i = 0, \ldots, M$, $j = 0, \ldots, N$, are to be determined from the information given by the data points $\mathbf{Q}_k = (x_k, y_k, z_k)$, $k = 1, \ldots, n_k$. Note that performing the component-wise minimization of these errors is equivalent to minimizing the sum, over the set of data, of the Euclidean distances between data points and corresponding points given by the model in 3D space. Note that, in addition to the coefficients of the basis functions, $\mathbf{C}_{ij}$, the parameter values, (u_k, v_k), $k = 1, \ldots, n_k$, associated with the data points also appear as unknowns in our formulation. Due to the fact that the blending functions $\phi_i(u)$ and $\psi_j(v)$ are nonlinear in u and v respectively, the least-squares minimization of the errors becomes a strongly nonlinear problem [149], with a high number of unknowns for large sets of data points, a case that happens very often in practice.

4.2. Previous Work

In general, surface reconstruction methods are classified in terms of the available input (2D slices, iso-parametric curves, clouds of points, mixed information, etc.). For instance, authors in [4, 5, 87, 110, 116] address the problem of obtaining a surface model from a set of given cross-sections, a classical problem in medical science, biomedical engineering and CAD/CAM (see our comments in Section 2 above). Other classical input data include iso-parametric curves on the surface [63] and even mixed information, such as scattered points and contours [38, 108, 136] or iso-parametric curves and data points [26, 81, 82].

In most cases, however, the available information about the surface is typically a dense set of (either organized or scattered) 3D data points obtained by using some sort of digitizing devices (see, e.g., [65, 66, 76, 103, 107]). In that case, the reconstructed surface can be described using three different representations providing different levels of accuracy, ranging from the coarsest (polygonal meshes) to the finest (free-form parametric surfaces):

- The simplest one is given by the polygonal meshes, where the data points are used as vertices connected by lines (edges) that work together to create a 3D model, comprised of vertices, edges and faces. This representation is the first choice for many computer graphics tasks, since it is very flexible and quicker to render and well suited for dealing with current graphical cards. However, polygonal meshes are never a truly faithful representation of a smooth surface. They are merely linear approximations of curved shapes; as such, they only provide a coarse representation of real objects: in a polygonal mesh, curves are approximated by linear segments, while surfaces are approximated by triangular or quadrilateral flat polygons. Although it is the coarsest representation, it is also the most popular because of its simplicity, flexibility and excellent performance with current graphical cards. Surface reconstruction methods with polygonal meshes can be found, for instance, in [34, 75, 76, 100, 115, 124, 159] and references therein.

- The next level is given by the CSG (Constructive Solid Geometry) models, where elementary geometries (such as spheres, boxes, cylinders, or cones) are combined in order to produce more elaborated shapes by applying some simple (Boolean) operators: union, intersection, difference. Although often CSG (Constructive Solid Geometry) presents a model or surface that appears visually complex, it is actually little more than a clever combination of simple objects by means of rather simple operations. As such, it is also limited in terms of the kind of objects it can represent: multibranched, self-intersecting or high-genus objects are very hard (if not impossible) to be constructed with this technology. This methodology works well but presents a low level of flexibility, being severely limited to very simple shapes [148]. However, their extreme simplicity is a limiting factor in order to recover non-trivial shapes.

- The most sophisticated and most accurate level consists of obtaining the real mathematical surface fitting the data points. This means to obtain a mathematical function describing the surface, such as $\mathbf{S}(u, v)$ in Eq. (3). Surface reconstruction by using mathematical surfaces has been analyzed from several points of view, such as parametric methods [9], subdivision surfaces [137], function reconstruction [35, 138], implicit surfaces [103], algebraic surfaces [125], etc. Among the different possibilities, free-form parametric surfaces are the most powerful and most common mathematical representation in real-world settings, because of their flexibility, versatility, and the fact that they represent well a wide variety of shapes in a very compact and intuitive mathematical form.

Unfortunately, obtaining the best approximating surface by using free-form parametric surfaces is much more troublesome than it may seem at first sight. The main reasons are:

- Free-form parametric surfaces may depend on many different parameters (data parameters, knots, control points, sometimes also weights) that are strongly interconnected each other, leading to a strongly nonlinear continuous optimization problem.

- It is also multivariate, as it typically involves a large number of unknown variables for a large number of data points, a case that happens very often in real-world examples.

- In addition, it is also over-determined, because we expect to obtain the approximating surface with many fewer parameters that the number of data points.

- Finally, the problem is known to be multimodal, i.e., the least-squares objective function can exhibit many local optima [88, 131], meaning that the problem might have several (global and/or local) good solutions.

In conclusion, we have to solve a very difficult multimodal, multivariate, high-dimensional continuous nonlinear optimization problem. In fact, previous methods indicated above solve the problem only for polygonal meshes but no real mathematical description of the fitting surface is actually obtained. To overcome this limitation, some methods based on artificial intelligence techniques have been developed during the last few years. Most of such methods rely on the *artificial neural networks* (ANN) formalism [69]. Since ANN methodology is actually inspired by the behavior of the human brain, it is able to reproduce some of its most typical features, such as the ability to learn from data. This explains why they have been so widely applied to data fitting problems. In general, ANN have also been applied to this problem [65, 70, 71, 72] mostly for arranging the input data in case of unorganized points. The goal of this step is to create a grid of control vertices with quadrilateral topology. After this pre-processing step, any other classical surface reconstruction method operating on organized points is subsequently applied. A work using a combination of neural networks and partial differential equation (PDE) techniques for the parameterization and reconstruction of surfaces from 3D scattered points can also be found in [6]. In that paper, two different schemes, SOM (self-organizing map) neural network and PDEs (partial differential equations), are used to cope with the surface parameterization issue, and GDA (gradient descent algorithm) is used to create a 3D base surface that is iteratively modified to get the reconstructed surface. Such a surface is described in terms of cubic polynomial B-splines with errors of about $10^{-1} \sim 10^{-2}$ for sets of about 10^4 data points. However, this method requires data points to be projected onto the base surface and therefore, only examples of neither self-intersecting nor high-genus surfaces are properly handled.

Although very popular, the ANN are however limited in many aspects. A major drawback is their inability to reproduce mathematically the functional structure of a given problem. This limitation can be overcome with the use of a new paradigm in artificial intelligence, the so-called *functional networks* (FN) (see [12, 13] for details). In short, functional networks are a generalization of the standard neural networks in which the scalar weights are replaced by neural functions. These neural functions can exhibit, in general, a multivariate character. Furthermore, different neurons can be associated with neural functions from different families of functions. These FN features allow us to reproduce exactly the functional structure of the problem by a careful choice of the functions involved, which can hereby be associated with one or several neurons of the network. This procedure yields a functional structure that is typically a replica of the underlying structure of the given problem.

Some previous papers have addressed the surface reconstruction problem by using functional networks [81, 80, 82]. Both works show, however, that the single application of functional networks is still unable to solve the general case. The work in [82] addresses the particular case of B-spline surface reconstruction when some additional information (iso-parametric curves) is available in addition to the data points. The fitting surfaces are a generalization of the Gordon surfaces [63]. The work in [39] combines functional networks with genetic algorithms in order to solve the (much simpler) polynomial Bézier case. The approach presented in [84] solves the general NURBS surface reconstruction problem based exclusively on neural and functional networks.

4.3. Metaheuristic Methods for Surface Reconstruction

There are fewer papers regarding surface reconstruction with metaheuristic techniques than those for curve reconstruction. Two of the first proposals are given by [90, 147], which propose the use of computational intelligence techniques (such as genetic programming and genetic evolution) for this issue. Following this idea, the method in [148] combines NURBS with Constructive Solid Geometry in a hybrid evolutionary algorithm/genetic programming approach. In practice, however, the method is very simple and not very powerful since no parameterization of data points is actually computed. Instead, it is assumed that the NURBS patch represents a surface of a solid which is infinite in the negative direction of the z-axis. This constraint, designed to avoid the parameterization process, has proved to be very limiting. In fact, the method is limited to very simple examples in which a planar base surface can be used. Other work related to this approach is that in [8].

A more recent approach is given in [145], where a Multi-Objective Evolutionary Algorithm (MOEA) is applied to reconstruct a simple smooth surface with different sets of data points. The method is limited in several ways: on one hand, authors assume that all weights are equal to one and the degree is 3, so the NURBS surface actually becomes a cubic polynomial B-spline surface. On the other hand, it is assumed that sampled points are uniformly spaced in the (u, v) domain, so clouds of scattered data points cannot be reconstructed. Finally, data points should also be projected in order to perform the evaluation within the MOEA. As a consequence, the method is restricted to rather simple examples.

The method in [150] applies simulated annealing for optimizing NURBS ship hull fitting. This work performs surface reconstruction from a set of cross-sections (called NURBS skinning) rather than from clouds of points. Given a set of data points, they are used to generate a set of cross-sections for surface fitting by making all those cross-sections compatible and joining them with one another. Then, surface optimization is accomplished on either Y or Z coordinate using simulated annealing (SA). In other words, SA is only applied to achieve surface optimization (not surface reconstruction), while non-evolutionary techniques are used for data points parameterization and surface fitting. In [139] artificial immune systems have been applied for B-spline surface approximation. However, the method is very simplified because the problem is addressed as a discrete problem and only simple cases can be solved. In [134] an evolutionary heuristic technique known as simulated evolution (SimE) is applied to curve and surface fitting problems using NURBS. This method is very limited in nature, since instead of computing the knot vectors and the parameterization of data points, their values are assumed *a priori*. Similarly, it is assumed that the number of control points is equal to the order of the NURBS, then control points are calculated by least-squares method directly.

The method in [62] is very different in conception, since its output is a polygonal mesh instead of a real mathematical surface. In that paper, evolutionary algorithms (namely, evolutionary search with soft selection and $1 + \lambda$) are used to recover the shape of tessellated surfaces such as a sphere, a fractal surface and a head (the Igea model). For a population size of $30 - 50$ particles, a polygonal mesh is obtained. However, the method is not able to reconstruct examples where a proper triangulation cannot be obtained. More recently, an example of the application of particle swarm optimization to the reconstruction of Bézier surfaces is given in [40]. The same type of surfaces is addressed with the firefly algorithm in [46] and in [51] with artificial immune systems. However, these papers can only be applied to global-support surfaces. The more difficult case of local-support surfaces is addressed in [43] by using an iterative two-steps genetic algorithm method to compute the data parameterization and the surface fitting respectively, and in [44], where particle swarm optimization is applied to compute a NURBS surface from a collection of data points.

5. Emerging Trends and Some Future Lines of Research

In spite of all research work carried out so far and reported in previous sections, the curve/surface reconstruction problem is still far from being solved in all its generality. The primary reason is that we are facing a very difficult optimization problem. Although the field has witnessed significant progresses during the last decades, there is still a long way to walk.

One of the major issues in the field is the determination of the best metaheuristic method to be applied to this problem. The "no free lunch" theorem taught us that we should not expect to find a universal "best method" for all optimization problems, as any two methods perform equivalently on average for all problems [151]. However, this property is not as limiting as it could appear, because it talks about the average. In this sense, we might arguably be able to identify a method that outperforms any other for a specific given problem. Clearly, it would be very helpful to be able to classify different metaheuristics in terms of their performance for this reconstruction problem. A sub-product of this approach would be to determine the "best metaheuristics" for this particular problem, provided that such a best method really exists. To this purpose, a first valuable step would be the creation of a reliable, standardized benchmark for the field. The primary goal of this benchmark is to facilitate a comparative analysis among the different metaheuristics, something that is not currently available to researchers and practitioners. Obviously, the second step in this process is the comparative analysis itself. This is not a trivial task, as it requires to carry out many different tasks, including the difficult one of parameter tuning.

Indeed, another challenging issue when working with metaheuristic algorithms is their inherent problem-dependent nature. It means that the parameter setting required for a method to work optimally is not universal either, but specialized for each particular problem. In this sense, the other factors being the same, the parameter setting leading to optimal performance for a given problem might be completely inadequate for other problems. At this moment, it is not even clear which are the best sets of parameters for a given metaheuristics to perform optimally for this problem.

Other exciting future line of research is the extension of this research to other families of curves and surfaces not addressed yet in the literature. Although there are very strong reasons to deal with free-form parametric functions, they are not the only ones with interest in applied and industrial fields. However, little has been done so far in this regard. We anticipate an increasing interest in this area for coming years.

Finally, there is still a promising field in the possible applications of these methods in many areas. With the popularization of sensor and capturing technologies such as 3D laser scanners and the wide availability of affordable 3D printers, we can envision a future of mass customization of products as a growing trend. As the complexity of shapes of customer products is increasing, more sophisticated methods for shape reconstruction will be required. At that time, we can expect a new golden era in the development of these reconstruction techniques.

Acknowledgments

This research has been kindly supported by the Computer Science National Program of the Spanish Ministry of Economy and Competitiveness, Project Ref. #TIN2012-30768, Toho University (Funabashi, Japan), and the University of Cantabria (Santander, Spain).

The authors are particularly grateful to the Department of Information Science of Toho University for all the facilities given to carry out this work.

References

[1] Ahn, C., An, J., Yoo, J.: Estimation of particle swarm distribution algorithms: combining the benefits of PSO and EDAs. *Information Sciences* (2010), doi: 10.1016/j.ins.2010.07.014

[2] Alhanaty, M., Bercovier, M.: Curve and surface fitting and design by optimal control methods. *Computer-Aided Design* 33 (2001) 167-182.

[3] Alvino, C.V., Yezzi, A.J.: Tomographic Reconstruction of Piecewise Smooth Images. In: Proceedings of Computer Vision and Pattern Recognition - CVPR'04. *IEEE Computer Society Press*, Los Alamitos, CA, Vol. 1 (2004) 576-581

[4] Bajaj, C., Bernardini, F., Xu, G.: Automatic Reconstruction of Surfaces and Scalar Fields from 3D Scans, *Proc. SIGGRAPH'95* (1995) 109-118

[5] Bajaj, C., Coyle, E.J., Lin, K.N.: Arbitrary topology shape reconstruction from planar cross sections. *Graphical Models and Image Processing*, 58 (1996) 524-543

[6] Barhak, J., Fischer, A.: Parameterization and reconstruction from 3D scattered points based on neural network and PDE techniques. *IEEE Trans. on Visualization and Computer Graphics*, 7(1) (2001) 1-16.

[7] Barnhill, R.E.: *Geometric Processing for Design and Manufacturing*. SIAM, Philadelphia (1992).

[8] Beielstein, T., Mehnen, J., Schnemann, L., Schwefel, H.P., Surmann, T., Weinert, K., Wiesmann, D.:. Design of evolutionary algorithms and applications in surface reconstruction. In: Schwefel, H.P., Wegener, I., Weinert, K. (editors): Advances in Computational Intelligence - Theory and Practice, Springer, Berlin (2003) 164-193

[9] Bolle, R.M., Vemuri, B.C.: On three-dimensional surface reconstruction methods. *IEEE Trans. on Pattern Analysis and Machine Intelligence*, 13(1) (1991) 1-13

[10] Brunnett, G., Kiefer, J.: Interpolation with minimal-energy splines. *Computer-Aided Design*, 26(2) (1994) 37-144.

[11] Burchard, H.G.: Splines (with optimal knots) are better. *Applicable Analysis,* 3 (1974) 309-319.

[12] Castillo, E., Iglesias, A.: Some characterizations of families of surfaces using functional equations. *ACM Transactions on Graphics*, 16(3) (1997) 296-318.

[13] Castillo, E., Iglesias, A., Ruiz-Cobo, R.: *Functional Equations in Applied Sciences*. Elsevier Science, Amsterdam (2005)

[14] Cobo, A., Glvez, A., Puig-Pey, J., Iglesias, A., Espinola, J.: Bio-inspired metaheuristic methods for fitting points in CAGD. *Int. Journal of Computer Information Systems and Industrial Management Applications*, 1 (2009) 36-47.

[15] Cosido, O., de José, J., Piquero, D., Iglesias, A., Sainz, E.: Implementation and Deployment of Geographical Information System Services in the Municipality of Santander. *Proc. of ICCSA 2011*, IEEE Computer Society Press, Los Alamitos CA (2011) 267-270.

[16] Cosido, O., Loucera, C., Iglesias, A.: Automatic calculation of bicycle routes by combining metaheuristics and GIS techniques within the framework of smart cities. *Proc. of Smartmile 2013*, IEEE Computer Society Press, Los Alamitos CA (2013) 259-266.

[17] Cosido, O., Iglesias, A., Gálvez, A., Catuogno, R., Campi, M., Terán, L., Sainz, E.: Hybridization of convergent photogrammetry, computer vision, and artificial intelligence for digital documentation of cultural heritage. A case study: the Magdalena Palace. *Proc. of Cyberworlds 2014*, IEEE Computer Society Press, Los Alamitos CA (2014) 369-376.

[18] Cox, M. G.: Algorithms for spline curves and surfaces. In: *Fundamental Developments of Computer-Aided Geometric Design*. Piegl, L. (Ed.) Academic Press, London, San Diego (1993) 51-76

[19] Crampin, M., Guifo, R., Read, G.A.: Linear approximation of curves with bounded curvature and a data reduction algorithm. *Computer Aided Design* 17(6) (1985) 257-261.

[20] de Boor, C.A.: *Practical Guide to Splines*. Springer-Verlag (2001).

[21] de Boor, C.A., Rice, J.R.: *Least squares cubic spline approximation. I: fixed knots*. CSD TR 20, Purdue University, Lafayette, IN (1968); *ibid: Least squares cubic spline approximation. II: variable knots*. CSD TR 21, Purdue University, Lafayette, IN (1968)

[22] Denison, D.G.T., Mallick, B.K., Smith, A.F.M.: Automatic Bayesian curve fitting. *Journal of the Royal Statistical Society, Series B*, 60(2), (1998) 330-350.

[23] Dierckx, P.: *Curve and Surface Fitting with Splines*. Oxford University Press, Oxford (1993).

[24] Draper, N. R., Smith, H.: *Applied Regression Analysis, 3rd ed*. Wiley-Interscience (1998).

[25] DiMatteo, I., Genovese, C.R., Kass, R. E.: Bayesian curve fitting with free-knot splines. *Biometrika*, 88 (2001) 1055-1071.

[26] Echevarría, G., Iglesias, A., Gálvez, A.: Extending neural networks for B-spline surface reconstruction. *Lectures Notes in Computer Science*, 2330 (2002) 305-314.

[27] Eck, M., Hadenfeld, J.: Local energy fairing of B-spline curves. In: Faring, G., Hagen, H., Noltemeier, H. (eds): *Computing* 10. Springer-Verlag (1995)

[28] Eck, M., Hoppe, H.: Automatic Reconstruction of B-Spline Surfaces of Arbitrary Topological Type, *Proc. SIGGRAPH'96* (1996) 325-334

[29] Engelbretch, A.P.: *Fundamentals of Computational Swarm Intelligence.* John Wiley and Sons, Chichester, England (2005)

[30] Fang, L., Gossard, D.C.: Multidimensional curve fitting to unorganized data points by nonlinear minimization. *Computer-Aided Design*, 27(1) (1995) 48-58.

[31] Farin, G.: *Curves and surfaces for CAGD (5th ed.).* Morgan Kaufmann, San Francisco (2002).

[32] Fister I., Yang, X.S., Brest, J., Fister Jr., I.: A comprehensive review of firefly algorithms. *Swarm and Evolutionary Computation*, 13 (2013) 34-46.

[33] Fister I., Yang, X.S., Brest, J., Fister Jr., I.: Memetic self-adaptive firefly algorithm. In: Yang, X.S., Cui, Z., Xiao, R., Gandomi, A.H., Karamanoglu, M. (Eds.): *Swarm Intelligence and Bio-Inspired Computation. Theory and Applications*, Elsevier (2013) 73-102.

[34] Floater, M.S.: Parameterization and smooth approximation of surface triangulations. *Computer Aided Geometric Design*, 14 (1997) 231-250

[35] Foley, T.A.: Interpolation to scattered data on a spherical domain. In: Mason, J.C., Cox, M.G. (Eds.) *Algorithms for Approximation II*, Chapman and Hall, London, New York (1990) 303-310

[36] Forsey, D.R., Bartels, R.H.: Surface fitting with hierarchical splines. *ACM Trans. Graph.* 14, (1995) 134-161

[37] Franke, R.H., Schumaker, L.L.: A bibliography of multivariate approximation. In: *Topics in Multivariate Approximation.* Chui, C.K., Schumaker, L.L., Utreras, F.I. (Eds.) Academic Press, New York (1986).

[38] Fuchs, H., Kedem, Z.M., Uselton, S.P.: Optimal surface reconstruction from planar contours. *Communications of the ACM*, 20(10) (1977) 693-702.

[39] Gálvez, A., Iglesias, A., Cobo, A., Puig-Pey, J., Espinola, J.: Bézier curve and surface fitting of 3D point clouds through genetic algorithms, functional networks and least-squares approximation. *Lectures Notes in Computer Science*, 4706 (2007) 680-693.

[40] Gálvez, A. Cobo, A., Puig-Pey, J. Iglesias, A.: Particle swarm optimization for Bézier surface reconstruction. *Lectures Notes in Computer Science*, 5102 (2008) 116-125.

[41] Gálvez, A., Iglesias A.: Efficient particle swarm optimization approach for data fitting with free knot B-splines. *Computer-Aided Design*, 43(12) (2011) 1683-1692.

[42] Gálvez, A., Iglesias A.: Particle swarm optimization for computer graphics and geometric modeling: recent trends. In: *Particle Swarm Optimization: Theory, Techniques and Applications*, Nova Science Publishers, New York, USA (2011) 169-192.

[43] Gálvez, A., Iglesias A., Puig-Pey J.: Iterative two-step genetic-algorithm method for efficient polynomial B-spline surface reconstruction. *Information Sciences*, 182(1) (2012) 56-76.

[44] Gálvez A., Iglesias A.: Particle swarm optimization for non-uniform rational B-spline surface reconstruction from clouds of 3D data points. *Information Sciences*, 192(1) (2012) 174-192.

[45] Gálvez A., Iglesias A.: A new iterative mutually-coupled hybrid GA-PSO approach for curve fitting in manufacturing. *Applied Soft Computing*, 13(3) (2013) 1491-1504.

[46] Gálvez A., Iglesias A.: Firefly algorithm for polynomial Bézier surface parameterization. *Journal of Applied Mathematics*, (2013) Article ID 237984, 9 pages.

[47] A. Gálvez, A. Iglesias, A. Avila, Discrete Bézier curve fitting with artificial immune systems. *Studies in Computational Intelligence*, 441 (2013) 59-75.

[48] Gálvez A., Iglesias A.: Firefly algorithm for explicit B-Spline curve fitting to data points. *Mathematical Problems in Engineering*, (2013) Article ID 528215, 12 pages.

[49] Gálvez A., Iglesias A.: From nonlinear optimization to convex optimization through firefly algorithm and indirect approach with applications to CAD/CAM. *The Scientific World Journal*, (2013) Article ID 283919, 10 pages.

[50] Gálvez, A., Iglesias, A. Puig-Pey, J.: Computing parallel curves on parametric surfaces. *Applied Mathematical Modelling*, 38 (2014) 2398-2413.

[51] Gálvez A., Iglesias A., Avila, A.: Immunological-based approach for accurate fitting of 3D noisy data points with Bézier surfaces. In: *Proc. of Int. Conference on Comp. Science-ICCS'2013, Procedia Computer Science*, 18 (2013) 50-59.

[52] Gálvez A., Iglesias A.: An electromagnetism-based global optimization approach for polynomial Bézier curve parameterization of noisy data points. *Proceedings of Cyberworlds 2013*. IEEE Computer Society Press, (2013) 259-266.

[53] Gálvez A., Iglesias A.: Firefly algorithm for Bézier curve approximation. *Proceedings of Int. Conf. on Computational Science and Its Applications - ICCSA'2013*. IEEE Computer Society Press, (2013) 81-88.

[54] Gálvez A., Iglesias A., Cabellos, L.: Discrete rule-based local search metaheuristic for Bézier curve parameterization. *Advances in Science and Technology Letters*, 22 (2013) 13-18.

[55] Gálvez A., Iglesias A., Cabellos, L.: Tabu search-based method for Bézier curve parameterization. *Int. Journal of Software Engineering and Applications*, 7(5) (2013) 283-296.

[56] Gálvez A., Iglesias A.: New memetic self-adaptive firefly algorithm for continuous optimization. *International Journal of Bio-Inspired Computation, (in press)*.

[57] Gálvez A., Iglesias A.: Cuckoo search with Lévy flights for weighted Bayesian energy functional optimization in global-support curve data fitting. *The Scientific World Journal*, (2014) Article ID 138760, 11 pages.

[58] Gálvez A., Iglesias A., Avila, A., Otero, C., Arias, R., Manchado, C.: Elitist clonal selection algorithm for optimal choice of free knots in B-spline data fitting. *Applied Soft Computing*, 26 (2015) 90-106.

[59] Gálvez, A., Iglesias, A., Avila, A.: Applying clonal selection theory to data fitting with rational Bézier curves. *Proc. of Cyberworlds 2014*, IEEE Computer Society Press, Los Alamitos CA (2014) 221-228.

[60] Goldberg, D.E.: *Genetic Algorithms in Search, Optimization, and Machine Learning*. Addison-Wesley (1989).

[61] Goldenthal, R., Bercovier, M.: Spline curve approximation and design by optimal control over the knots. *Computing* 72 (2004) 53-64.

[62] Goinski, A.: Evolutionary surface reconstruction. In: *Proc. IEEE Conference on Human System Interactions*, Krakow, Poland (2008) 464-469.

[63] Gordon, W. J.: Spline-blended surface interpolation through curve networks. *J. Math. Mech.*, 18(10) (1969) 931-952

[64] Greiner, G.: Variational design and fairing of spline surfaces. *Computer Graphics Forum*, 13(3) (1994) 143-154

[65] Gu, P., Yan, X.: Neural network approach to the reconstruction of free-form surfaces for reverse engineering. *Computer-Aided Design* 27(1) (1995) 59-64.

[66] Guo, B.: Surface Reconstruction from Points to Splines, *Computer-Aided Design* 29(4) (1997) 269-277

[67] Guo, Q., Zhang, M.: A novel approach for multi-agent-based intelligent manufacturing system. *Information Sciences*, 179(18) (2009) 3079-3090.

[68] Hagen, H., Santarelli, P.: Variational design of smooth B-spline surfaces. In: Hagen, H. (ed.): *Topics in Surface Modeling*. SIAM 85-94 (1992)

[69] Hertz, J., Krogh, A., Palmer, R.G.: *Introduction to the Theory of Neural Computation*. Addison Wesley, Reading, MA (1991).

[70] Hoffmann, M., Varady, L.: Free-form surfaces for scattered data by neural networks. *Journal for Geometry and Graphics*, 2 (1998) 1-6

[71] Hoffmann M.: Modified Kohonen neural network for surface reconstruction. *Publicationes Mathematicae*, 54 (1999) 857-864.

[72] Hoffmann M.: Numerical control of Kohonen neural network for scattered data approximation. *Numerical Algorithms*, 39, (2005) 175-186.

[73] Holland, J.H.: *Adaptation in Natural and Artificial Systems*. Ann Arbor: The University of Michigan Press (1975)

[74] Hölzle, G.E.: Knot placement for piecewise polynomial approximation of curves. *Computer Aided Design*, 15(5) (1993) 295-296.

[75] Hoppe, H., DeRose, T., Duchamp, T., McDonald, J., Stuetzle, W.: Surface reconstruction from unorganized points. *Proc. of SIGGRAPH'92, Computer Graphics*, 26(2) (1992) 71-78

[76] Hoppe, H.: *Surface Reconstruction from Unorganized Points*. Ph. D. Thesis, Department of Computer Science and Engineering, University of Washington (1994)

[77] Hoschek, J.: Smoothing of curves and surfaces. *Computer Aided Design*, 2 (1985) 97-105.

[78] Hoschek, J., Lasser, D.: *Fundamentals of Computer Aided Geometric Design*. A.K. Peters, Wellesley, MA (1993).

[79] Iglesias, A., Echevarría, G., Gálvez, A.: Functional networks for B-spline surface reconstruction. *Future Generation Computer Systems*, 20(8) (2004) 1337-1353.

[80] A. Iglesias, A. Gálvez, Applying functional networks to fit data points from B-spline surfaces. In: *Proceedings of the Computer Graphics International, CGI'2001*, Hong-Kong (China). IEEE Computer Society Press, Los Alamitos, California (2001) 329-332.

[81] Iglesias, A., Gálvez, A.: A new artificial intelligence paradigm for computer aided geometric design. *Lectures Notes in Artificial Intelligence*, 1930 (2001) 200-213.

[82] Iglesias, A., Echevarría, G., Gálvez, A.: Functional Networks for B-spline Surface Reconstruction. *Future Generation Computer Systems*, 20(8) (2004) 1337-1353.

[83] A. Iglesias, A. Gálvez, Curve fitting with RBS functional networks. In: *Proc. of International Conference on Convergence Information Technology-ICCIT'2008*, Busan (Korea). IEEE Computer Society Press, Los Alamitos, California (2008) 299-306.

[84] Iglesias, A., Gálvez, A.: Hybrid functional-neural approach for surface reconstruction. *Mathematical Problems in Engineering*, (2014) Article ID 351648, 13 pages.

[85] Isheila, A. Gonneta, J.P., Joannica, D., Fontaine, J.F.: Systematic error correction of a 3D laser scanning measurement device. *Optics and Lasers in Engineering*, 49(1) (2011) 16-24.

[86] Jing, L., Sun, L.: Fitting B-spline curves by least squares support vector machines. In: Proc. of the 2nd. Int. Conf. on Neural Networks & Brain. Beijing (China). IEEE Press (2005) 905-909.

[87] Jones, M., Chen, M.: A new approach to the construction of surfaces from contour data. *Computer Graphics Forum*, 13(3) (1994) 75-84

[88] Jupp, D.L.B.: Approximation to data by splines with free knots. *SIAM Journal of Numerical Analysis*, 15 (1978) 328-343.

[89] Kaufman, E., Klass, R.: Smoothing surfaces using reflection lines for families of splines. *Computer Aided Design*, 20 (1988) 312-316

[90] Keller, R.E., Banshaf, W., Mehnen, J., Weinert, K: CAD surface reconstruction from digitized 3D point data with a genetic programming/evolution strategy hybrid. In: *Advances in Genetic Programming 3*, MIT Press, Cambridge, MA, USA (1999) 41-65

[91] Kennedy, J., Eberhart, R.C.: Particle swarm optimization. *IEEE International Conference on Neural Networks*, Perth, Australia (1995) 1942-1948

[92] Kennedy, J., Eberhart, R.C., Shi, Y.: *Swarm Intelligence*, San Francisco: Morgan Kaufmann Publishers (2001)

[93] Kirkpatrick, S., Gelatt, C.D., Vecchi, M.P.: Optimization by simulated annealing. *Science*, 220(4598) (1983) 671-680.

[94] Knopf, G.K., Kofman, J.: Adaptive reconstruction of free-form surfaces using Bernstein basis function networks. *Engineering Applications of Artificial Intelligence*, 14(5) (2001) 577-588.

[95] Kodama, T., Li, X., Nakahira, K., Ito, D.: Evolutionary computation applied to the reconstruction of 3-D surface topography in the SEM. *Journal of Electron Microscopy*, 54(5) (2005) 429-435

[96] Kumar, S.G., Kalra, P.K., Dhande, S.G.: Parameter optimization for B-spline curve fitting using genetic algorithms. Proc. of *Congress on Evolutionary Computation*, 3 (2003) 1871-1878

[97] Kumar, S.G., Kalra, P.K., Dhande, S.G.: Curve and surface reconstruction from points: an approach based on self-organizing maps. *Applied Soft Computing*, 5(5) (2004) 55-66

[98] Lee, T.C.M.: On algorithms for ordinary least squares regression spline fitting: a comparative study. *J. Statist. Comput. Simul.* 72(8) (2002) 647-663.

[99] Leu, M.C., Peng, X., Zhang, W.: Surface Reconstruction for Interactive Modeling of Freeform Solids by Virtual Sculpting. *CIRP Annals - Manufacturing Technology*, 54(1) (2005) 131-134

[100] Levoy, M. Pulli, K., Curless, B., Rusinkiewicz, S., Koller, D., Pereira, L., Ginzton, M., Anderson, S., Davis, J., Ginsberg, J., Shade, J., Fulk, D.: The Digital Michelangelo Project: 3D scanning of large statues. In *SIGGRAPH 2000*, New Orleans, (2000) 131-144

[101] Li, W., Xu, S., Zhao, G., Goh, L.P.: Adaptive knot placement in B-spline curve approximation. *Computer Aided Design* 37 (2005) 791-797.

[102] Li, M., Yan Y.: Bayesian adaptive penalized splines. *Journal of Academy of Business and Economics*, 2 (2006) 129-141.

[103] Lim, C., Turkiyyah, G., Ganter, M., Storti, D.: Implicit reconstruction of solids from cloud point sets. *Proc. of 1995 ACM Symposium on Solid Modeling*, Salt Lake City, Utah (1995) 393-402

[104] Lindstrom, M.J.: Penalized estimation of free-knot splines. *Journal of Computational and Graphical Statistics*, 8(2) (1999) 333-352

[105] Loucera, C., Gálvez, A., Iglesias, A.: Simulated annealing algorithm for Bezier curve approximation. *Proc. of Cyberworlds 2014*, IEEE Computer Society Press, Los Alamitos CA (2014) 182-189.

[106] Lyche T, Morken K. A data-reduction strategy for splines with applications to the approximation of functions and data. *IMA Journal of Numerical Analysis*, 8 (1988) 185-208.

[107] Ma, W.Y., Kruth, J.P.: Parameterization of randomly measured points for least squares fitting of B-spline curves and surfaces. *Computer-Aided Design*, 27(9) (1995) 663-675.

[108] Maekawa, I., Ko, K.: Surface construction by fitting unorganized curves. *Graphical Models* 64, (2002) 316-332.

[109] Martinsson, H., Gaspard, F., Bartoli, A., Lavest, J.M.: Energy-based reconstruction of 3D curves for quality control. *Lecture Notes in Computer Science*, 4679 (2007) 414-428.

[110] Meyers, D., Skinnwer, S., Sloan, K.: Surfaces from contours. *ACM Transactions on Graphics,* 11(3) (1992) 228-258

[111] Mitchell, M.: *An Introduction to Genetic Algorithms (Complex Adaptive Systems)*. MIT Press (1998).

[112] Molinari, N., Durand, J.F., Sabatier, R.: Bounded optimal knots for regression splines. *Computational Statistics & Data Analysis*, 45(2) (2004) 159-178.

[113] Moreton, H.P., Sequin, C.H.: Functional optimisation for fair surface design. *Computer Graphics*, 26(2) (1992) 167-176.

[114] Mukai, T.: Latent nonuniform splines for animation approximation. *ACM Siggraph Asia 2012 Technical Briefs*, (2012) Article 3.

[115] Oblonsek, C., Guid, N.: A fast surface-based procedure for object reconstruction from 3D scattered points. *Computer Vision and Image Understanding*, 69(2) (1998) 185-195

[116] Park, H., Kim, K.: Smooth surface approximation to serial cross-sections. *Computer Aided Design*, 28(12) (1997) 995-1005

[117] Park, H.: An error-bounded approximate method for representing planar curves in B-splines. *Computer Aided Geometric Design* 21 (2004) 479-497.

[118] Park, H., Lee, J.H.: B-spline curve fitting based on adaptive curve refinement using dominant points. *Computer-Aided Design* 39 (2007) 439-451.

[119] Patrikalakis, N.M., Maekawa, T.: *Shape Interrogation for Computer Aided Design and Manufacturing.* Springer Verlag, Heidelberg (2002).

[120] Piegl, L., Tiller, W.: *The NURBS Book*, Springer Verlag, Berlin Heidelberg (1997).

[121] Piegl, L., Tiller, W.: Least-square B-spline curve approximation with arbitrary end derivatives. *Eng Comput.* 16 (2000) 109-116.

[122] Pottmann, H., Leopoldseder, S. Hofer, M., Steiner, T., Wang, W.: Industrial geometry: recent advances and applications in CAD. *Computer-Aided Design*, 37 (2005) 751-766.

[123] Powell, M.J.D.: Curve fitting by splines in one variable. In: Hayes, J.G. (editor): *Numerical approximation to functions and data.* Athlone Press, London (1970).

[124] Prasad, M. , Zisserman, A., Fitzgibbon, A. W.: Single View Reconstruction of Curved Surfaces. In: Proceedings of the IEEE Conference on Computer Vision and Pattern Recognition, *IEEE Computer Society Press*, Los Alamitos, CA (2006)

[125] Pratt, V.: Direct least-squares fitting of algebraic surfaces. *Proc. of SIGGRAPH'87, Computer Graphics*, 21(4) (1987) 145-152.

[126] Puig-Pey, J., Gálvez, A., Iglesias, A., Rodríguez, J., Corcuera, P., Gutiérrez, F.: Polar isodistance curves on parametric surfaces. *Lectures Notes in Computer Science*, 2330 (2002) 161-170.

[127] Puig-Pey, J., Gálvez, A., Iglesias, A.: Helical curves on surfaces for computer-aided geometric design and manufacturing. *Lectures Notes in Computer Science*, 3044 (2004) 771-778.

[128] Puig-Pey, J., Gálvez, A., Iglesias, A.: Some applications of scalar and vector fields to geometric processing of surfaces. *Computers & Graphics*, 29(5) (2005) 723-729.

[129] Puig-Pey, J., Gálvez, A., Iglesias, A., Corcuera, P., Rodríguez, J.: Some problems in geometric processing of surfaces. In: *Advances in Mathematical and Statistical Modeling* (Series: Statistics for Industry and Technology, SIT) Birkhauser, Boston (2008) 293-304.

[130] Razdan, A.: *Knot Placement for B-spline curve approximation.* Tempe, AZ: Arizona State University (1999).

[131] Rice, J.R.: *The Approximation of Functions. Vol. 2*. Addison-Wesley, Reading, MA (1969).

[132] Rice, J.R.: *Numerical Methods, Software and Analysis. 2nd. Edition*. Academic Press, New York (1993).

[133] Sarfraz, M., Raza, S.A.: Capturing outline of fonts using genetic algorithms and splines. *Proc. of Fifth International Conference on Information Visualization IV'2001*, IEEE Computer Society Press (2001) 738-743.

[134] Sarfraz, M.: Computer-aided reverse engineering using simulated evolution on NURBS. *Virtual and Physical Prototyping*, 1(4) (2006) 243-257

[135] Sarioz, E.: An optimization approach for fairing of ship hull forms. *Ocean Engineering*, 33 (2006) 2105-2118.

[136] Savchenko, V., Pasko, A., Okunev, O., Kunii, T.: Function representation of solids reconstructed from scattered surface points and contours. *Computer Graphics Forum*, 14(4) (1995) 181-188

[137] Schmitt, F., Barsky, B.A., Du, W.: An adaptive subdivision method for surface fitting from sampled data. *Proc. of SIGGRAPH'86, Computer Graphics*, 20(4) (1986) 179-188.

[138] Sclaroff, S., Pentland, A.: Generalized implicit functions for computer graphics. *Proc. of SIGGRAPH'91, Computer Graphics*, 25(4) (1991) 247-250

[139] Ulker, E., Isler, V.: An artificial immune system approach for B-spline surface approximation problem. *Lecture Notes in Computer Science*, 4488 (2007) 49-56.

[140] Ulker, E., Arslan, A.: Automatic knot adjustment using an artificial immune system for B-spline curve approximation. *Information Sciences*, 179 (2009) 1483-1494.

[141] Varady, T., Martin, R.: Reverse Engineering. In: Farin, G., Hoschek, J., Kim, M. (eds.): *Handbook of Computer Aided Geometric Design*. Elsevier Science (2002).

[142] Varady, T., Martin, R.R., Cox, J.: Reverse engineering of geometric models - an introduction. *Computer Aided Design*, 29(4) (1997) 255-268.

[143] Vassilev, T.I.: Fair interpolation and approximation of B-splines by energy minimization and points insertion. *Computer-Aided Design*, 28(9) (1996) 753-760.

[144] Veltkamp, R.C., Wesselink, W.: Modeling 3D curves of minimal energy. *Computer Graphics Forum*, 14(3) (1995) 97-110.

[145] Wagner, T., Michelitsch, T., Sacharow, A.: On the design of optimizers for surface reconstruction. *Proceedings of the 2007 Genetic and Evolutionary Computation Conference-GECCO2007* London, England (2007) 2195-2202

[146] Wang, W.P., Pottmann, H., Liu, Y.: Fitting B-spline curves to point clouds by curvature-based squared distance minimization. *ACM Transactions on Graphics*, 25(2) (2006) 214-238.

[147] Weinert, K., Mehnen, J., Albersmann, F., Dreup, P.: New solutions for surface reconstruction from discrete point data by means of computational intelligence. *Proceedings of Intelligent Computation in Manufacturing Engineering-ICME'98*, Capri, Italy (1998) 431-438.

[148] Weinert, K., Surmann, T., Mehnen, J.: Evolutionary surface reconstruction using CSG-NURBS-hybrids. *Proceedings of the 2001 Genetic and Evolutionary Computation Conference-GECCO2001*, San Francisco, USA (2001) 1456-1463.

[149] Weiss, V., Or, L., Renner, G., Varady, T.: Advanced surface fitting techniques. *Comput.-Aided Geomet. Design* 19 (2002) 19-42.

[150] Wen, A.S., : New solutions for surface reconstruction from discrete point data by means of computational intelligence. *Proceedings of Intelligent Computation in Manufacturing Engineering-ICME'98*, Sydney, Australia, IEEE CS Press (2006) 431-438.

[151] Wolpert, D.H., Macready, W.G.: No free lunch theorems for optimization. *IEEE Transactions on Evolutionary Computation*, 1(1) (1997) 67-82.

[152] Yang, H.P., Wang, W.P., Sun, J.G.: Control point adjustment for B-spline curve approximation. *Computer-Aided Design* 36 (2004) 639-652.

[153] Yang, X.S.: Firefly algorithms for multimodal optimization. *Lectures Notes in Computer Science*, 5792 (2009) 169-178.

[154] Yang, X.S.: Firefly algorithm, stochastic test functions and design optimisation. *Int. Journal of Bio-Inspired Computation*, 2(2) (2010) 78-84.

[155] Yang, X.-S.: *Nature-Inspired Metaheuristic Algorithms (2nd. Edition)*. Luniver Press, Frome, UK (2010).

[156] Yang, X.-S.: *Engineering Optimization: An Introduction with Metaheuristic Applications*. Wiley & Sons, New Jersey (2010).

[157] Yoshimoto F., Moriyama, M., Harada T.: Automatic knot adjustment by a genetic algorithm for data fitting with a spline. *Proc. of Shape Modeling International'99*, IEEE Computer Society Press (1999) 162-169.

[158] Yoshimoto F., Harada T., Yoshimoto Y.: Data fitting with a spline using a real-coded algorithm. *Computer-Aided Design*, 35 (2003) 751-760.

[159] Yu, Y.: Surface reconstruction from unorganized points using self-organizing neural networks. In: *Proceedings of IEEE Visualization 99* (1999) 61-64.

[160] Zhang, C., Zhang, P., Cheng, F.: Fairing spline curves and surfaces by minimising energy. *Computer-Aided Design*, 33(13) (2001) 913-923.

[161] Zhao, X., Zhang, C., Yang, B., Li, P.: Adaptive knot adjustment using a GMM-based continuous optimization algorithm in B-spline curve approximation. *Computer-Aided Design*, 43 (2011) 598-604.

In: Horizons in Computer Science Research. Volume 11   ISBN: 978-1-63482-499-6
Editor: Thomas S. Clary, pp. 63-143   © 2015 Nova Science Publishers, Inc.

Chapter 3

STREAM-BASED PARALLEL COMPUTING METHODOLOGY AND DEVELOPMENT ENVIRONMENT FOR HIGH PERFORMANCE MANYCORE ACCELERATORS

Shinichi Yamagiwa[1,*], *Gabriel Falcao*[2,†], *Koichi Wada*[3,‡] *and Leonel Sousa*[4,§]

[1]Faculty of Engineering, Information and Systems,
University of Tsukuba, JAPAN
[2]Instituto de Telecomunicações, Department of Electrical
and Computer Engineering, University of Coimbra, Portugal
[3]Faculty of Engineering, Information and Systems,
University of Tsukuba, JAPAN
[4]INESC-ID, Instituto Superior Técnico,
Universidade de Lisboa, Portugal

Abstract

The latest supercomputers incorporate a high number of compute units under the form of manycore accelerators. Such accelerators, like GPUs, have integrated processors where a massively high number of threads, in the order of thousands, execute concurrently. Compared to single-CPU throughput performance, they offer higher levels of parallelism. Therefore, they represent an indispensable technology in the new era of high performance supercomputing. However, the accelerator is equipped via the peripheral bus of the host CPU, which inevitably creates communication overheads when exchanging programs and data between the CPU and the accelerator. Also, we need to develop both programs to run on these processors that have distinct architectures. To make it simpler for the programmer to use the accelerator and exploit its potential throughput performance, this chapter describes the Caravela platform. Caravela provides a simple programming interface that overcomes the difficulty of developing and

---
*E-mail address: yamagiwa@cs.tsukuba.ac.jp
†E-mail address: gff@uc.pt
‡E-mail address: wada@cs.tsukuba.ac.jp
§E-mail address: las@inesc-id.pt

running parallel kernels not only on single but also on multiple manycore accelerators. This chapter describes parallel programming techniques and methods applied to a variety of research test case scenarios.

PACS: 07.05.Bx, 07.05.Wr

Keywords: stream-based computing, dataflow, massively parallel computing, graphics processing units, Manycore Processors, Caravela

AMS Subject Classification: 94-04, 94-02, 94C

1. Introduction

Many of the advanced supercomputers listed in the Top500 utilize the huge performance enhancement provided by manycore accelerators such as GPUs. The application programmer targeting the use of a supercomputer needs to be able of performing hybrid programming, not only for the conventional parallel computing code development and optimizations on the CPU side, using for example MPI-based message passing techniques, but also for the parallelization of algorithms in the accelerators, using massively parallel programming environments like the stream-based computing OpenCL framework and language. The key to exploit the potential performance of supercomputers lies in programming techniques for heterogeneous systems, with the capacity of distributed processing nodes augmented with accelerators.

This chapter introduces *Caravela* [48][41][49], a novel programming environment for high performance computing using accelerators. Caravela virtualizes the interface for multiple accelerators and invokes the task with thousands of threads in parallel. The task unit of Caravela, denoted flow-model, includes the I/O data streams and the program code for the particular task. The program code is written in a stream-based programming language such as originally DirectX, OpenCL and CUDA. By connecting multiple flow-models, a large task can be organized.

The chapter introduces the programming environment using Caravela and presents the performance evaluation for massively systems with parallel accelerators. Caravela provides both a C-based programming library and a command line execution interface called *CarSh* [53].

The chapter also shows the readers a parallel extension technique used for stream-based computing with multiple accelerators, by applying the conventional message passing techniques using MPI [50].

Moreover, the chapter introduces I/O optimization techniques when the recursive or iterative flow-models are included in the processing task, designated as swap method [52][25]. It is extended to a pipelined execution model using multiple accelerators organized in a meta-pipeline structure [51]. By using the swap method, this chapter also introduces a new execution mechanism for accelerators called the scenario-based execution [46]. It is capable of executing multiple flow-models of recursive or iterative nature on the accelerator side without burdening the CPU with unnecessary communications. Therefore, it invokes multiple flow-models without introducing communication overheads among the accelerator and GPUs, and thus achieves very high performance.

Regarding the application of the referred techniques on Caravela, the chapter reports performance evaluations using simple applications and kernels. Finally, the chapter proposes future work and the expected direction of these technologies in high performance stream-based computing for supercomputers.

1.1.   Stream Computing

Multicore/manycore architectures have gained traction due to the saturation of Moore's law related to the growth of transistor count per silicon platform. The manycore architecture originates from graphics processing demands that need fast computations to achieve a high frequency framing on dynamic graphics, especially for entertainment markets [32]. It requires the concurrent processing of multiple pixels computed by hundreds of processing units. It also exploits the potential fine-grained parallelism from application programs [36]. Thus, the GPU has become an indispensable tool to implement a high performance computing platform.

In the manycore architecture, each processing unit identifies its target computing element regarding a processor index. For example, assuming a vector summation $r_c = r_a + r_b$, a programmer needs to consider that the calculation is separated into each element of vectors like $r_c[id] = r_a[id] + r_b[id]$, where id represents the index of the vector element. Each calculation of $r_c[id]$ is assigned to a compute unit, thus the summations of elements in the vector are performed in parallel. Optimistically, the vector summation needs only the processing time to calculate the "+" operation when the number of computing units is larger than the length of r_c. Thus, a programmer certainly needs to consider the indexing of computing elements and also independent processing for each computing element assigned to a unit. Because of the processing style based on the indexed processors, it is called *stream computing*.

An accelerator in the manycore architecture works as a co-processor of a host CPU connected via the peripheral bus. Therefore, for programming the accelerator, the host CPU is indispensable and controls the configuration and behavior of the accelerator. Thus, the programmer must write both computing programs on the accelerator side and the controlling program on the host CPU side unavoidably. To reduce the difficulty of such double programming situation, there are available programming languages and the respective runtimes. For example, the recent standard ones are NVIDIA's CUDA [33] and OpenCL [31].

1.2.   Computing Power of Graphics Processing Units

Graphical applications, especially 3D graphics visualization techniques, have drastically advanced in this decade. Even a commodity personal computer now supplies very high quality graphics processed in real-time. This is mainly due to the GPU connected to the personal computer. The power of GPUs is growing drastically: for example, floating-point processing performance on nVIDIA's Geforce7 achieves 300 GFLOPS, which compares very well to 8 GFLOPS of Intel Core2Duo processors. This is a remarkable computational power available for applications that demand high workloads.

Nowadays, researchers of high performance computing are also focusing their efforts on the performance of GPUs, and investigating the possibility for its usage as a substitute of CPUs. For example, GPGPU (General-purpose processing on GPU) allows achieving

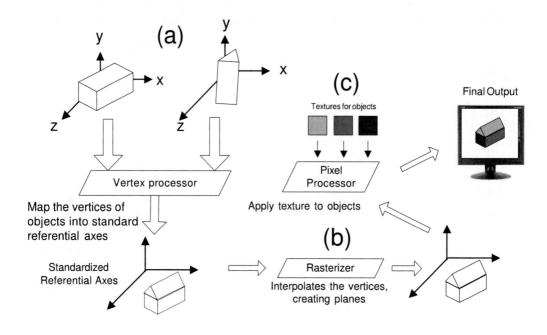

Figure 1. Processing steps for graphics rendering.

a high level of performance [24] [29]. A cluster-based approach using PCs with high performance GPUs has been reported in [9]. Moreover, compiler-oriented support for GPU resources has also been proposed [6].

1.3. The Conventional Graphics Processing on GPU

This subsection introduces the processing steps and architecture that allows GPUs to generate graphics objects in order to display them on a screen. The GPU acts as a co-processor of the CPU via a peripheral bus, such as the AGP or the PCI Express. A Video RAM (VRAM) is connected to the GPU, which reads/writes graphics objects from/to the VRAM. The CPU controls the GPU operation by sending the object data to the VRAM and a program to the GPU.

Figure 1 shows the processing steps performed by the GPU to create a graphical image and store it in a frame buffer in order to be displayed in a screen. First, the graphics data is prepared as a set of normalized vertices of objects on a referential axis defined by the graphics designer (Figure 1(a)). The vertices are sent to a vertex processor, in order to change the size or the perspective of the object, which is performed by calculating rotations and transformations of the coordinates. In this step all objects are mapped to a standardized referential axis. In the next step, a rasterizer interpolates the coordinates and defines the planes that form the graphics objects (Figure 1(b)). Finally, a pixel processor receives these planes from the rasterizer, calculates the composed RGB colors from the textures of the objects and sends this color data to the frame buffer (Figure 1(c)). Then, the color data in the frame buffer can be finally displayed in the screen.

1.4.   General-purpose Computing on Graphics Processing Units

In recent GPUs, the vertex and pixel processors are programmable. The designers of graphics scenes can make programs for the processors specific for the desired graphics effects. It is very important that the programs run fast in order to achieve a huge number of processed frames per second. Therefore, GPUs have dedicated floating-point processing pipelines in these processors and GPGPU applications make strong use of these processors. However, the rasterizer is composed of fixed hardware, and its output data cannot be controlled. Moreover, the output data from the rasterizer is just sent to the pixel processor and cannot be fetched by the CPU. Thus, it is reasonable for GPGPU applications to use the computing power of the pixel processor due to its programmability capabilities and flexibility for I/O data control.

The focus of this chapter is not restricted to the performance of GPUs, but also addresses the execution paradigm on GPUs. As shown above, the pixel processor does not touch any resources and the data sent to it is input as a stream of massive data elements. Then it processes each data unit (pixel color data) and outputs a data stream. This means that the program on the GPU works in a closed environment. Moreover, it is possible to write programs in standard languages such as DirectX assembly language, High Level Shader Language (HLSL) [1] and OpenGL Shading Language [23]. Thus, the program can run on any GPU connected to any computer.

According to the discussion above, it can be concluded that security concerns about the resources touched by programs on a GRID platform can be solved by the GPU's execution mechanism, due to its stream-based processing nature. Thus, we aim to develop an execution mechanism on the GRID environment based on stream-based computing using GPUs' power.

2.   Caravela: A Stream Computing Environment

2.1.   Preface

Worldwide distributed computing has become one of the remarkable possible ways to use anonymous processing power, due to the development of distributed execution platforms. The platforms can be based on message passing computing, using a server software such as Globus [2], or a mobile agent-based one that migrates@among the resources organized as a virtual network [12]. According to the research reports of those platforms [5, 20], worldwide distributed computing is effective in achieving an ultra computing power, by taking advantage of huge amounts of unused computing power from over the world. This computing style is named GRID computing [40].

For a GRID computing platform, one of most important issue that the developer must address is security, both for users and for contributors of the computing resources. For example, the users of the platform do not desire that someone steals programs or data dispatched to a computing resource, in the communication channel to the resource or in the resource itself. On the other hand, contributors of the computing resources also do not desire that a program assigned by the users touch their private resources, such as protected data, hardware and network connections. The contributors may call such a program executing in their computers a *virus*. It must be paid a lot of attention to avoid such situations in a GRID.

This section describes the design and implementation of the *Caravela* platform that provides a novel mechanism to execute programs in a GRID environment, which provides a suitable security level of execution.

The *Caravela* defines a data structure for a unit of execution named *flow-model* unit, which is composed by input data streams, output data streams and a program to process those I/O data streams. The Caravela will assign the flow-model unit(s) to resources in the GRID environment. The program in the flow-model unit processes the input data in a stream-based processing flow, such as in a dataflow processor. According to the proposed execution model, the program in the flow-model unit is not allowed to touch the resources around the processing unit to which the flow-model is assigned, except for its I/O data streams.

The flow-model execution method fits well into a Graphics Processing Unit (GPU) because the GPU supports stream-based computation using texture inputs. Moreover, the performance of GPU is much higher when compared with that of a CPU [35]. Therefore, this section also shows an implementation of the Caravela platform which maps the flow-model on a GPU. Moreover, this section describes an example where flow-model units execute distributed on remote GPU resources.

2.2. The GRID Computing Environment

Among the platforms for GRID computing, there exist several methods to implement mechanisms to release resources for users and to remotely use those resources. One of them is Globus [2], a well known message passing-based platform for GRID computing. The users of the Globus platform can write programs as MPI-based parallel applications [22]. Therefore, applications which have been parallelized with MPI functions can easily migrate from a local cluster, or a supercomputer-based environment to the Globus platform. Another platform example is the agent-based implementation Condor-G [12]. This kind of implementation is mainly used for managing resources in a GRID. The tasks performed in remote computing resources using such platforms are assigned anonymously. It is very difficult for users and contributors to trust each other and be sure that the tasks never damage the computing resource and are not damaged by some malicious access. Therefore, in any implementation of GRID platforms the security must be considered as one of the important issues.

To achieve trustful communication among users and contributors of computing resources, any GRID platform must address the following security issues:

1. **Data security exchanged among processing resources via network**
   When a program is assigned to a remote processing unit, it must be sent to the resource and, also, the data must be received by the program. The data transferred via the network can be snooped by a third person using tools such as `tcpdump`. This means that the users do not trust the system. This problem is also a security matter in web-based applications. Therefore, data encryption such as SSL (Secure Socket Layer) is applied to the connections between computing resources [11].

2. **Program and data security on remote resources**

On GRID environments, users would assign their programs to unknown machines anywhere in the world. Therefore, the users don't want that the program content or data be snooped or stolen by the resource owners. For overcoming this problem, the GRID platforms force the creation of an account for the user which is managed by the administrator.

3. **Resource security during program execution**

This is the most dangerous security problem in the platform. When a program is dispatched by the user to a remote computing resource, it may make use anything in there. This is just the behavior of a computer *virus*. The GRID environment must have capabilities to restrict the permissions of user programs. Therefore, a GRID platform generally has resource management tools such as GRMS [3].

The first security problem above is solved by encrypting the data exchanged among resources and users. The second problem can be solved by the administrator of the computing resources, for example creating user accounts. However, in what respects the third problem, although some solutions tackle the user program access to resources, such as Java's RMI (Remote Method Invocation) mechanism [16] by restricting the available resources to the program in the virtual machine, it is very hard to configure the restrictions for all the applications. For this reason, in some applications which need to touch special resources on a remote host, Java allows the user program to open a security hole by using JNI (Java Native Interface) [27]. This is inconsistent with the security wall of the virtual machine. Therefore, we need to address the third problem by using a new execution mechanism for the programs.

2.3. Design of Caravela Platform

The execution unit of the Caravela platform is defined as the *flow-model*. As shown in Figure 2, the flow-model is composed of input/output data streams, of constant parameter inputs and of a program which processes the input data streams and generates output data streams, by fetching each input data unit from the input streams. The application program in Caravela is executed as stream-based computation, such as the one of a dataflow processor. However, the input data stream of the flow-model can be accessed randomly because the input data streams are just memory buffers for the program that uses the data. On the other hand, the output data streams are sequences based on the unit of data in the stream. Thus, the execution of the program embedded in the flow-model is not able to touch other resources beyond the I/O data streams.

The presentation of the flow-model is one of the issues for the discussion. Although the same available representation for the PetriNet graph can be used, due to its dataflow-like processing style, the flow-model admits finite loops supported by the Caravela runtime. The Caravela runtime operates as a resource manager for flow-models. To implement a loop with the flow-model, the output data stream(s) are connected to the input data stream(s), providing data migration among the stream buffers.

The flow-model provides the advantage when applied in distributed environments of encapsulating all the methods to execute a task into a data structure. Therefore, the flow-

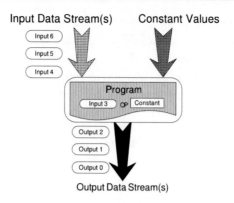

Figure 2. Structure of the flow-model.

model can be managed as a task object distributed anywhere, and can be fetched by the Caravela runtime. For example, when a flow-model is placed in a remote machine, an application over Caravela platform can fetch and reproduce the execution mechanism from the remote flow-model.

Regarding the processing unit to be assigned to a flow-model program, any software-based emulator, hardware data-flow processor, dedicated processor hardware, or others, can be applied.

2.4.   Caravela Runtime Environment

The flow-model execution requires a managing system, which assigns and loads the flow-model program into a processing unit, allocates memory buffers for input/output data streams, copies the input data streams to the allocated buffers and triggers the start of the program. In addition, after program execution, the runtime may need to read back the output data from the output stream buffers to forward it to the next flow-model or to store it. The Caravela runtime defines two functionalities for flow-model execution: the local and the remote execution functions.

The execution in a local processing resource corresponds to following the steps referred above. The runtime checks if the program in the flow-model matches the specification of a local processing unit.

To support the remote execution of the flow-model, the Caravela runtime needs a function to respond to requests sent by Caravela platforms located in other remote resources. The servers placed in the remote resources are categorized into two types: *worker* and *broker* servers.

- Worker server

  The worker server acts as a processing resource that assigns one flow-model to its local processing unit. This server communicates with its client to send/receive output/input data of the flow-model. If an execution request from a client does not include the flow-model itself but an information of the location of the flow-model, the server will fetch it from the address. Then, the server will assign the flow-model to the local processing unit.

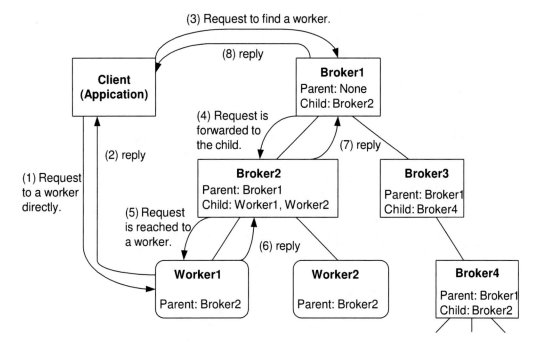

Figure 3. Caravela network example.

- Broker server

  The broker server performs as a router to reach the worker servers. The worker servers, after activation, send a request to register its route to one of broker servers. The broker server can have a parent broker server that accepts to register the route to a child broker. This mechanism creates a tree shaped worker network with broker servers as trunks of a tree. We call this tree-based virtual network the *Caravela network*.

Figure 3 shows an example of the Caravela network. The workers (Worker1 and Worker2) "belong" to the Broker1 and Broker2. Assume that the client tries to find a worker in the Caravela network and sends a request to the Worker1 directly (Figure 3 (1)). In this case, the client must know the route to the Worker1. The reply will be returned to the client directly (Figure 3 (2)). On the other hand, when the client sends the same request to the Broker1 (Figure 3 (3)), the Broker1 will forward the request to the Broker2 according to the routing information about the child(Figure 3(4)). The Broker2 knows that the Worker1 is its children and forwards the request to it (Figure 3 (5)). Finally, the request is processed and an answer returns by the opposite direction of the request and reaches the client(Figure 3(6)(7)(8)).

Regarding resource limitation for security matters, the broker and the worker servers may not accept flow-models that specify larger data streams than the limits configured by the servers. This mechanism protects the contributors' environment from the trouble caused by memory consumption. Moreover, the worker servers may specify a time limitation based on a unit of a flow-model execution. When the time spent by our application exceeds the limit, the worker server may cancel the subsequent flow-model execution. This mechanism allows the resource contributors to quantify the percentage of his/her contribution for anonymous computing on Caravela network. Thus, these capabilities of the worker and the broker servers implement a secure environment for GRID computing.

2.5. Application Interface in Caravela Platform

The interface for applications of Caravela platform is defined as a collection of functions to manage computing resources and to assign flow-models to the available computing resources. Applications on the Caravela platform need to follow the steps below:

1. **Initialization of the platform**
   In the beginning, the application initializes its context in the Caravela platform. This step creates a local temporal space for the subsequent management tasks.

2. **Reproduction of flow-model(s)**
   The Application fetches flow-model which may be in a remote location.

3. **Acquisition of processing unit(s)**
   To assign the flow-model, the application needs to acquire a processing unit that matches the conditions needed for the flow-model execution. If the application targets execution in a local processing unit, it queries directly the local resource. On the other hand, if the application needs to query the processing units of remote resources, for example when the requirements for the flow-model execution do not match the specification of the local processing unit, it sends a query request to worker or broker servers. If the application queries the worker, the worker will return its availability for flow-model execution. In this case, the application will send the requests directly to it. If the server is a broker, it will tell about all the available processing units it knows. In this case, the application will communicate to the broker server to execute the flow-model. Then the broker server will propagate the following requests to the worker server using its routing information.

4. **Mapping flow-model(s) to processing unit(s)**
   The application needs to map the flow-model to the processing unit reserved in the previous step. In the current step it will assign a program, I/O buffers and constant parameter inputs included in the flow-model. If the targeted processing unit is remote, the application exchanges requests with the worker servers.

5. **Execution of flow-model(s)**
   Before the execution in the processing unit starts, input data streams must be initialized. The execution of the flow-model is called "firing", which corresponds to activating a program in the flow-model and generating output data.

6. **Releasing processing unit(s) and flow-model(s)**
   After the execution of the flow-model, it is unmapped from the processing unit. Because the flow-model and the processing unit are not necessary in the next steps, they are released by the application.

7. **Finalization of the platform**
   Finally, the application needs to be terminated to exit from the Caravela environment.

The design considerations mentioned above are able to build a distributed processing platform using the flow-model framework. Because the flow-model includes enough information for independent execution, it performs stream-based processing without touching the resources in the host machine. Application in the Caravela platform is able to execute flow-models in a processing unit through secure execution mechanisms.

2.6. Implementation of Caravela Based on GPUs

The Caravela platform has been implemented using GPU as the processing unit. First, we need to consider the content of the flow-model.

2.6.1. Packing Flow-model

When GPUs are used as processing units of the Caravela platform, the flow-model unit includes a pixel shader program, textures as the input data streams, constant values of the shader program as the input constants and the frame buffers for output of the shader program as places to put the output data streams.

The flow-model unit needs to include also other important items related to the requirements for the program execution. The requirements consist mainly of the program's language type, its version and accepted data types, and an assembly version that shows significant differences, such as loop instruction available on Pixel Shader Model 3.0 or floating-point-based frame buffers.

We use the name "pixel" for a unit of the I/O buffer because the pixel processor processes input data for every pixel color. For example, a multiplication is performed with two registers that include ARGB elements as its operands, and outputs a register formed by ARGB elements.

In conclusion, the flow-model defines the number of pixels for the I/O data streams, the number of constant parameters, the data type on the I/O data streams, the pixel shader program and the requirements for the aimed GPU. To give portability to the flow-model, these items are packed into an Extensible Markup Language (XML) file. This mechanism allows the application in a remote computer to fetch just the XML file and easily execute the flow-model unit.

To help defining the flow-model, we have implemented a GUI-based tool, called *FlowModelCreator*, that is available in the Caravela package.

2.6.2. Applying GPU to Processing Unit

The application in the Caravela platform is supported by the Caravela runtime environment referred in section 2.4, which is running on the CPU of a commodity computer. Therefore, the application is a program which transfers and fires the flow-model unit execution in the GPUs according to the steps referred in section 2.5. For executing the flow-model in the GPU we need to define the resource hierarchy in the computer. Figure 4 shows a classification of the resource hierarchy in a computer. The group composed by the CPU and peripheral components, such as the host memory and the graphics boards, is defined as the "machine". A graphics board in the machine is defined as the "adapter". A GPU's pixel processor on the adapter is defined as the "shader". In summary, a *machine* may have

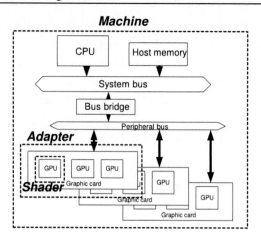

Figure 4. Resource hierarchy in a processing unit.

multiple *adapters*, and the adapter may have multiple *shaders*. The application needs to get the shader to map the flow-model to be executed on a pixel processor.

To control the pixel processor we need runtime software. Our first implementation of the Caravela platform uses Direct3D of the DirectX9 API and OpenGL. These runtimes provide functions to control the pixel processor. However, the interface is dedicated for graphics applications. Therefore, a rectangle plane object must be defined to present the output data streams of the pixel shader program. The plane acts as output target for multiple output data streams from the pixel shader program. However, on VRAM the buffers are separated into individual memory space. To save the output data stream, the runtime software fetches the spaces from the VRAM. According to this technique, a loop of a flow-model, or the connections of multiple flow-models, can be implemented with copy operations from the output data streams to the input data streams.

2.6.3. The Caravela Library

To control the flow-model execution, implicitly controlling the GPU, the application uses the Caravela library functions programmed in C language as listed in Table 1.

The CARAVELA_Initialize() function performs the initialization of one of the graphics runtime specified by the argument and prepares the context to use the Caravela platform, while CARAVELA_Finalize() is called to release those resources.

The CARAVELA_CreateFlowModelFromFile() function is called to build a flow-model from an XML file. An address of a flow-model is defined as a URL. Therefore, the function accesses a flow-model placed in a remote resource by using the Hypertext Transfer Protocol (HTTP).

The CARAVELA_CreateMachine() function is called when the application needs to define a machine data structure. If the function returns successfully, the CARAVELA_QueryShader() function is called to acquire a shader.

After application has prepared a flow-model and a shader, it can call the CARAVELA_MapFlowModelFromShader() function. This function assigns the program in the flow-model unit to the pixel shader, allocates the I/O streams to the VRAM

Table 1. Basic functions of Caravela library

`CARAVELA_CreateMachine(...)`	
	creates a machine structure
`CARAVELA_QueryShader(...)`	
	queries a shader on a machine
`CARAVELA_CreateFlowModelFromFile(...)`	
	creates a flow-model structure from XML file
`CARAVELA_GetInputData(...)`	
	gets a buffer of an input data stream
`CARAVELA_GetOutputData(...)`	
	gets a buffer of an output data stream
`CARAVELA_MapFlowModelIntoShader(...)`	
	maps a flow-model to a shader
`CARAVELA_FireFlowModel(...)`	
	executes a flow-model mapped to a shader

and returns a "fuse" to be used for triggering the flow-model execution. After receiving the "fuse", the `CARAVELA_FireFlowModel()` function sends commands to the pixel processor to execute the flow-model.

The `CARAVELA_GetInputData()` function prepares an input data stream in the host memory and the VRAM as texture data that will be input to the pixel processor. This function returns a buffer pointer for the input data stream which is used by the application to initialize the input data. On the other hand, the `CARAVELA_GetOutputData()` function returns an output data stream allocated in the VRAM.

Using the functions explained above, an application in the Caravela platform can locally execute a flow-model using the GPU's computation power. When the application needs more shaders, or the shader acquired does not match the requirements of the flow-model unit, it needs to query other shaders in the remote worker servers. In this case, the functions described in the next section are used.

2.6.4. The Remote Execution Mechanism

The broker and the worker servers are implemented by a piece of software called *CaravelaSnoopServer*, runnning on a remote CPU. The CaravelaSnoopServer can be configured as a broker or as a worker server.

The requests for CaravelaSnoopServer are received by the WebServices via Simple Object Access Protocol (SOAP). The address of the WebServices is specified by a WSDL file placed in an predefined address of the server. Two service functions are provided by the server: `putRequest()` and `getReply()`. The request and the reply exchanged between the server and an application are formatted in XML. The `putRequest()` function saves the XML description into a file where the CaravelaSnoopServer can pick it. According to this mechanism, requests are sent by the application. The `getReply()` function returns the reply from the CaravelaSnoopServer after processing the corresponding request. The application, or other servers, call this function periodically to receive the reply.

When the application sends a request about shaders to a broker server, the request is saved in the server and processed by the CaravelaSnoopServer. If the server is a worker, the request will be processed and the `getReply()` function is called. If the server is a broker, the request will be forwarded to the next server until it reaches a worker server. Then, a reply from the worker will be fetched by the previous requester. Thus, the reply will be propagated till the application. When a broker server is invoked in a bridge between a Wide Area Network (WAN) and a Local Area Network (LAN), the request and the reply are also able to be exchanged among the servers connected to the different networks and the application successfully.

The Caravela library implements the mechanism mentioned above to execute the process remotely.

When the application calls the `CARAVELA_CreateMachine()` function with `REMOTE_MACHINE` or `REMOTE_BROKER` arguments, which indicates a worker or a broker server respectively, the function creates a machine structure of remote resources. If it is a `REMOTE_MACHINE`, the execution steps of the flow-model follow the same steps as the ones in the local execution. If it is a `REMOTE_BROKER`, the application tries to acquire workers by executing the `CARAVELA_GetRemoteMachines()` function and by using the broker machine structure. This function returns all the worker machines that are "seen" by the broker. Then, the application can select the appropriate worker machines and can map the flow-model(s) into the selected worker(s). After this step the application is able to follow the steps appropriate for local execution.

Requests and replies from and to the worker server are directly exchanged if the application selected a worker server. On the other hand, if it is a broker server, all the requests and replies are exchanged via the broker server. This mechanism has the advantage of being transparent for the applications.

2.7. Experimental Example

Now, let us examine an experimental example that consists in a two dimensional Finite Impulse Response (2D FIR) filter algorithm. The 2D FIR filter is mainly used to perform image or video processing, like sharpening, or edge detection of an image/frame. The type of filtering is changed by using different taps values in the coefficient matrix, where common dimensions are 3x3 or 7x7. Here, we illustrate the programming of a filter with a 3x3 coefficient matrix:

$$y_{k,l} = \sum_{i=0}^{2} \sum_{j=0}^{2} h_{i,j} x_{k+i,l+j} \tag{1}$$

h is the 3x3 coefficient matrix and x is the input matrix, size MxN, with k and l being integers in the range from 0 to M-3 and to N-3, respectively.

The calculation steps followed in this example are shown in Figure 5(a) for $M = N = 4$. The first step consists in multiplying each element of the sub-matrix (window) with corners in x_{00} and x_{22} with the correspondent elements of the coefficient matrix, and then adding all of them to get the output as the result y_{00}. This arithmetic operation is usually called *Multiply and ACcumulate* (MAC). In the second step, the input matrix' window is shifted to the right, and this step is repeated with the output going to y_{01}. Repeating this operation for every element of the input matrix, except for the elements belonging to the

Table 2. Environment for local execution.

CPU	AMD Opteron 170 @ 2Ghz
Host memory	2x1GB DDR
GPU	MSI NX7300GS
VRAM	256MB DDR2
OS	WindowsXP SP2
Graphics API	DirectX9c

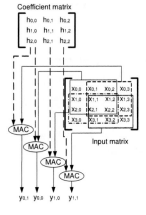

(a) 2D FIR filter with 4x4 input matrix

```
sampler s0;
float4x3 c;

void main(
  in float2 t0: TEXCOORD0, // dcl t0.xy

    out float4 oC0: COLOR0 )
    {
  float inv = 1/c[3][0];
  float4 input_row0;
  float4 input_row1;

  int i,j;
  float2 coord = t0;
  oC0 = 0;
  for(i=0;i<3;i++,coord.y+=inv){
    input_row0 = tex2D(s0, coord);
    coord.x += inv;
    input_row1 = tex2D(s0, coord);
    oC0.x += (input_row0.x * c[0][i] + input_row0.y * c[1][i] + input_row0.z * c[2][i]);
    oC0.y += (input_row0.y * c[0][i] + input_row0.z * c[1][i] + input_row0.w * c[2][i]);
    oC0.z += (input_row0.z * c[0][i] + input_row0.w * c[1][i] + input_row1.x * c[2][i]);
    oC0.w += (input_row0.w * c[0][i] + input_row1.x * c[1][i] + input_row1.y * c[2][i]);
    coord.x= t0.x;
  }
}
```
(1)

(b) Program embedded in flow-model

Figure 5. The calculation steps and the program of a flow-model corresponding to a 2D FIR filter.

last two columns or rows, the application calculates the result of applying the filter to the input matrix.

Figure 5(b) shows the program to be embedded into a flow-model. This program is written in the DirectX' HLSL whose syntax is very similar to the C language. To be fit into the GPU's hardware architecture, the program assumes that M equals to $4 \times N$ due to the register characteristics, but it can be generalized.

The `main()` function is the routine executed in the GPU. We need to be careful about the arguments of the function, because the input to the pixel processor are the coordinates of the texture's pixels (`t0`). The output contains the pixel colors on the buffer for the screen (`oC0`). This function will be executed in parallel on the multiple pixel processors because the pixel values are independent, and outputs a pixel color by each input texture's coordinate.

The code shown in Figure 5(b)(1) corresponding to the calculation of equation (1), and accesses not sequentially the texture data by adding the offset `inv` to `coord` for each texture pixel. The `coord` is the 2D address of the texture (i.e., input matrix) and the `tex2D` function fetches the texture values. Therefore, the input data of this application is randomly accessed.

The values of the texture returned by `tex2D` function (i.e., the input matrix), the output oC0 and the coefficient matrix c include four floating point values and calculates four elements of the output matrix oC0. Thus, the pixel processor also performs parallel processing.

2.7.1. A Local Execution Example

The code using the runtime functions of the Caravela for local execution of the flow-model of 2D FIR filter is shown in Figure 6(a). At the beginning, the machine is created in step (1). The flow-model will be reproduced in step (2), from a path to an XML file defined in the FLOWMODEL_FILE macro. Using the machine structure, step (3) queries a shader from the local machine. If it is successful, the flow-model will be mapped to the shader in step (4). Here the input data stream is initialized as shown in step (5). After initialization, the flow-model will be fired in step (6). This function will block the subsequent execution until its execution has been finished. Therefore, the code for getting the output in step (7) is executed right after the firing. Finally, the flow-model and the shader are released in step (8).

   Thus, the interface for executing the flow-model execution in the local machine is simple and transparent. Therefore, the programmer can write application for the Caravela platform without accounting for the details of the processing unit which is used.

2.7.2. A Remote Execution Example

There exist two ways for remote execution of the flow-model. One of them requests a processing unit to a specific worker server as shown in step (9) of Figure 6(b). In this case, a remote machine is created as REMOTE_MACHINE with the URL for the remote worker. All the processes, such as querying shaders and mapping the flow-model, are performed by the machine structure returned by CARAVELA_CreateMachine(). On the other hand, when the request for acquiring a processing unit is performed via a broker server, as shown in step (10) of Figure 6(b), the machine structure will be created by passing REMOTE_BROKER to the CARAVELA_CreateMachine() function with the URL for a remote broker server, and the machine structure returned by the function will be passed to the CARAVELA_GetRemoteMachines() function. Finally, the available machines returned by the function will be used by the application, but the communication itself will be performed via the broker server.

   In both cases, the processing steps after machine creation are the same as those presented in the description of local execution in Figure 6(a). Thus, it is easy for the application designer to migrate it from a local execution situation to a remote execution situation by changing only a small part of the code for machine creation.

2.7.3. Performance Considerations

To evaluate the performance of the local execution of the FIR filter depicted in Figure 5(b), we measured execution times when using the computing environment referred in Table 2, with 100 iterations on a 1024x1024 pixel input matrix (i.e., 1024x4096 floating point values at the input of the 2D FIR filter). In order to have a comparison reference, we have also

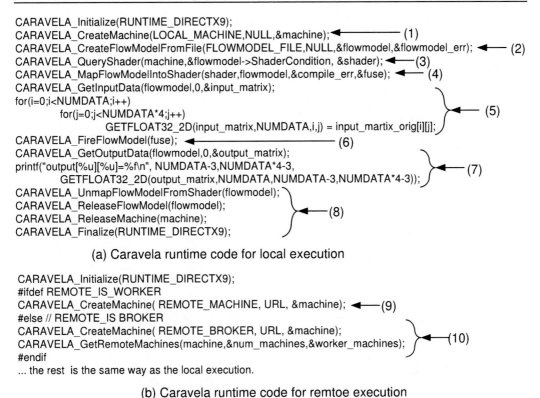

```
CARAVELA_Initialize(RUNTIME_DIRECTX9);
CARAVELA_CreateMachine(LOCAL_MACHINE,NULL,&machine);            (1)
CARAVELA_CreateFlowModelFromFile(FLOWMODEL_FILE,NULL,&flowmodel,&flowmodel_err);    (2)
CARAVELA_QueryShader(machine,&flowmodel->ShaderCondition, &shader);   (3)
CARAVELA_MapFlowModelIntoShader(shader,flowmodel,&compile_err,&fuse);    (4)
CARAVELA_GetInputData(flowmodel,0,&input_matrix);
for(i=0;i<NUMDATA;i++)
        for(j=0;j<NUMDATA*4;j++)                                          (5)
            GETFLOAT32_2D(input_matrix,NUMDATA,i,j) = input_martix_orig[i][j];
CARAVELA_FireFlowModel(fuse);                    (6)
CARAVELA_GetOutputData(flowmodel,0,&output_matrix);
printf("output[%u][%u]=%f\n", NUMDATA-3,NUMDATA*4-3,
        GETFLOAT32_2D(output_matrix,NUMDATA,NUMDATA-3,NUMDATA*4-3));     (7)
CARAVELA_UnmapFlowModelFromShader(flowmodel);
CARAVELA_ReleaseFlowModel(flowmodel);
CARAVELA_ReleaseMachine(machine);                (8)
CARAVELA_Finalize(RUNTIME_DIRECTX9);
```

(a) Caravela runtime code for local execution

```
CARAVELA_Initialize(RUNTIME_DIRECTX9);
#ifdef REMOTE_IS_WORKER
CARAVELA_CreateMachine( REMOTE_MACHINE, URL, &machine);    (9)
#else // REMOTE_IS_BROKER
CARAVELA_CreateMachine( REMOTE_BROKER, URL, &machine);
CARAVELA_GetRemoteMachines(machine,&num_machines,&worker_machines);   (10)
#endif
... the rest is the same way as the local execution.
```

(b) Caravela runtime code for remtoe execution

Figure 6. An example of application code on the Caravela platform for performing local and remote flow-model execution.

implemented the 2D FIR filter on the CPU side. The input matrix size and the number of iterations are the same in both experiments.

The calculation time on the Caravela platform is 10.6 s, which compares with 23.5 s on the CPU-based version. The Caravela platform achieves about 2.2 times higher performance than the host CPU. Thus, we can conclude that, by providing a secure environment and a transparent interface for programmers and resource contributors, the current implementation of the Caravela platform smoothly assigns the flow-model to the pixel processor on a GPU for example. It also implements a high performance stream-based computing environment.

3.   Commandline Based Execution of Flow-models

3.1.   Stream-oriented Programming Environment

To reduce the difficulty of the double programming situation, there exist programming languages and the runtimes. The recent de fact standard ones are NVIDIA's CUDA [33] and OpenCL [34][31][47].

The CUDA assumes an architecture model as illustrated in Figure 7 (a). The model defines a GPU which is connected to a CPU's peripheral bus. A VRAM maintains data used

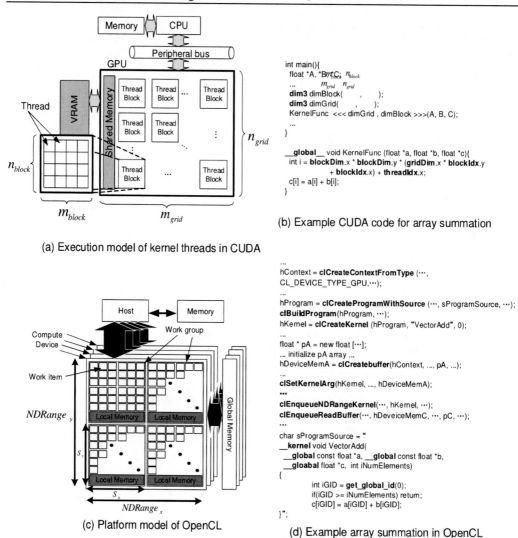

(a) Execution model of kernel threads in CUDA

(b) Example CUDA code for array summation

(c) Platform model of OpenCL

(d) Example array summation in OpenCL

Figure 7. CUDA and OpenCL architecture models and its vector summation examples.

for calculation on the GPU. The kernel program is downloaded by the host CPU to GPU and the data is also copied from the host memory. The program is executed as a thread in a thread block grouped with multiple threads. The thread blocks are tiled in a matrix of from one to three dimensions. In the figure, thread blocks are tiled in two dimensions which size is $n_{grid} \times m_{grid}$. Each thread block consists of $n_{block} \times m_{block}$ threads. The program shown in Figure 7 (b) is an example of vector summation written by using CUDA. The kernel program is defined with the __global__ directive so that it is executed on GPU. In the function, the global variables named `gridDim`, `blockDim`, `blockIdx`, `threadIdx`, implicitly declared by the CUDA runtime, are available to be used to specify the size of the grid and the thread block, the indices of the thread block and of the thread respectively. The function is called by the host CPU program specifying the number of threads with <<< >>>.

The OpenCL defines a common platform model that includes the processing element and the memory hierarchy. Figure 7(c) illustrates the platform model for the processing element. The host CPU is connected to the *OpenCL device*. The OpenCL device consists of the individual processing element called *compute unit*. The compute unit includes one or more *work groups* that include the *work items*. The work item is identified by the unique ID and processes the corresponding result using the related input data associated by the ID. The total number of work items is given by the program using a parameter called *NDRange* that can be defined in from one to three dimensions. The example in the figure includes $NDRange_x \times NDRange_y$ work items. The OpenCL program is written in C as the host CPU side shown in Figure 7(d). The resources in the OpenCL are obtained by the *context* created by the runtime function. In the figure, the context for a GPU is defined by specifying CL_DEVICE_TYPE_GPU as its argument. The argument is variable to select different types of accelerators. The kernel program is provided by a source string defined as an array of char. The string is passed to the runtime functions to compile and prepare the executable code in the accelerator. The buffers for I/O data streams are allocated using the conventional functions such as "new" or "malloc" in the CPU side. The programmer can select if the buffers are accessed directly from the accelerator or if the buffer mirrors are allocated in the accelerator's memory. And then, the argument pointers of the kernel function that point to the actual buffers in the host and/or in the compute device are passed to the accelerator. Finally, the kernel is executed by the clEnqueueNDRangeKernel function and the output data streams in the accelerator's memory are copied to the host CPU side.

The assumed architectures in CUDA and OpenCL are very similar. The major difference between those is the kernel compilation mechanism. The CUDA program is compiled whole code including the kernel function by using the *nvcc* compiler. Then the executable for the host CPU downloads the program implicitly to the GPU. Besides, the OpenCL one passes the source string of the kernel code to the runtime function. To separate the kernel code in CUDA as performed by OpenCL, *nvcc* can output the assembly language (PTX) of the kernel code. The assembly language code is also able to be loaded by a runtime function of CUDA. To keep the code compatibility among both runtimes, it is important to develop a unified interface for the accelerator that loads and executes the kernel code without developing the host side program using different runtime functions.

The stream-based computing environment provided by the accelerators brings a powerful parallel processing environment due to the exploited concurrency implicitly from the program. Moreover the runtime environments such as OpenCL and CUDA let the programmer easily develop the application on the accelerators. However, the programmer needs to design and implement both the host CPU program and the kernel program for the accelerator. Caravela platform provides a model-based execution mechanism using flow-model. However, it still has the duty for the double programming separating the CPU program using the Caravela library and the flow-model with the kernel program. So that the programmer concentrates to write the kernel program on the accelerator, it is indispensable to invent a new programming environment where avoids to develop the host CPU program. As the related work, *barracuda* [4] on ruby extension for OpenCL provides wrapper methods for hiding the difficulty of the host CPU program. And StreamIt [43] provides a unified language to resolve the double programming difficulty at compiling time. However those also need to code the scenario for the kernel execution timings. If the programmer needs

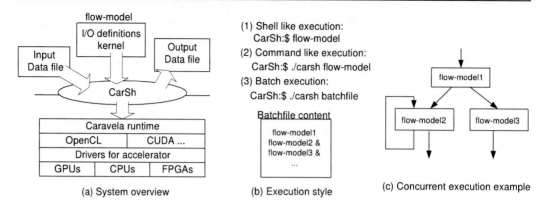

Figure 8. CarSh system overview.

to invoke multiple kernel programs concurrently, those programs must include a detailed schedule for multi-thread execution on the CPU side. Therefore, it is important to develop a kernel execution environment for intuitive programming of complex applications utilizing accelerator's power, where the programmer only considers the kernel program, the I/O kernels and parallelization parameters. And then the execution timings should be automatically and implicitly decided at running time. In this section, using the flow-model definition to resolve the problem, we propose a novel shell-like and commandline-based programming environment for the stream-based accelerators called *CarSh*.

3.2.   Design of CarSh

When we execute any kind of commands in a conventional CPU-based system, we often use a shell such as *bash*. We just rely on the execution timings and managements of the processes such as background/foreground execution. We consider the same execution mechanism on the stream-based programs for accelerators.

Figure 8(a) shows the system overview of CarSh. CarSh receives flow-models and the corresponding input data files. After the execution of the flow-model the output data are also stored into files. As shown in Figure 8(b) CarSh executes flow-models directly (1) from the commandline of CarSh like a shell prompt, (2) from an argument of CarSh and (3) from a batch file of an execution schedule of multiple flow-models. The batch file implements a pipeline execution of multiple flow-models, for example, shown in Figure 8(c). The data I/O for the pipeline execution are provided by files or internally allocated buffers in CarSh. In the pipeline, *flowmodel2* and *flowmodel3* can be invoked simultaneously. Here, CarSh needs a background concurrent execution mechanism of the flow-models. If a flow-model defines the recursive I/O using the swap pair, CarSh needs automatically to detect the property and executes the iteration for the swap pair. According to the consideration for the interface, we introduce the design considerations below for CarSh.

3.3.   Management of Flow-model Execution

CarSh needs to execute a flow-model automatically detecting the definitions and execute it over the Caravela framework. It needs to define an executable format for the execution.

The format includes 1) I/O buffer definition with the data type, 2) flow-model XML file, 3) target lower level runtime such as OpenCL, 4) optional functionality definitions such as the *swap function*. CarSh prepares the input data from the I/O definitions, executes the flow-model applying the optional functions and finally saves the result of the output data from the flow-model. This scenario is packed in a single executable format and passed it to CarSh.

In addition to the single execution of a flow-model, CarSh needs a batch execution mode for supporting the pipeline execution of multiple flow-models as shown in Figure 8(c). The batch execution follows a formatted scenario with the execution steps of the flow-models. To implement this batch execution, CarSh needs a background execution mode and a synchronization function for the previous flow-model executions. For example, to invoke the pipeline in the figure, CarSh executes *flowmodel1* and wait the execution. After that, *flowmodel2* and *flowmodel3* can be concurrently executed as the background tasks. CarSh also needs to have a synchronization function to wait for finishing previously executed flow-models.

The flow-model does not define any behavior regarding iterative execution. Moreover, a set of flow-model (i.e., batch) execution must have possibility to be repeated as it would get the results after specified steps such as the LU decomposition algorithm. Therefore, CarSh needs a function to repeat execution of a flow-model or a batch scenario for a specified times.

3.4. Management of I/O Data Streams

The flow-model execution needs input data and after the execution it saves the output data. CarSh introduces two mechanisms for saving/restoring the I/O data. One is a simple mechanism reading/writing the input/output data from a file. In this case, CarSh sets the data read from the file to the corresponding input buffer and uses it for the flow-model execution. The output data are also saved into a file that can be used as the input again. Thus, through one flow-model execution to another in a pipeline structure the files are passed and received. Another mechanism is *virtual buffer* that works as a virtual space for I/O data provided by CarSh inside. The virtual buffer is first prepared by CarSh before the flow-model execution. During the execution, it is used as the place for saving the I/O data of flow-models. The content data of the virtual buffer can be loaded from a file or saved to a file. To manage the virtual buffer, CarSh needs the management functions for *creating*, *deleting* the buffer, and also functions for *filling* and *dumping* data in the buffer from/to files.

According to the functions for flow-model execution and the I/O data, CarSh will provide a shell-like stream computing environment just giving the kernel programs and the execution scenario is packed into the executable or the batch. During execution of the scenario, CarSh fulfills the input data from files or the virtual buffer and passes the execution result to the next file or the virtual buffer. The next flow-model can read the result from the buffer to continue the execution. Thus, the flow-model execution conveys data from one buffer to the next ones. CarSh provides also the iteration of flow-model or batch. Thus, the programmer who uses CarSh does not consider the host CPU program at all. He/she finally becomes available to focus on designing just the kernel programs and the dataflow scenario.

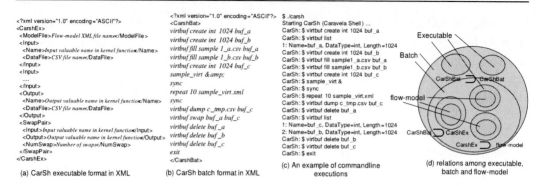

Figure 9. Implementation of CarSh.

3.5. Implementation of CarSh

Our first implementation of CarSh employs *process*-based task management using *fork* system call on Linux environment. Thread-based implementation is also possible and would achieve better performance. A process is assigned to each flow-model execution by giving an executable XML file as shown in Figure 9(a) to CarSh commandline. When '&' is added in the last of the commandline, the process is executed in background. This implements the concurrent execution of multiple flow-models. For the synchronization of one or more process executions our implementation introduces *sync* command to wait all the process execution including the background processes using `waitpid` system call. The batch scenario is written in an XML file with `<CarshBat>` tag. Given in the commandline in CarSh, the batch XML file includes the steps of the scenario like the example of Figure 9(b).

I/O data for the flow-model are loaded and saved from/to CSV files. The file is directly assigned by `<DataFile>` tag in `<Input>` and `<Output>` tags. The `<DataFile>` tag accepts also the virtual buffer name as the input for the flow-model. The I/O arguments of the kernel code in the flow-model are linked in the executable file of CarSh. Thus, the virtual buffers are connected to the I/O in the flow-model. This means that the I/O data inputted/outputted to/from accelerator will be passed to/from the CSV files.

The virtual buffer is implemented by the POSIX shared memory object. The first process of CarSh (here calls this process *master*) creates the shared objects that correspond to the virtual buffers using `shm_open` system call and the buffer sizes are truncated by `ftrancate` system call. The master process folks other children processes of flow-models that open the shred memory objects, and then the children processes use the shared memory object as the I/O buffers. The content of the shared object is saved into a file in CSV format. While the flow-model execution processes are working, the virtual buffers are never removed because those are used for the flow-model execution. Then the master process can delete the buffers using `shm_unlink` system call. Thus the shared object is created and deleted by the master process.

Figure 9(c) shows an example of CarSh commandline execution. First the *virtbuf* command manages the virtual buffers with the argument *list* that shows all allocated virtual buffers and the argument *create* that allocates a virual buffer. After executing an executable or a batch file named *sample_virt.xml* in the background and synchronizes it by *sync* com-

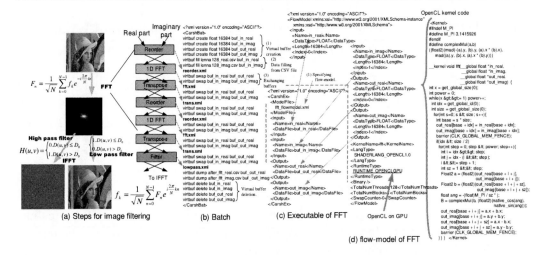

Figure 10. Implementation of image filtering using FFT on CarSh.

mand. *repeat* performs the iterative execution of the same XML file for 10 times. The *virtbuf* command can save the buffer contents to files using *dump* argument. The *swap* argument of the command exchanges buffer names. Finally the *delete* argument deletes all the allocated virtual buffers.

The inclusion relations among the flow-model, the executable and the batch are illustrated in Figure 9(d). The executable only includes the flow-model directly. The batch includes the executables and the other batches. If a programmer needs to repeat execution of a processing pipeline with flow-models, he/she can pack the pipeline to a batch and then prepares another batch that includes the batch. Therefore, nesting the executable and the batch, we can implement any combination of processing flows.

3.6.   Evaluations

Let us explain evaluations of CarSh focusing on the performance and the programmability. Here we use a typical image filtering using 2D FFT performed often in the image operations. Figure 10(a) shows the processing steps used in the evaluation. An image (*Lena*), which is transformed by the FFT, is passed to a high or low pass filter, and finally transposed by IFFT. This simple process is composed by five flow-models: *reorder* performs butterfly exchanges, *transpose* inverses the rows and the columns, *filter, FFT and IFFT*. the whole calculation is defined by a CarSh batch XML file listed in Figure 10(b). It uses virtual buffers for the real and imaginary parts inputted/outputted to/from the subsequent processes managed by *virtbuf* command such as Figure 10(b)-(1)(2). After every flow-model execution, those buffers are exchanged such as Figure 10(b)-(3). After the executions of the flow-models, the virtual buffers are deleted. Here, each flow-model execution is called from the CarSh executable XML file, for example, FFT shown in Figure 10(c). The I/O data for initialization/resulting values are passed via the virtual buffers. The flow-model of the FFT is shown in Figure 10(d). The I/O arguments of the kernel program correspond to the real and imaginary parts. Those match each other among the executable and the flow-model. Finally, CarSh will execute the batch XML file to get a filtered image.

Table 3. Performance of Image filtering using FFT on CarSh over OpenCL runtime.

Image size (GPU)	FFT	Filter	IFFT	Total (sec)	Image size (CPU)	FFT	Filter	IFFT	Total (sec)
128^2	0.766	0.128	0.764	1.658	128^2	1.969	0.281	1.971	4.221
256^2	0.78	0.128	0.779	1.687	256^2	2.002	0.266	1.999	4.267
512^2	0.825	0.135	0.826	1.786	512^2	2.029	0.302	2.032	4.363
1024^2	0.985	0.153	0.988	2.126	1024^2	2.216	0.329	2.218	4.763

3.6.1. Programmability of CarSh

This example is a typical pipelined application with multiple flow-models. The pipeline is organized by passing buffers from one kernel program to the next. This must be implemented by buffer management functions on the host CPU side if we apply the conventional double programming method using the OpenCL runtime for accelerators. Moreover, CarSh provides the virtual buffer. It is easy for the programmer to allocate buffers used for the I/O data from/to the flow-model. Thus, buffers are easily defined in the batch XML file by specifying the names. Those are fulfilled from CSV files to the buffer, and simply passed via the names of the buffer among flow-models in the executables.

Without considering the timings for kernel executions and also the buffer management among the host CPU and the accelerator, the programmer can perform a straightforward programming using CarSh framework. The programmer is able to focus on brushing up the stream-based algorithm written in the kernel program. Moreover, because whole code for CarSh is written in text, it is very highly portable among different combinations of a host CPU and an accelerator. This enables a remote development environment where the code compatibility is guaranteed. For example, when we use different kinds of accelerators over OpenCL, we can just change `RuntimeType` tag in flow-model as shown in Figure 10(d). This mechanism makes the performance check much easy as we just change the string in the flow-model XML description.

3.6.2. Performance of CarSh

We have measured performances of the image filtering example with varying the accelerator types and the image sizes. Our platform of the performance test is a PC with a Corei7 930 2.80GHz with an Nvidia Tesla M2050 GPU. Table 3 shows the comparison among the GPU-based and the CPU-based executions of the image filtering batch file on CarSh. Both executions use the same kernel functions and the CarSh related XML files. The number of parallelism in OpenCL is set to 1024 where the OpenCL runtime distributes 1024 concurrent threads on the GPU and the CPU. The CPU-based execution is performed on the Intel OpenCL runtime using the multiple cores of the CPU. According to the performances listed in the table, the GPU-based performance achieves almost double of the CPU-based one. This implies that we can control the performance of a set of CarSh executable XMLs. Therefore, if we introduce a new powerful accelerator, we can easily upgrade the performance changing the runtime type description in the flow-model.

As we explained in this section, CarSh brings a simple and transparent programming style for the high programmability on the stream computing employing XML-based packaging for the kernel function invoked in the accelerator. It is easy to control the performance by changing the runtime type description defined in flow-model. Thus, we have confirmed that CarSh overcomes the programming complexity on the current stream-based accelerators that enforces the double programming. Moreover, CarSh provides the novel commandline interface for executing the kernel function. This promotes high productivity of programs on manycore architectures.

4. Parallel Execution of Multiple Flow-models

4.1. CaravelaMPI

4.1.1. Parallel Computation with MPI

There are two major paradigms for programming and implementing parallel applications: *i*) *message passing paradigm* that exchanges messages between processes that run concurrently; and *ii*) *shared memory paradigm* that shares data between processes through physical, or virtual, shared memory. Interfaces and libraries such as the Parallel Virtual Machine (PVM) [13] and the MPI [44] have been developed to support parallel programming based on message passing. The OpenMP [19] has been designed to program shared memory systems. This section is focused on parallel programming based on the message passing paradigm, namely the MPI.

To program an efficient parallel application based on message passing, the programmer has to consider both the computation and communication aspects of processing algorithms and systems. Therefore, when performance of parallel applications running on an MPI-based cluster has to be improved, two main approaches can be adopted: *i*) upgrading the system, namely upgrading the processor hardware, increasing the amount of memory and upgrading the network platform (not only at the hardware level but also in the software layers [21]) whenever parallel applications require intensive communication; and *ii*) redesigning algorithms to exploit further parallelism in applications, increasing computation instead of communication time, or by overlapping these two parts. In the latter approach, programmers must try to find parts of application where communication can be overlapped with computation, using MPI asynchronous communication functions such as MPI_Isend and MPI_Irecv. These functions do not block the subsequent computation and implicitly send/receive messages to/from the receivers/senders. For instance, as illustrated in Figure 11, the MPI_Irecv() function in Proc0 executes its communication implicitly while computations are performed. After the computation is finished, the communication is synchronized by using the MPI_Wait() function. This mechanism works with a communication request data structure that is received from the communication function (i.e., MPI_Irecv()) and is passed into the synchronization function (MPI_Wait()). According to the implicit communication operation, the communication time can be concealed by the computation time and consequently the processing efficiency increases. Thus, it is very important to try to overlap communication with computation when using message passing paradigms, so that performance of entire system can be increased without having to invest more powerful hardware resources.

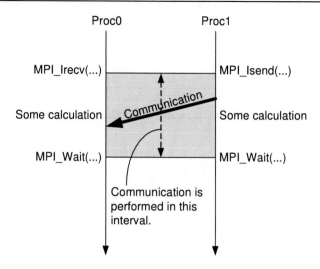

Figure 11. Overlapping communication with computation.

4.1.2. Discussion

With the huge computing capacity of GPUs it is likely that GPU-based clusters will become important to design high performance computing platforms. The experience of building a GPU cluster [9] has already been reported as a breakthrough in cluster computing platforms. Although the parallel algorithms originally devised for conventional cluster computers will have to be reworked for GPU-based clusters, it can be quite advantageous in terms of gains, if we are able to exploit the huge computing power provided by GPU clusters.

In spite of such exciting forecast, the programming of GPU-based clusters has to become feasible, and a de facto standard Application Programming Interfaces (API) will have to be developed in order to make usage of those parallel systems accessible while achieving high processing efficiency. Programming on such raw system is a very complex task, which requires mixing GPU control functions provided by graphics runtime with MPI functions executed by CPU under control of operating system.

Herein, we propose a unified library named *CaravelaMPI* that encapsulates communication and GPU control procedures and functions. CaravelaMPI combines MPI and Caravela library, hiding the details of the graphics runtime environment and allowing the programmer to concentrate himself in a goal of achieving an efficient parallel implementation for his application.

Design and implementation aspects of the CaravelaMPI and associated software library will be presented and discussed in the next section.

4.1.3. Design of CaravelaMPI

Parallel processing based on message passing paradigm has three different stages: message reception, computation and message transmission. Exact timing for receiving messages is usually statically unpredictable, since it is dependent on characteristics of systems and of running programs. Programmer uses asynchronous receiving function to reserve data reception and puts other calculation in waiting time for the reception. For the transmission after the calculation, the same technique can be used to send result data applying asynchronous transmission function, without synchronizing to finish data transmission in network hardware.

According to the patterns between communications and calculations in message passing of parallel application mentioned above, we propose the following interface models in CaravelaMPI: *i) Recv-Calculate-Send; ii) Recv-Calculate; iii) Calculate-Send*; and *iv) Synchronization for asynchronous communication.*

Recv-Calculate-Send interface model provides a mechanism to receive I/O data streams as messages from remote processes, to execute a flow-model using the messages and to send results from the flow-model execution to remote processes. This interface model is provided with both synchronous and asynchronous versions. In the synchronous version, this interface model blocks the subsequent program operations until arrival of input data messages, where the flow-model execution resumes and the transmission of the output data is performed. On the other hand, if the calling mode is asynchronous, this interface model does not block the subsequent operations. Therefore, the asynchronous version of this interface model just reserves communications and computation with flow-model, issuing a request. To confirm the request completion, programmer uses the synchronization interface model that will be explained later.

Recv-Calculate interface model receives I/O data messages for a flow-model and executes it using the received data. When an application needs to perform both reception and calculation, such as the case when it must gather all results from other processes and calculate the final result, programmer can use this kind of interface model. This interface has also two versions: synchronous and asynchronous. The synchronous version blocks the subsequent operations until the flow-model execution has been completed, while the asynchronous version does not block, issuing a request. To check the request completion, the synchronization interface model mentioned later is invoked.

Calculate-Send interface model corresponds to complementary part of the Recv-Calculate-Send interface model. The flow-model execution is immediately performed after this interface model is invoked. This interface model has synchronous version and asynchronous one. For sending output data streams to other processes, the former one performs the flow-model execution and the communication without returning from the corresponding interface function. The latter version returns immediately only issuing a request. Therefore, to confirm completion of the request, synchronization interface model must be invoked.

Finally, in addition to MPI functions for synchronization such as `MPI_Wait()` or `MPI_Test()`, a synchronization interface model is required for managing the completion of communication and calculations performed by the interface models proposed above. This interface blocks all the subsequent calculations until the corresponding request has been completed.

In all models, except the synchronization one, to perform recursive execution of the flow-model, the interfaces can accept the I/O pair data structure for the buffer swapping functions in Caravela, and also the number of iterations. This allows to loop a flow-model for a given number of times, while exchanging the I/O data streams specified in the swap I/O pairs.

By using the proposed interface models, application can thus efficiently implement

Table 4. CaravelaMPI functions

Management functions
`CaravelaMPI_Init(...)`   Initialization of CaravelaMPI environment.
`CaravelaMPI_Finalize(...)`   finalization of CaravelaMPI environment.
Synchronous communication functions
`CaravelaMPI_Recvsend(...)`   Synchronous Recv-Calculate-Send interface.
`CaravelaMPI_Recv(...)`   Synchronous Recv-Calculate interface.
`CaravelaMPI_Send(...)`   Synchronous Calculate-Send interface.
Asynchronous communication functions
`CaravelaMPI_Irecvsend(...)`   Asynchronous Recv-Calculate-Send interface.
`CaravelaMPI_Irecv(...)`   Asynchronous Recv-Calculate interface.
`CaravelaMPI_Isend(...)`   Asynchronous Calculate-Send interface.
Synchronization functions
`CaravelaMPI_Wait(...)`   Synchronization interface to complete a request.
`CaravelaMPI_Test(...)`   Synchronization interface to check a request completion.

communications and parallel execution with the GPU's resources. When programmer tries to overshadow GPU calculations with communications, the interfaces can be moved to the other timings. During the migrations of communication timings, calculations on GPUs will be moved together because the GPU calculations are encapsulated into the interface models using the flow-model framework. Moreover, because the completion of GPU calculations can be checked by the synchronization interface model, flexible control for execution timings on GPUs becomes available, considering communication timings simultaneously. Thus, the interface disparity between communications and program execution on GPU discussed in the previous section will be addressed by the CaravelaMPI, and also the performance tuning regarding communication timing will cause an speedup of parallel applications.

4.1.4. Implementation of CaravelaMPI

CaravelaMPI was implemented by using both MPI and Caravela library functions. The set of functions provided by CaravelaMPI to program parallel applications is presented in Table 4. Four main categories of functions are implemented: *i*) management functions, *ii*) synchronous communication functions, *iii*) asynchronous communication functions, and *iv*) synchronization functions for *iii*).

Because the synchronous functions in CaravelaMPI are implemented with combining the asynchronous functions, let us explain the asynchronous and the synchronization functions first.

`CaravelaMPI_Irecvsend()` corresponds to the Recv-Calculate-Send interface model. Its arguments are arrays of I/O data streams, arrays of source/destination ranks, arrays of sending/receiving messages, a communicator for the MPI runtime, a flow-model, an array of swap I/O pairs, the number of iteration for flow-model execution and a request data structure. The arrays of I/O data streams can be specified as NULL when the subsequent calculations do not need that intermediate data. The arrays of ranks are used for receiving input data streams and for sending output data streams to/from the flow-model. The communicator is applied for defining communication group in MPI runtime such as `MPI_COMM_WORLD`. `CaravelaMPI_Irecvsend()` receives messages that correspond to given input data streams of the flow-model and executes the flow-model using the swap I/O pair data structure and sends the output data streams to the remote processes. The send and receive operations are implemented by `MPI_Isend()` and `MPI_Irecv()`. By including the argument information for the function, the request also obtains the MPI-related request data structure. The function never blocks the subsequent calculations. Therefore, the function returns immediately after saving the request data structure which obtains type of requested interface and the argument information. Each operation performed in the function (message reception, calculation on GPU and message transmission) is completed when the synchronization functions are called.

`CaravelaMPI_Irecv()` and `CaravelaMPI_Isend()` correspond to the asynchronous versions of the Recv-Calculate and the Calculate-Send interfaces respectively. These functions perform a part of `CaravelaMPI_Irecvsend()` except buffer management for I/O data streams in flow-model. The former function needs to receive an array of memory areas as its arguments for the output data streams because it returns the results of the flow-model execution. On the other hand, the latter function needs to receive an array for the input data streams. Moreover, these functions also do not block the subsequent calculations and just saves argument information to a request data structure. The completion is also performed in the same way as the one of `CaravelaMPI_Irecvsend()`.

The synchronization functions have interface to receive request as its argument which is returned by the asynchronous functions. These functions immediately return after checking the completion of the request. However, while checking the request's status, when some operations have been finished even if the operations are not related to the request, it executes the next operations of those requests. For example, if receiving messages for input data streams related to `CaravelaMPI_Irecv()` has been finished, flow-model execution that is the next step of the function is performed in `CaravelaMPI_Test()`. The function returns a status data structure that contains arrays of I/O data streams used by the flow-model execution and status data structure for MPI functions. On the other hand, `CaravelaMPI_Wait()` blocks the subsequent calculations, until all operations related to its requested arguments have been completed. While checking the completion, this function also tries to finish other pending requests which may have been issued by other functions.

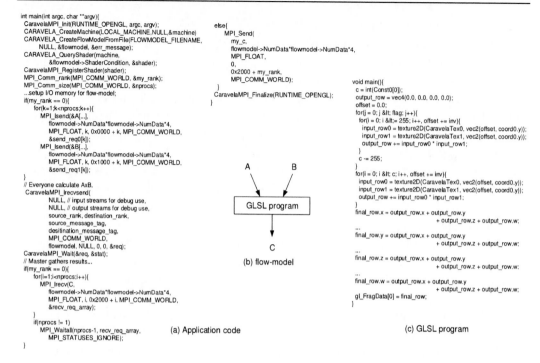

Figure 12. C code and flow-model for matrix multiply.

The communication operations included in the request are synchronized with MPI_Test() and MPI_Wait(), applying the MPI-related request data structure to the functions.

Finally, the synchronous functions are implemented by using the asynchronous functions and the synchronization ones.

By using the CaravelaMPI functions that combine communications for exchanging data with MPI functions and calculations based on GPUs, an application programmer can concentrate to construct a target algorithm of application without taking into consideration the details for the graphics runtime. Moreover, the application can fully and transparently use the massive computational power of GPUs. Thus, the CaravelaMPI will act as an efficient and high performance message passing library on a GPU cluster.

4.1.5. Experimental Performance and Evaluation

To experimentally validate the proposed interface and to evaluate performance of the CaravelaMPI, experimental results were obtained and are presented in two ways: one evaluates performance using a simple parallel kernel for matrix multiplication; another evaluates the programmability aspect. We used a small cluster computer environment that is made of two computers composed of AMD Opteron 2GHz with 2GB DDR memory where NVIDIA GeForce 7300 with 256MB DDR VRAM and ATI RADEON1950 with 512MB DDR VRAM are equipped, with Linux and connected by 10M Ethernet. The LAM [26] implementation of the MPI is adopted in both machines and the OpenGL runtime environment is used as the graphics runtime of the Caravela library.

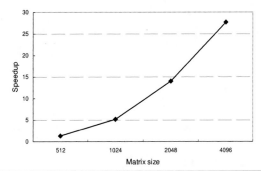

Execution time (sec)				
Matrix size	512^2	1024^2	2048^2	4096^2
CPU-based	0.84	6.05	44.66	345.85
GPU-based	0.65	1.15	3.19	12.49

Figure 13. Execution times and speedups with 4 processes.

In this experiment, the calculation corresponds to the multiplication of matrices with $N \times N$: $C_{N,N} = A_{N,N} \times B_{N,N}$. For parallelizing the computation, the workload is equally distributed to each processor, by initially computing $n = N/nprocs$. Process with rank 0 distributes n rows of the matrix A and n columns of the matrix B to the processes that become responsible for them. After receiving the rows and columns, each process calculates $n \times N$ dot products for the elements it is responsible in the matrix C, and returns n rows of the matrix C to the process 0. Using `CaravelaMPI_Irecvsend()` and `CaravelaMPI_Wait()`, the parallel algorithm was implemented by C code listed in Figure 12(a). The process 0 sends the parts of matrices A and B to other processes. Then, those processes call `CaravelaMPI_Irecvsend()` using a flow-model that calculates dot products for correspondent elements of matrix C. The flow-model is designed as illustrated in Figure 12(b), which has two input data streams (A and B) and generates an output data stream (C). Figure 12(c) shows the shader program generated by the Caravela library in GLSL, which is embedded in the flow-model. This shader program reads four elements A and B in each access to the VRAM, calculates dot products of those elements and outputs results for C by outputting the result to the VRAM.

To compare the performance of the GPU version, we also implemented a CPU version that the dot products were implemented by for-loops and the code was compiled by *mpicc* with *O3* option.

We experimentally measured elapsed time from the initial data distribution initiated by processor 0 to return of result to the processor, parallelizing with four processes, where two processes are assigned to each computer. Figure 13 shows the execution times and the speedup for different matrix sizes, for N equal to 512, 1024, 2048 and 4096. The speedup is computed as the ratio that the execution time of the CPU-based implementation is divided by the one of the GPU-based. The GPU-based implementation is 27 times faster than the GPU-based one when N is 4096. Thus, the cluster of GPUs achieves much higher performance than the CPU-based cluster. Therefore, we confirmed that the CaravelaMPI is very important factor of providing transparent and flexible API for GPU cluster.

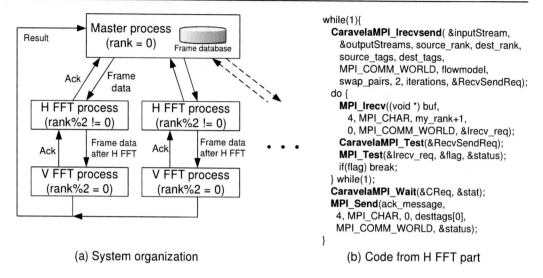

(a) System organization

```
while(1){
    CaravelaMPI_Irecvsend( &inputStream,
        &outputStreams, source_rank, dest_rank,
        source_tags, dest_tags,
        MPI_COMM_WORLD, flowmodel,
        swap_pairs, 2, iterations, &RecvSendReq);
    do {
        MPI_Irecv((void *) buf,
            4, MPI_CHAR, my_rank+1,
            0, MPI_COMM_WORLD, &Irecv_req);
        CaravelaMPI_Test(&RecvSendReq);
        MPI_Test(&Irecv_req, &flag, &status);
        if(flag) break;
    } while(1);
    CaravelaMPI_Wait(&CReq, &stat);
    MPI_Send(ack_message,
        4, MPI_CHAR, 0, desttags[0],
        MPI_COMM_WORLD, &status);
}
```

(b) Code from H FFT part

Figure 14. Structure and application code for FFT system.

4.1.6. Evaluation for Programmability

We implemented a parallel image processing system as illustrated in Figure 14(a). This system performs two dimensional FFT (Fast Fourier Transform) using several image frames saved in a database. The master server picks up every image from the frame database and sends it to the processing pipeline while searching for an idle processing pipeline. The processing pipeline is structured in an H FFT and a V FFT processes. The H FFT process computes a one dimensional FFT for the horizontal direction. The V FFT does the same for the vertical direction. The H FFT process receives a frame from the master, computes FFT using a flow-model, and sends the result to the V FFT process. The V FFT process receives the results from the H FFT process, computes FFT with the flow-model, and sends the result back to the master. When the H or V FFT process finishes its computation, it sends a notification to indicate that the process is idle. As soon as the FFT processes receive and compute the frames, they send the results to the next processes. Thus, the processing pipeline receives the input data and generates the output data asynchronously. Therefore, each process must manage dynamically sending/receiving messages and calculations on the FFT processes.

We applied a GPU-based one dimensional FFT algorithm reported in [14] for the FFT processes. Those are implemented into flow-models and passed to the CaravelaMPI functions on the processes.

Let us focus on the code for H FFT process as listed in Figure 14(b), comparing the coding style with the conventional one applied to programming on a GPU cluster. In the code of the figure, `CaravelaMPI_Irecvsend()` function manages the receiving/sending data and the GPU's computation implicitly. The GPU's computation is managed by `CaravelaMPI_Test()` function, and the communication is implicitly performed. Therefore, the code size can become small and the processing flow becomes transparent. If we use the MPI functions and the graphics runtime functions directly, we would have to consider the calling order of both functions arranging the timings of GPU's calculation and com-

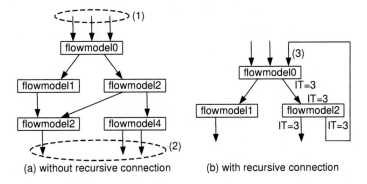

(a) without recursive connection   (b) with recursive connection

Figure 15. Examples of pipeline-models with and without recursive connection.

munications simultaneously. Thus, we can clearly say that CaravelaMPI achieves better programmability on parallel application for GPU cluster than the conventional method that would require the hand-scratched scheduling of GPU's calculations and communications separately.

4.2. Meta-pipeline

Thus, using the flow-model framework, the Caravela platform has implemented a stream-based computing environment, applying GPUs as the processing units. However, the application must manage flow-model execution and data forwarding between the flow-models. Even if flow-models for a target algorithm can be executed in a pipeline manner, a large communication overhead is imposed to feedback the reply to the application. This section is focused on an extension of the execution mechanism to a pipelined processing mechanism, directly connecting flow-models assigned to multiple processing units distributed across the Caravela platform.

The mechanism in the Caravela platform that executes the multiple flow-models connected through I/O data streams is called *meta-pipeline*. The meta-pipeline applies the *pipeline-model* to execute the flow-model units.

4.2.1. Pipeline-model

As depicted in Figure 15, flow-models whose I/O data streams are connected can create a pipeline-model. The pipeline-model assumes that a meta-pipeline as a whole may have its own I/O *ports*: input data streams (1) in Figure 15 are received in *ENTRANCE* ports and output data streams (2) are provided in *EXIT* ports. Since it is a pipeline-model, and it has been defined to compute applications, it must fulfill the following conditions: 1) one or more EXIT ports must exist; 2) one or more flow-models are included; and 3) all the flow-models are connected by at least one I/O data stream. The first condition means that at least a data stream is provided at the output of the pipeline-model, otherwise the computation would be useless. The second and third conditions impose that a meta-pipeline can not include other independent meta-pipelines, otherwise it has to be split in multiple individual meta-pipelines, according to the pipeline-model. Note that no condition is imposed for the number of input ports, because the pipeline-model can have a self-generated feedback input stream data that results from the output data stream. This is a common situation for algorithms that generate special data streams, for example the recursive generation of the Fibonacci number sequence.

When all input data streams of a flow-model unit are ready, this unit is executed. For example, in the pipeline model depicted in Figure 15(a), if data for the ENTRANCE ports (1) has become ready, 'flowmodel0' is executed and generates the output data stream needed to 'flowmodel1'. At this time, the readiness of the 'flowmodel1' input data stream triggers its execution, and the process is repeated for the subsequent flow-model units. In the example of Figure 15(b), at the beginning of the execution the input data streams of 'flowmodel0' never become all ready, unless the data stream in the feedback connection (3) is artificially initialized. Without this initialization, a deadlock can occur in the pipeline-model's execution. This particular type of input port, called *INITONCE* port, must be initialized with an input data stream to trigger the execution of the pipeline.

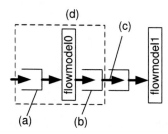

Figure 16. Buffers to avoid serial execution of multiple flow-models connected in a meta-pipeline.

To increase the flexibility of the model, we also define a limit number of iterations (depicted in Figure 15 as IT) without initializations of input data for INITONCE port. For example, if the input data stream (3) is defined as an INITONCE port and the *iteration limit* is three, as illustrated in Figure 15(b), the port must be initialized every three times the output data is generated by the 'flowmodel2'. The concept of iteration limits is not only applied to INITONCE ports but also to ENTRANCE and EXIT ports. In the case of ENTRANCE port, an iteration limit restricts input data initialization, which means the ENTRANCE port is only initialized when the number of executions is multiple of the IT. The same role is applied to the EXIT ports, also to efficiently get the generated output data streams. Moreover, we call *INTERMEDIATE* ports to the flow-model's I/O which are not in any one of the categories referred above (i.e., a port that connects an output stream of a flow-model to an input stream of another flow-model that does not require any assignment of initial data, on the contrary to the INITONCE port). The concept of iteration limit is also applied to the INTERMEDIATE ports: for instance, when the iteration limits illustrated in Figure 15(b) are set, the output data from 'flowmodel0' is generated every three executions and the input/output data of 'flowmodel2' is initialized/generated every three iterations of 'flowmodel2'. A merit of the iteration limit is to define an execution set; for example in Figure 15(b), 'flowmodel2' can be iterated without initializing the input data stream and without generating the output data stream. This allows the remote processing unit assigned to a flow-model not to send/receive data at every execution, thus avoiding redundant data communication.

In summary, flow-model execution in a pipeline-model is repeated whenever sets of initial data are provided for ENTRANCE port(s) and INITONCE port(s). Moreover, different iterations of the flow-models can be executed in parallel in independent processing units, with the required communication reduced to the minimum by parameterizing the model with the limit numbers of iterations. Thus, the meta-pipeline execution mechanism will behave in a distributed environment as a suitable autonomous stream-based computing unit.

4.2.2. Runtime Environment

Meta-pipeline requires a runtime execution mechanism, which is able to check if all input data streams of any flow-model are ready, maintaining the maximum number of processing units (GPUs) busy, executing the respective flow-models. Although a connection between flow-models' input and output data streams can be established through a shared buffer that receives the output data stream and allows it to be used as the next input data stream, this approach can serialize the execution of a meta-pipeline. It can prevent the execution of a flow-model that can not output data because the buffer is occupied with data required by the subsequent flow-model. To avoid this serialization, we define an execution model as depicted in Figure 16. Each flow-model has individual buffers for its input and output data streams (Figure 16(a)(b)). When the input data streams are initialized and 'flowmodel0' is invoked, its output data streams are stored in the output buffer once (Figure 16(b)). When the subsequent flow-model's input buffer becomes empty, the content of the output buffer will be moved to the input buffer (Figure 16(c)). This usage of independent buffers for input and output data streams avoids serial execution, in Figure 16 of 'flowmodel0' and 'flowmodel1'.

A single flow-model with input/output data stream(s) and its buffers, such as depicted in Figure 16(d) can be instantiated as a single flow-model execution using the Caravela library functions shown in Table 1. Therefore, it can be mapped and executed in any processing unit of the Caravela platform. When in a connection the output and input buffers have different sizes, data is copied by adopting the smaller buffer size. For example, when the buffer size of Figure 16(c) is smaller than the one of Figure 16(b), data is resized to fit in the buffer of Figure 16(c), and is copied from one buffer to the other. Therefore, even if different sized buffers are connected in a pipeline-model, the I/O data will be smoothly propagated.

4.2.3. Application Programming Interface

An Application Programming Interface for the meta-pipeline is defined and additional functions are included in the Caravela library for implementing it. To invoke a pipeline-model, an application follows the eight steps presented below.

1. **Looking for processing units**
   This step uses the conventional Caravela functions shown in Table 1 to acquire processing units. The processing units can be located locally or remotely.

2. **Creating flow-models**
   This step is also available through the functions associated to the conventional Car-

avela platform. Flow-models that are used in a pipeline-model are reproduced from local or remote flow-model's XML files in this step.

3. **Creating a pipeline-model data structure**

   A pipeline-model is represented in a single data structure in the Caravela system. In this step, the application creates the data structure.

4. **Registering flow-models and processing units to pipeline-model**

   This step registers into the pipeline-model data structure the flow-models produced in the 2nd step and the processing units queried in the 1st step. A pair flow-model/processing unit is named *stage* of the pipeline. The application needs to create all the stages in a pipeline-model in this step.

5. **Creating connections among flow-models**

   This step defines connections between I/O data streams of flow-models registered to the different stages of the pipeline-model. To fulfill the conditions to be a valid pipeline-model, the application must connect appropriate I/O data streams of flow-models.

6. **Defining INITONCE ports and iteration limits**

   Regarding to the connections defined in the previous step, if a connection creates a loop, it must be marked as an INITONCE port at the corresponding input data stream of the flow-model. Iteration limits associated to ports in the pipeline-model must be also specified in this step.

7. **Implementing pipeline-model**

   This step checks if the pipeline-model satisfies the conditions and if the pipeline-model is available to be executed. If so, all the processing units registered to the pipeline-model are reserved. If the resources are located in remote machines, connections to communicate data among stages are established. Moreover, the flow-models associated to the processing units are sent to them. Thereafter, each flow-model becomes ready to be executed waiting for input data via INITONCE/ENTRANCE ports.

8. **Invoking pipeline-model**

   The invocation of the pipeline-model is automatically made by sending input data to its ENTRANCE/INITONCE ports. This operation must be performed on the application side. When input data is provided to the first stage of a pipeline-model, its flow-model is executed and provides output data to the next stage. This execution mechanism is propagated until EXIT ports appear in a stage. The application needs to keep sending input data as long as ENTRANCE/INITONCE ports are waiting for input data. Stages are executed while data is received and when data reaches the EXIT ports it must be received by the application. Due to the pipeline execution mechanism, while the output data is not completely received by the application the stages associated with the EXIT ports will stall. Therefore, as soon as the output data is ready at the EXIT ports, it must be received by the application.

Following the steps above, the application sets up a pipeline-model and distributes flow-models registered to be part of the pipeline-model through remote resources. Moreover, the pipeline-model is implicitly executed by the meta-pipeline's runtime environment, as the application provides input data to the ENTRANCE/INITONCE ports. Thus, pipeline-model programmers do not need to explicitly schedule flow-model execution.

4.2.4.   Library Functions

The meta-pipeline is implemented as a set of C-based functions, which extends the original Caravela library with the basic functions. For example, machine creation and shader acquisition are performed by instantiating the basic functions as listed in Table 1.

After acquiring the shaders, a set of other functions has to be used. Firstly the CARAVELA_CreatePipeline function is instantiated to create a data structure for the pipeline-model. At the next step, CARAVELA_AddShaderToPipeline function adds a shader, acquired by CARAVELA_QueryShader function of the original Caravela library, to the pipeline-model data structure. To associate a shader to the pipeline-model, a flow-model previously created by the CARAVELA_CreateFlowModelFromFile is introduced by using the CARAVELA_AttachFlowModelToShader function. Thus, a pair of a shader and a flow-model has been registered in the pipeline-model, which means stages of the meta-pipeline have been individually defined.

The CARAVELA_ConnectIO function is used to setup connections between pipeline stages, receiving as arguments a flow-model previously registered in a pipeline-model and input/output data streams' indices. As a consequence, the I/O data streams are marked as INTERMEDIATE ports. If needed, CARAVELA_SpecifyInitOncePort is called after making a connection, to specify that an INTERMEDIATE port is an INITONCE port. The iteration limit (IT) parameter, whose meaning was defined in the previous section, is specified after creating the connections by instantiating the CARAVELA_SpecifyEntrancePort, the CARAVELA_SpecifyExitPort, and the CARAVELA_SpecifyIntermediateInput/Output functions. The setup of the pipeline-model is the last step before the application can start implementing the meta-pipeline.

The function CARAVELA_ImplementPipelineModel implements the pipeline-model. It assigns flow-model/shader pairs (i.e., stages) to machines equipped with shaders. This function returns the identifiers of the ENTRANCE and EXIT ports in an array. This function does not execute any stage of the pipeline-model. The execution is triggered by the CARAVELA_SendInputDataToPipeline, that sends input data to ENTRANCE ports, and CARAVELA_ReceiveOutputDataFromPipeline function that receives output data from the EXIT ports. These functions have internally a function for executing the stages whenever the established conditions are fulfilled. This execution mechanism can perform local execution or remote execution.

4.2.5.   Implementation of the Execution Mechanism

Since the meta-pipeline execution is triggered by inputting data into the ENTRANCE ports, data must be provided to the ports periodically to maintain pipeline operation. Moreover, data streams generated on the EXIT ports must be read by the application as soon as they are generated in order to avoid stalls. Figure 17 shows, as an example, a piece of code for

```
// Preparing input data
Input_data = ...;
While(1){
        // Sending input data to pipeline-model.
        if(CARAVELA_SendInputDataToPipeline(
                pipelinemodel,  // a pipeline-model
                port,           // an ENTRANCE port to be initialized.
                input_data,
                number_of_data) == CARAVELA_SUCCESS){
                        // Preparing the next input data
                        Input_data = ...;
        }
        // Getting output data from pipeline-model.
        if(CARAVELA_ReceiveOutputDataFromPipeline(
                pipelinemodel,  // a pipeline-model
                port,           // an EXIT port to be initialized.
                &flowmodel,     // a flow-model of the port (output from function)
                &index,         // an index of output stream of flow-model
                                                        (output from function)
                &output_data,   // (output from function)
                &number_of_data // (output from function)
                ) == CARAVELA_SUCCESS){
                        // Processing output data
        }
}
```

Figure 17. Code for pipeline-model execution, which provides input data to ENTRANCE port(s) and receives output data from EXIT port(s) of a meta-pipeline.

executing a pipeline-model, where new data is sent in each iteration to ENTRANCE ports and new results are received from EXIT ports.

For executing stages in local shaders, CARAVELA_SendInputDataToPipeline and CARAVELA_ReceiveOutputDataFromPipeline functions have the chance to execute stages by repeatedly executing the code shown in Figure 17. In our implementation, for executing stages on remote shaders, CARAVELA_ImplementPipelineModel function distributes flow-models associated to stages in a pipeline-model to worker servers (see Figure 3). Worker servers prepare its shader resources for receiving flow-models and wait for data to the respective ENTRANCE ports. When the worker servers receive input data for flow-models and execute it, they forward the output data to the other worker servers that have the subsequent flow-models in the pipeline-model. Execution of the flow-model in a worker server is triggered by input data. Therefore, the application does not need to explicitly activate each flow-model's distributed remote shaders. To conclude, we can state that the meta-pipeline mechanism allows applications to define stages, which are implicitly executed in local or in remote machines.

4.2.6. Designing a Modeling Tool for Meta-pipeline Applications

The meta-pipeline mechanism allows the definition and execution of the pipeline-model with complex interconnection patterns, which can easily lead to deadlock situations. For example, the flow-model unit (1) in Figure 18 can never start execution, because not all the input data streams are available, and consequently the whole pipeline execution will be stalled. To avoid this situation, the application programmer needs to identify the edges

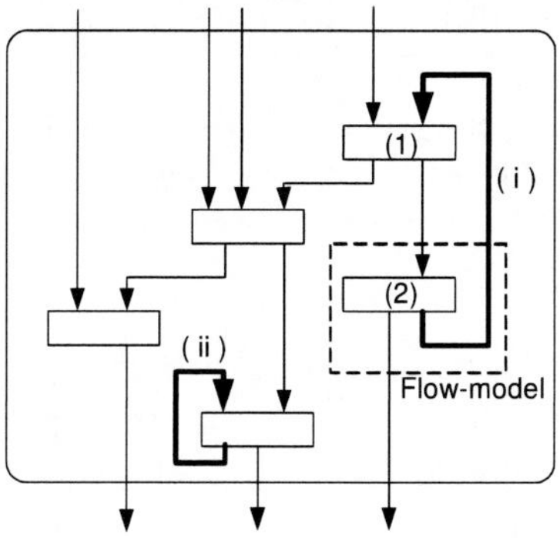

Figure 18. Flow-model and Pipeline-model in Caravela platform where a deadlock occurs in the loop (i) consisting of (1)→(2)→(1) and loop (ii).

in the feedback connections that require initialization. If the feedback connections in a pipeline-model are simple and in small number, such as the connection (i) or (ii) illustrated in Figure 18, it is an easy task for the programmer to identify them. However, when the pipeline-model is more complex, this task when done by hand becomes hard and susceptible to introduce errors.

To program an application according to the pipeline-model one has to define the meta-pipeline and program the communication between flow-model units using a set of Caravela C functions. The programmer has to register flow-model units to a pipeline-model using CARAVELA_AttachFlowModelToShader function, and to establish the connections between the flow-models through the CARAVELA_ConnectIO function. A GUI-based modeling tool that abstracts the details needed to develop this code, which is quite useful in practice, is described in the next sections.

4.2.7. GUI-based Modeling Tool for the Pipeline-model

The main purpose of the modeling tool is to provide: *i*) a GUI for defining the pipeline structure; *ii*) save and restore mechanisms for establishing meta-pipelines; and *iii*) tools to verify the pipeline-model and to generate the executable program. Component *ii*) encapsulates pipeline-model into a file, which enables to share it with other applications and programmers. The last component checks the validity of pipeline-models, by identifying connections on the computational loops that can cause execution deadlock. Moreover, this component generates the required source code for implementing the defined meta-pipeline application. This last task is accomplished by instantiating the required Caravela C functions in the proper order. A typical design flow with these three components is: programmer graphically creates a pipeline-model by establishing the flow-models and connections between them; whenever a programmer wants to save or interrupt the design, the defined pipeline-model is stored into a file, which can be reused by other programmer or application; finally, the tool verifies the design and generates the C code required to implement the specified meta-pipeline. The component *i*) can be implemented with conventional graphics libraries, such as *Windows control* and *Tcl/Tk*. The GUI shows a pictorial diagram of the flow associated to the pipeline-model. To save and restore flow-models to/from files,

---

Algorithm 1 Algorithm for identifying computational loops in pipeline graphs.

1: Identification of all cyclic paths in the pipeline graph
2: Sorting cyclic paths in ascending order regarding the number of nodes
3: Reducing the sorted cyclic path list to the minimum cyclic paths
4: Composing a list exclusively with edges to be initialized

---

standard languages such as XML can be used. However, the component requires the development of a method to detect computational loops in the pipeline. Therefore, a new general and efficient algorithm was developed to detect computational loops in pipeline graphs, in order to avoid deadlock situations.

4.2.8. Algorithm to Detect Execution Deadlock

Loop identification is an essential step in high-level programming languages for performing loop transformation and optimization in computers. Among the algorithms that have been proposed for loop identification, the Tarjan's algorithm [42] is the most well known for identifying loops for the case of reducible graphs, while the Havlak's algorithm [18] corresponds to an extension of the Tarjan's algorithm also to handle irreducible graphs. However, both algorithms are mainly targeted to reducible graphs that only contain loops with a single entry, in opposition to the irreducible graphs that accommodate loops with more than one entry. Therefore a new efficient algorithm is required to solve the deadlock problem by identifying the uninitialized inputs in any pipeline-model structure with a general topology and no restrictions.

Servers/programs and the data streams in the pipeline-model can be represented by a directed graph (DG). In such DG, a node represents a flow-model while input and output data streams are represented by directed edges. These DGs are designated in this particular application *pipeline graph*s. Conditions to compute a node are the ones required by the flow-model: the node is computed *iff* data in all the input edges is ready, and data is only generated in output edge(s) after computing the respective node.

The problem to be solved here is to find the minimum set of edges that needs to be initialized to start computing the pipeline graph, in order to avoid a deadlock situation. To find such edges, the algorithm has to identify loops like (i) and (ii) in Figure 18. These loops are called *cyclic paths* because they are cyclically executed, such as node (2)→node (1)→node (2) in Figure 18.

4.2.9. Proposed Algorithm

Since the pipeline graph accepts that a single node may have multiple input and output edges, without imposing any restrictions, multiple cyclic paths can exist in such a graph. For example, a pipeline graph might contain two or more cyclic paths between two given nodes, including the case when these paths are composed by the same nodes. Supposing the cyclic path node0→node1→node2→node1, the connection between node2 and node1 can be presented in two or more cyclic paths (e.g., node1→node2→node1 and node2→node1→node2), and therefore cyclic paths have to be identified not only by the nodes but also by the edges.

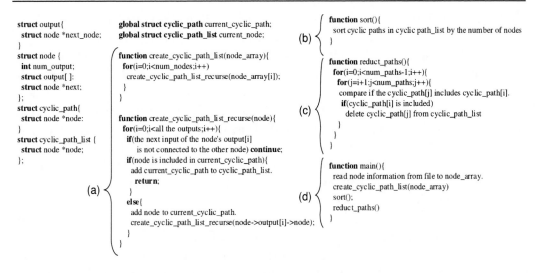

Figure 19. The algorithm phases represented in pseudo-code: each number in the figure indicates the corresponding phase number in the loop detection algorithm.

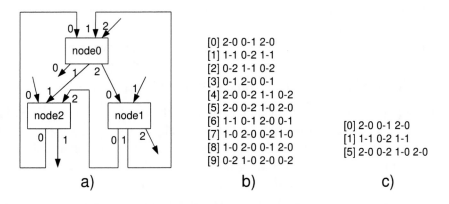

Figure 20. Application example of the algorithm (x-y denotes node x-edge$y$): a) pipeline graph; b) list generated after phase 1 and phase 2; c) list after phase 3.

Four main phases can be considered in the proposed Algorithm 1. Phase 1 of Algorithm 1 generates a *cyclic path list* with all existent cyclic paths, each one represented by the nodes that compose it and the corresponding output edges. Phase 2 of Algorithm 1 sorts the cyclic paths identified in phase 1 in ascending order according to the number of nodes. After the sorting process, longer cyclic paths may include other shorter cyclic paths existent in the list. Phase 3 of Algorithm 1 finds a minimum set of cyclic paths that are exclusive, in the sense that they do not accommodate common shorter cyclic paths. This means that when a cyclic path exactly matches a part of another cyclic path in the list, the larger one is removed from this list. From this phase it results a set of exclusive cyclic paths, herein designated by *true cyclic paths*. In the last phase, phase 4 of Algorithm 1, a list of true cyclic paths without common edges is produced, and then a list with the edges that need to be initialized is built. For example, when the following two true cyclic paths exist, node1(edge1) $\rightarrow$ node2(edge3) $\rightarrow$ node1 and node0(edge1) $\rightarrow$ node1(edge1) $\rightarrow$ node2(edge3) $\rightarrow$ node1, and the edge node1(edge1) → node2 is selected to be initialized, the later cyclic path is removed because the required initialization was already performed in the former.

Figure 19 presents pseudo-code of the proposed algorithm as well as related data structures required to implement it. The naif implementation of phase 1 in Figure 19 directly identifies cyclic paths in a recursive way. For example, a fast mergesort algorithm can be used in Figure 19 to sort the cyclic paths. In Figure 19, the third phase reduces the cyclic path list by considering the already initialized edges. Finally, Figure 19 represents the main functions that execute the phases in order to produce the final list of edges not initialized. A lemma, and the respective proof, is provided in appendix to prove that phases 3 and 4 of the proposed algorithm reduce the cyclic path list and compose a list exclusively composed by edges not initialized.

Figure 20 illustrates an application of the proposed algorithm to a pipeline graph with only three nodes. After identifying loops in phase 1 and phase 2, the cyclic path list shown in Figure 20 b) is achieved. It includes all the cyclic paths ranked by the number of nodes (ascending order). From the top of the list to the base, the cyclic path list is reduced in phase 3 of the algorithm by comparing all cyclic paths. The "true" list of cyclic paths is presented in Figure 20 c). The paths in the list are the ones that really have to be initialized in order to avoid deadlock. For example, when we choose the input0 of node0 and the input0 of node1 as the edges to be initialized, the condition to avoid deadlock is satisfied, because all the cyclic paths listed in Figure 20 includes one of these edges.

4.2.10.　Complexity Analysis and Optimization Techniques

The complexity of the proposed algorithm depends on the number of the cyclic paths, and in particular on the number of true cyclic paths. The complexity of phase 1, by considering V vertices and E edges, is $O(V + E)$. By assuming that C cyclic paths are identified, the complexity of fast sorting algorithm for the phase 2 is $O(C \log C)$, and the complexity of phase 3 is, in the worst case, $O(CV)$. $O(CV)$ can also be considered the worst case complexity for the fourth and last phase. In practice, the optimization technique decreases, from the second to the last phase, the number of cyclic paths that has to be analyzed to C. By considering the number of cycles proportional to the number of vertices $O(V)$, the total complexity is $O(V^2)$, even for a pipeline graph with a high number of edges E, in the order of $O(V^2)$. The complexity of the Havlak's algorithm is $\theta(V^2)$, even for graphs with a number of edges proportional to the number of vertices $O(V)$.

Some aspects can be optimized for achieving a more efficient implementation of the proposed algorithm. Although phase 1 of the proposed algorithm is based on the Dijkstra's algorithm, we can simplify it for our particular problem. One of the main changes was to dismiss all cycle paths that include other cyclic paths inside, such as, for example, the case with node0→node1→node2→node1→node0 doesn't have to be considered. This optimization reduces not only the memory required to store the list of cyclic paths but also the number of comparisons required in phase 2 for sorting the cyclic paths.

Together with the phase 1, phase 3 is the most computational demanding part of the algorithm, when the number of cyclic paths is reduced based on an all-to-all comparison. This computational burden can be lightened by taking advantage of the fact that the cyclic paths are ordered according to the number of nodes, and that with the previous optimization technique it can be assured that a cyclic path A can not match any other paths with a larger number of nodes than the path A. Therefore, for any path A, the comparisons in phase 3 can stop when the number of nodes in a cyclic path is larger than the one of path A. This last optimization significantly reduces the number of comparisons required for performing phase 3 of the algorithm.

4.2.11. Implementation and Experimental Results

Let us show a realistic application example programmed by applying the proposed meta-pipeline execution mechanism. The Discrete Wavelet Transform (DWT) [7] was chosen as the application to show the effectiveness of the meta-pipeline execution mechanism. We have also programmed, in C# language, a GUI-based *PipelineModelCreator* entry tool for programming meta-pipeline applications. To assess this tool and the deadlock detection function, we will evaluate the efficiency of the proposed algorithm to extract the cyclic paths in the pipeline-model and compare it with the algorithm without the optimization techniques discussed in the previous section.

1. 2D Discrete Wavelet Transform

   Discrete Wavelet Transform (DWT) [7] is a powerful tool for image processing applications, such as compression used in JPEG2000 standard, denoising, edge detection and feature extraction. The 1D DWT decomposes an input signal $S(i)$ into two sub-band coefficient sets: a set of low frequency coefficients $L(i)$ and a set of high frequency ones $H(i)$. After applying a linear low-pass and high-pass filter to the input signal $S(i)$, a decimation process is pipelined. Representing a k-th low-pass filter coefficient by $l(k)$ and a high-pass filter one by $h(k)$, the i-th DWT coefficient in the corresponding sub-band is computed by:

$$L(i) = \sum_{k=0}^{K-1} S(2i+k)l(k), H(i) = \sum_{k=0}^{K-1} S(2i+k)h(k)$$

   where K is the number of filter taps. The decimation process is already embedded in the equations above, thus the number of coefficients per sub-band becomes half the number of samples of the input signal.

   Due to the separable property of the DWT, two dimensional DWT (2D-DWT) can be performed by sequentially applying the equations above across the horizontal and vertical image directions. It generates 4 sub-bands (i.e., LL, HL, LH and HH as shown in Figure 21(a)). Each sub-band corresponds to a possible combination of direction (horizontal/vertical) and filter response (low/high-pass). To generate four new sub-bands, the same calculation is applied to the LL sub-band previously computed. This recursive calculation is iterated until the given number of decomposition levels is achieved (typically 3 to 5 levels). Figure 21(c) shows a result of 2D-DWT with 2 decomposition levels calculated from the input image in Figure 21(b).

2. Pipeline-model for 2D-DWT

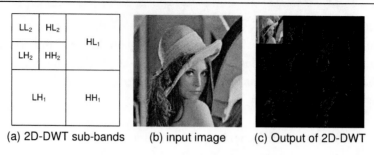

(a) 2D-DWT sub-bands   (b) input image   (c) Output of 2D-DWT

Figure 21. 2D-DWT example with 2 decomposition levels.

The recursive nature of N-level DWT decomposition suggests a pipeline-model organization, with each pipeline stage corresponding to one decomposition level. Each stage in this pipeline can be a single kernel program that generates the LL_n sub-band to be used in the next stage:

$$LL_n(i,j) = \sum_{k=0}^{K-1} \sum_{m=0}^{M-1} LL_{n-1}(2i+k, 2j+m)l(m)l(k),$$

and also the remaining sub-bands (HL_n, LH_n and HH_n), using the correspondent filter combinations. Therefore, a flow-model with an input stream and two output streams is applied to each stage in the pipeline: one of the output streams corresponds to LL_n and the remaining sub-bands compose the other output stream.

The program included in the flow-model is shown in Figure 22(a). The program is written in GLSL. It receives an LL sub-band as the input data stream and generates two output data streams. Using this flow-model, the pipeline-model illustrated in Figure 22(b) can be defined. Each stage in the pipeline-model consists in a flow-model (kernel program in Figure 22(a)). From one level to the next, the size of the input data streams are reduced to 1/4. The input data stream in the ENTRANCE port triggers the flow-model in level 1. One of the output data streams of this flow-model is connected to the next stage (i.e., INTERMEDIATE port). The other output data streams carry the sub-bands at the corresponding decomposition levels, through the EXIT ports.

After implementing the pipeline-model and by feeding the image data to the EN-TRANCE port, the Caravela runtime executes the flow-model in each stage when the input data becomes available. If the pipeline-model is computed in a single local shader, each stage is assigned to the shader and automatically replaced by the next stage. When it is executed in remote worker servers, each flow-model is assigned to a worker, and waits for the input data that is propagated from the previous flow-model in the pipeline.

4.2.12. GUI-based Tool with Automatic Deadlock Detection

The time to compute phase 1 to phase 3 of Algorithm 1 is measured by considering randomly generated pipeline graphs. The pipeline graphs are generated considering a number

```
uniform sampler2D CaravelaTex0;
uniform sampler2D CaravelaTex1;
uniform vec4 const0;
uniform vec4 const1;

void main()
{
  float delta = 1/NUMDATA;
  int i;
  vec4 tmp, tmp0, tmp1;
  vec2 coord = gl_TexCoord[0].xy;
  vec2 caux;
  coord += coord;  caux = coord;
  tmp.x = texture2D(CaravelaTex0, coord).x; coord.x += delta;
  tmp.y = texture2D(CaravelaTex0, coord).x; coord.x += delta;
  tmp.z = texture2D(CaravelaTex0, coord).x; coord.x += delta;
  tmp.w = texture2D(CaravelaTex0, coord).x;
  tmp0.x = dot(tmp, const0); tmp1.x = dot(tmp, const1);

  coord.x = caux.x; coord.y += delta;
  tmp.x = texture2D(CaravelaTex0, coord).x; coord.x += delta;
  tmp.y = texture2D(CaravelaTex0, coord).x; coord.x += delta;
  tmp.z = texture2D(CaravelaTex0, coord).x; coord.x += delta;
  tmp.w = texture2D(CaravelaTex0, coord).x;
  tmp0.y = dot(tmp, const0); tmp1.y = dot(tmp, const1);

  coord.x = caux.x; coord.y += delta;
  tmp.x = texture2D(CaravelaTex0, coord).x; coord.x += delta;
  tmp.y = texture2D(CaravelaTex0, coord).x; coord.x += delta;
  tmp.z = texture2D(CaravelaTex0, coord).x; coord.x += delta;
  tmp.w = texture2D(CaravelaTex0, coord).x;
  tmp0.z = dot(tmp, const0); tmp1.z = dot(tmp, const1);

  coord.x = caux.x; coord.y += delta;
  tmp.x = texture2D(CaravelaTex0, coord).x; coord.x += delta;
  tmp.y = texture2D(CaravelaTex0, coord).x; coord.x += delta;
  tmp.z = texture2D(CaravelaTex0, coord).x; coord.x += delta;
  tmp.w = texture2D(CaravelaTex0, coord).x;
  tmp0.w = dot(tmp, const0); tmp1.w = dot(tmp, const1);

  result.x = dot(tmp0, const0);
  result.y = dot(tmp0, const1);
  result.z = dot(tmp1, const0);
  result.w = dot(tmp1, const1);

  gl_FragData[0] = result;
  gl_FragData[1] = result;
}
```

(a) kernel program of flow-model

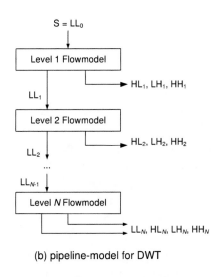

(b) pipeline-model for DWT

Figure 22. Flow-model and pipeline-model for the 2D-DWT.

of nodes that varies from 2 to 10. For each node, a number of output edges, that also varies from 2 to the number of nodes, and a number of input edges equals to the number of nodes. For evaluating the algorithm and the optimization techniques proposed in section 4.2.10, the corresponding program was compiled with GCC 3.3.5 and executed on the Linux operating system. A personal computer with a 3.2GHz Pentium4 with 1GB DDR400 memory was used for obtaining the experimental results.

Figure 23 shows the obtained results for different numbers of true cyclic paths. Without applying any optimization technique, the execution time varies with $C \times logC$. However, when the number of valid cyclic paths grows the execution time significantly increases, mainly due to the memory accesses. Therefore, the reduction of the number of memory accessed is important to execute the algorithm with a good performance. The execution time is drastically reduced (see Figure 23), mainly by applying the optimization technique in phase 3. Moreover, the execution time has become predictable due to the decreasing of

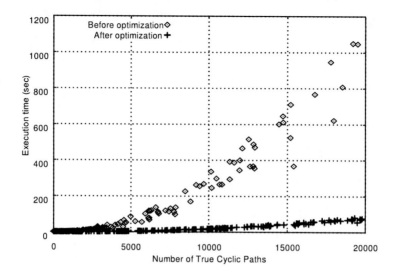

Figure 23. Experimental results with and without the optimization techniques.

the number of memory accesses in phase 1.

Figure 24 shows a design verification example with the pipeline-model illustrated in Figure 20. A screen-shot of the tools with the automatically detected computational loops is presented in Figure 20 a); the dotted lines represent the connections that have to be initialized in order to avoid deadlock. We implemented an additional function to specify initialization dataset for each marked input edge. After specifying the initialization dataset for all the marked inputs (repeating the steps as performed in Figure 20), the tool results show the connections with just solid lines. Then the programmer can give order to the tool to generate the C code for the designed pipeline-model and to execute it on the Caravela platform.

With the PipelineModelCreator tool, programmer is able to graphically design a meta-pipeline application through simple steps and to automatically check the existence of computational loops in order to avoid deadlocks.

4.3.   Automatic Parallelization of a Pipeline-flow Based on Flow-models

4.3.1.   GUI-based Stream-based Computing

We have developed a GUI of Caravela platform as shown in Figure 25. The programmer just defines the flow-models and connection among those flow-models graphically. It generates executables and batches needed for CarSh. The GUI is very helpful for automatic programming for accelerators. However, it is very hard to generate an execution scenario for the processing pipeline. For example, given a processing pipeline as depicted in Figure 26 (a), it is easy for us to identify the execution order. While the input data for *flowmodel1* is given successively, the overall calculation is invoked in the order from *flowmodel1* to *flowmodel4*.

When we consider the concurrency of the execution of multiple flow-models, it is also conceivable for us by writing the execution order with the considerations: 1) The *flowmodel1* and *flowmodel2* are not executable in parallel because the connected I/O are inter-

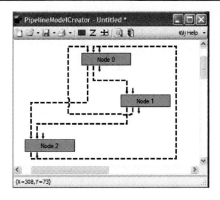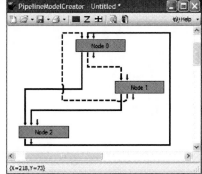

(a) After verifying the pipeline-model. Three loops are detected.

(b) After giving initialization dataset to the connection from node2 to node0. Two computational loops are solved.

Figure 24. Example of design and verification with the PipelineModelCreator.

fered with each other because it is assigned to the same physical buffer. 2) The *flowmodel2* must be executed after the *flowmodel1* because the input data must be prepared (we call this *initialized*) before the flow-model execution. Such as the right side of Figure 26 (a), after the executions of *flowmodel1* and *flowmodel2*, we can think intuitively that the combinations of *flowmodel2 & 4* and *flowmodel1 & 3* are executed concurrently.

However, given the processing flow of Figure 26 (b), how do you specify which is the flow-model initially executed when the first input data is given to *flowmodel1*? How is the parallelism if multiple flow-models could be invoked concurrently? It is impossible to implement the perfect GUI-based programming method before solving these problems. As an objective of this section, we propose an algorithm that mechanically exploits the deterministic execution order and the parallelism from any kind of pipeline execution flow.

4.3.2. Spanning Tree

Challenges for execution ordering and exploiting parallelism from a program are studied in the decades by researchers of compilers. The High Performance Fortran (HPF) is a well-known solution to exploit potential parallelism from a numerical program description. *Spanning Tree* introduced in [45] is a technique to determine the control flow of a program description.

Given a directed graph $G(V, E)$, where V is a set of vertices (nodes) of G, and E is the set of edges of G, $S(V, T)$ is called the $G(V, E)$'s *spanning tree*, when a subset of edges T satisfies $T \subseteq E$ and the graph $S(V, T)$ forms a tree. Here, $S(V, T)$ does not include loops. When spanning tree is defined, the edges in G is categorized into four types: 1) *Tree edges* form the spanning tree. 2) *Advancing edges* are a set of edges of $X \to Y$ that are not the tree edges. Y is a descendant of X. The edges jump to vertices in the lower structure of the tree. 3) *Retreating edges* are also a set of edges of $X \to Y$ that are not the tree edges. Y is an ancestor of X. That is, the edges jump to vertices in the upper structure of the tree. Finally, 4) *Cross edges* are the rest of the edges which are not belong to 1) - 3). Those are a set of edges of $X \to Y$, where Y is neither ancestor nor a descendant of X. Here, there exists a condition regarding the root vertex of the spanning tree. From a

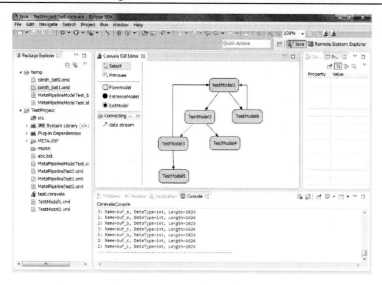

Figure 25. The Caravela GUI implemented as an Eclipse plugin that generates XML files of the flow-model, CarSh executables and batches.

Algorithm 2 Depth-first spanning tree (DFST) algorithm.

```
void DFST(int x){
pre_num ++;
NPre[x] = pre_num;
for(int y=0; y<N; y++){
  if(edges[x][y].connect){
    if(NPre[y] == 0){
      //x → y is a tree edge
      DFST(y);
    }
    else if(Npre[x] < Npre[y]) { // x → y is an advancing edge }
    else if(NRPost[x] == 0){ //x → y is an retreating edge }
    else { // x → y is an cross edge }
  }
}
NRPost[x] = rpost_num;
rpost_num --;
}
```

---

root vertex, the graph must have a reachable path to all other vertices. If the path does not include all vertices of G, it does not have a spanning tree. However, note that a spanning tree generated from a node is uniquely found in G. Therefore, a different root constructs a different spanning tree from the same graph.

Algorithm 2 lists the steps to categorize the edges of a directed graph into four categories above, when a root vertex is given to the DFST function. This algorithm is developed based on the Tarjan's depth-first search algorithm [42]. In this meaning, we call it *Depth-First Spanning Tree* (DFST) algorithm. Regarding the tree edges generated by the algorithm, we can find the spanning tree.

The algorithm is a combination of the preorder numbering $NPre()$ and the reverse post numbering $NRPost()$. In the former numbering, if $NPre(X) < NPre(Y)$, X is either a preorder ancestor of Y in the tree, or the left of Y. In the latter numbering, if $NRPost(X) < NRPost(Y)$, X is either a preorder ancestor of Y in the tree, or the

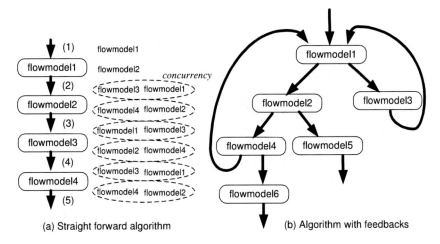

(a) Straight forward algorithm

(b) Algorithm with feedbacks

Figure 26. Pipeline flow examples of a) straight forward algorithm and b) algorithm with feedbacks.

right of Y. First, in the step performing the preorder numbering , the DFST is checking the preorder number of the next connected node after the current node. If it is zero, it is detected as a tree edge. When the search reaches a leaf of the tree, it performs the reverse post numbering, returning to the tree edges. In the backward searching, it marks one of retreating, advancing and cross edges.

Figure 27 shows an example of a spanning tree generated by the DFST. The pairs of numbers in the figure are $(NPre, NRPost)$. We select A as the root vertex. First the preorder numbering is performed in the order of $A \rightarrow B \rightarrow C \rightarrow I \rightarrow J \rightarrow D \rightarrow E \rightarrow G \rightarrow H \rightarrow F$. During the numbering of the backward searching, the reverse post numbering is performed in the order of $J \rightarrow I \rightarrow H \rightarrow G \rightarrow E \rightarrow F \rightarrow D \rightarrow C \rightarrow B \rightarrow A$. In the former step, the tree edges are found like the path marked with the thick arrows. The retreating edges and the crossing edges are also found during the backward search.

4.3.3. Discussion

Spanning tree method is also applied in the communication network field. The Spanning Tree Protocol (STP) is a network protocol that ensures a loop-free topology for any bridged Ethernet-based local area network. The basic function of STP is to prevent bridge loops and the broadcast radiation that results from them. The spanning tree also allows a network design to include spare (redundant) links to provide automatic backup paths if an active link fails, without the danger of bridge loops, or the need for manual enabling/disabling of these backup links. Spanning Tree Protocol (STP) is standardized as IEEE 802.1D. As the name suggests, it creates a spanning tree within a network of connected layer-2 bridges (typically Ethernet switches) and disables those links that are not part of the spanning tree, leaving a single active path between any two network nodes [37]. Perlman applied STP to a routing algorithm in a communication path, considering the network connections among switches and communication nodes as edges and nodes of a directed graph [38]. The algorithm finds the shortest network path with the smallest number of links that eliminates loops.

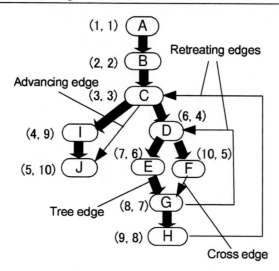

Figure 27. Spanning tree examples.

To break loops in the LAN while maintaining access to all LAN segments, the program in each bridge that allows it to determine how to use the protocol is known as the spanning tree algorithm. The algorithm is specifically constructed to avoid bridge loops (multiple paths linking one segment to another, resulting in an infinite loop situation). The algorithm is responsible for a bridge using only the most efficient path when faced with multiple paths. If the best path fails, the algorithm recalculates the network and finds the next best route.

The Dijkstra's algorithm [8] is also another well-known graph search algorithm that solves the single-source shortest path problem for a graph with non-negative edge path costs, producing a shortest path tree [28]. For a given source node in the graph, the algorithm finds the shortest path and the reaching cost between a vertex and another vertex. For example, if the vertices of the graph represent cities and edge path costs represent driving distances between pairs of cities connected by a direct road, the Dijkstra's algorithm can be used to find the shortest route between one city and all other cities. As a result, the shortest path first is widely used in network routing protocols, most notably IS-IS [15] and OSPF (Open Shortest Path First) [30].

In the Dijkstra's algorithm, the node at which it starts is called the initial node, and the distance of node Y is the one from the initial node to the node Y. The algorithm will assign some initial distance values and will try to improve them step by step. The steps of the algorithm are summarized below; 1) assigning every node a temporary distance value, 2) marking all nodes unvisited, for the current node, 3) considering all of its unvisited neighbors and calculating their temporary distances, 4) marking the current node as visited and removing it from the unvisited set, and 5) finishing the algorithm if the destination node has been marked as visited or if the smallest temporary distance among the nodes in the unvisited set is infinity, 6) selecting the unvisited node that is marked with the smallest temporary distance, and setting it as the new current node then go back to step 3).

The Dijkstra's algorithm is usually the working principle behind link-state routing protocols, OSPF and IS-IS being the most common ones. The process that underlies the Dijkstra's algorithm is similar to the greedy process used in Prim's algorithm [39]. Prim's purpose is to find a minimum spanning tree [10] that connects all nodes in the graph. Meanwhile, the Dijkstra's is concerned only between two nodes. The Prim's does not evaluate the total weight of the path from the starting node, only the individual path.

The spanning tree algorithm is to discover a loop-free subset of the topology dynamically. For example, if a network topology does not change, the network is not partitioned temporarily while nodes switch over to other routes. If the backup root is very near the old root, the topology will not change significantly even when the old root dies. On the other hand, in the case of the Dijkstra's algorithm, when any cost is changed, it inevitably needs to recalculate it. Therefore, the search result of Dijkstra's algorithm is not adaptive to the dynamic route path.

According to the discussion above, the spanning tree algorithm is powerful for finding a route path between the nodes in a tree. When we consider a pipeline with processing tasks (i.e., flow-models) connected by the I/O data streams, it can be treated as a tree. Therefore, the spanning tree algorithm can be applied to define a unique processing order. Additionally it also finds the feedback I/Os. In the spanning tree, the nodes with the same depth from the root node do not have edges among them. This means that those nodes (flow-models) can be independently executed. The groups of the nodes induce a definition of stages in the processing pipeline because we can define an execution order of the groups. Thus, the spanning tree algorithm can define an effective pipeline order with all tasks included in the processing flow. This section will focus on the characteristics of the pipeline flow exploited by the spanning tree algorithm and proposes a novel algorithm using the spanning tree that extracts the best parallelism.

4.3.4. Parallelism Extraction Algorithm with Spanning Tree

In order to address the execution order and finds the concurrency, we need to develop an algorithm for 1) finding a flow-model executed first, 2) finding a deterministic execution order without I/O buffer collisions and 3) exploiting an available concurrency from the processing flow. We also define the CarSh batch scenario from the algorithm. Let us map the processing flow to a directed graph. The flow-models correspond to the nodes. The I/O data streams correspond to the edges.

1. Finding the first execution flow-model

   First, we define an *executable node* and a *root node*. When all edges point to a node that is given, we call the node *executable*. The edges that come out from the node are *initialized* after the execution of the node. Here, these nodes are found by the algorithm explained in section 4.2.9. Selecting one of the nodes in the minimum cyclic paths as the root node, we can find a spanning tree. It includes a unique path of the tree when the execution steps follow the tree edges from the root node to downward. This path becomes the execution flow of the directed graph of the flow-models.

2. Extracting parallelism and determining execution order

   The number of nodes in a cyclic path is not only one in general. Any node in a minimum cyclic path can be the root node of the spanning tree. Therefore, it is

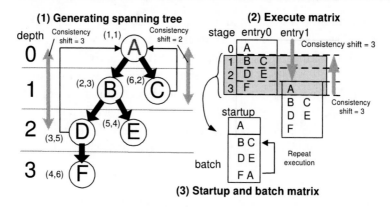

Figure 28. Processing steps of the PEA-ST.

available for all nodes to be selected as the root node in the spanning tree. Here, we assume that the processing flow builds a strongly connected directed graph.

The goal of this section is to exploit parallelism of the processing flow. With the parallelism, we perform a processing order of concurrent execution of multiple flow-models in a pipeline manner by using the parallelism extraction algorithm with spanning tree (PEA-ST). Here, let us consider the case of Figure 28. We assume that the edges $D \rightarrow A$ and $C \rightarrow A$ are initialized. Then we select A as the root node. The spanning tree of the graph becomes like Figure 28(1). The initialized edges are categorized as the retreating edges. Others are the tree edges.

To exploit the parallelism from the spanning tree, we define *depth* and *stage* of a processing pipeline. The depth of a node is defined as the number of tree edges from the node to the root node. The stage is defined as a set of nodes (kernel programs of flow-models) which can be invoked concurrently without the I/O buffer conflicts. Let us generate the depths and stages of the spanning tree in Figure 28. Here, we define that a tree edge has a single depth of the pipeline. For instance, the depth of E is 2 because there are two tree edges in the path of $A \rightarrow B \rightarrow E$. As another example, the depth of F is 3 because there are three tree edges in the path of $A \rightarrow B \rightarrow D \rightarrow F$. Thus, the total depth of the example graph becomes four.

According to the definitions of the stage and the depth, it is obviously to find that the nodes with the same depth can be added to the same stage. For example, the nodes B and C or the ones D and E can be invoked concurrently because there is no I/O conflict among those nodes in the same stage. Therefore, we can build the pipeline as $A \rightarrow (B, C) \rightarrow (D, E) \rightarrow F$. Shifting a stage, we can organize a pipeline like $A \rightarrow (B, C, A) \rightarrow (D, E, B, C) \rightarrow (F, D, E) \rightarrow (A, F) \rightarrow (B, C, A)...$

In the explanation above, we ignore the retreating edges. Here, we consider the effect of the retreating edges (i.e., loops) in the graph. If we completely ignore a retreating edge, the pipeline works incorrectly due to I/O conflicts caused by the loops. For example, the stage (B, C, A) can not be executed correctly because A must be invoked after C. Moreover, A must be invoked after D in the next execution. To resolve the problems we define *consistency shift*. First we find a retreating edge. In the loop where the two nodes connected by that retreating edge, we calculate the number of nodes connected by tree edges. In the example case, the edge $D \rightarrow A$ includes three nodes (i.e., A, B and D). The edge $C \rightarrow A$ includes two nodes (i.e., A and C). The consistency shift is that number we just calculated. For example, if the consistency shift is two, the pipeline becomes $A \rightarrow (B, C) \rightarrow (D, E, A) \rightarrow (F, B, C) \rightarrow (A, D, E)$... by shifting two stages. However A be invoked before D which causes I/O conflict. Therefore, it must be maximized. Taking the largest number of consistency shift among all retreating edges. Thus, if the stages are shifted by the max consistency shift, all nodes related to retreating edges are invoked correctly. The correct pipeline should become $A \rightarrow (B, C) \rightarrow (D, E) \rightarrow (F, A) \rightarrow (B, C) \rightarrow (D, E) \rightarrow (F, A)$...

Although the condition that a graph has no retreating edge, we need to consider the consistency shift. For example, we consider a straightforward processing flow $A \rightarrow B \rightarrow C$. The pipeline would become $A \rightarrow (B, A) \rightarrow (C, B) \rightarrow (A, B)$... However, this is wrong because may occur I/O conflict. To resolve this case, we assume that nodes connected by an edge also have a retreating edge. Therefore, the default number of the consistency shift must be two.

In the correct pipeline, we can find two parts. One is the initial stage(s) executed once called *startup*. The other is the contiguous repeating stage(s) called *repeat batch*. In the example case, the stage of (A) is the former. In the case of Figure 28, a set of stages of $(B, C) \rightarrow (D, E) \rightarrow (F, A)$ is the latter. The startup stages include the beginning ones of the pipeline after the consistency shift is performed. Therefore, the number of stages of the startup is calculated by $depth - max\_consistency\_shift$. In the example case, it is $4 - 3 = 1$. Therefore the first stage with A is included in the startup. Other three stages organize the repeat batch. Thus, while the correct pipeline is configured, the startup is invoked once. Then the repeat batch is repeated.

Regarding the cross edges, PEA-ST ignores them because the edge can be treated as tree edge. Cross edge has two or more ancestors. An edge from one of the ancestors should become tree edge.

Let us summarize the processing steps of the PEA-ST explained above. First, one of the root nodes is selected. This makes a graph executable. Second, a spanning tree is created from the root node. Only a tree is generated. Third, the consistency shift is calculated from the retreating edges. Finally, the startup and the repeat batch are generated.

4.3.5. Implementation

Algorithm 3 shows the PEA-ST written by a C-like code. The *main* function processes 1) spanning tree creation, 2) consistency shift calculation, 3) startup and batch creation and finally 4) updating the startup and the repeat batch according to the user-defined requirements. The function checks all available spanning trees by selecting available root nodes. The process 4) will break the loop of selecting the root nodes and return the best startup and repeat batch.

The spanning tree creation is performed by *DFST_Modified* function. In the function

Algorithm 3 Parallelism extraction algorithm applying spanning tree (PEA-ST).

```
struct edge {                         struct node {          void main(){
   bool connect;                         char name;             for(int result=0; result<N; result++){
} edges[N][N];                           int depth;                node_init();
                                         bool update;              edge_init();
                                      } nodes[N];                  root_test(result);
                                                                  if(node can reach all other nodes){
void DFST_Modified(int x){                                           node[result].depth=0;
 pre_num ++;                                                         DFST_Modified(result);
 NPre[x] = pre_num;                                                }
 for(int y=0; y<N; y++){                                           else continue;
   if(edges[x][y].connect){        ◄————Tree edge                 if(there is no retreating edges)
     if(NPre[y] == 0){                                               consistency_shift=2;
       nodes[y].depth=nodes[x].depth+1;                            else
       DFST_Modified(y);                                             consistency_shift = max_retreat_offset;
     }                                                             for(i=0;i*move<max_stage;i++){
     else if(NPre[x] < NPre[y]) ◄———— Advancing edge                 for(int j=0; j<N; j++){
       edges[x][y].connect = false;                                    stage= nodes[j].depth+i*move;
     else if(NRPost[x] == 0){  ◄———— Retreating edge                   if(stage < max_stage){
       If(max_retreat_offset<nodes[x].depth - nodes[y].depth)            excute[stage][count[stage]] = nodes[j].name;
         max_retreat_offset=nodes[x].depth - nodes[y].depth +1;         count[stage]++;
       edges[x][y].connect = false;                                   }
     }                                ┌— Cross edge                 }
     else  Edges[x][y].connect = false; ◄                          }
   }                                                              if(Parallelism is better than the previous one)
 }                                                                  update(startup and batch);
 NRPost[x] = rpost_num;                                            else continue;
 rpost_num --;                                                   }
}                                                              }
```

all edges are categorized to the ones defined by the spanning tree. When an edge is categorized, it updates the *edges* matrix that obtains the tree edge. If an edge is categorized as a retreating edge, it updates the *max_retreat_offset* that obtains the largest offset of stages in the retreating edge (i.e., consistency shift).

After the spanning tree creation, the *main* function calculates the consistency shift. If any consistency shift exists, the *max_retreat_offset* is used. If not, it is two because of the case of straightforward processing flow. Then finally the execute matrix is created. It obtains the stages and the node combinations at each stage. Using the example of Figure 28, let us explain how to calculate the startup and the repeat batch. At the first iteration of *execute* matrix creation, it fills each stage with the nodes of the same depth illustrated by *entry0* in the figure. In the second iteration, it shifts the column index by the consistency shift and fills the nodes of stages again like *entry1*. If the shifted index is larger than the depth of the graph, the iteration ends. The final *execute* matrix is the startup and the repeat batch. The repeat batch is the last n rows of the matrix where n is the consistency shift. The remaining row(s) are the startup.

Finally, user-defined conditions are checked. The conditions depend on the maximum/minimum parallelism, the average parallelism, the number of stages and the smallest consistency shift, etc. In our implementation, we apply the condition to find the largest parallelism of $MIN\_AVR < parallelism < MAX\_AVR$ and $parallelism < MAX$, where MIN_AVR and MAX_AVR are the minimum and maximum parallelisms respectively, and where the MAX is the maximum parallelism. MAX is given by the programmer because of the limitation of the resources (the number of accelerators).

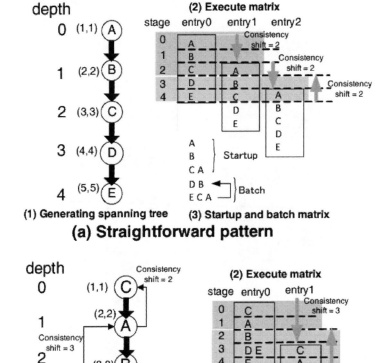

Figure 29. Examples of batch generation using the PEA-ST. A straight forward pattern (a) and the pattern with feedforward edges of Figure 28 when C is selected to the root vertex(b).

Regarding the complexity of the PEA-ST, it is similar to the spanning tree algorithm. The preorder and the reverse post order numberings takes $O(NE)$ time respectively, where N is the number of nodes and E is the number of edges in the graph. However, the PEA-ST needs to try all available spanning tree creations of the root nodes. Therefore, it becomes $O(NEM)$ where M is the number of available root nodes.

4.3.6. Examples

Here, let us introduce two additional examples as depicted in Figure 29. The straightforward pattern shown in Figure 29(a) needs three iterations to generate an *execute* matrix. The maximum parallelism becomes three. Figure 29(b) shows another example of the same processing flow as Figure 28. But the root node is C. This case shows that the maximum parallelism becomes three. It is two when we selected A as the root node. Thus, PEA-ST is

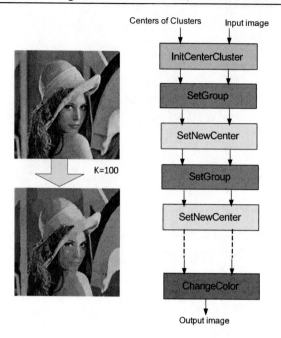

Figure 30. k-means example applying PEA-ST.

very flexible to select an ideal parallelism defined by a programmer according to the limited number of accelerator resources.

4.3.7. Performance Evaluation

To validate the PEA-ST, we have made two applications related to image processing. The first one shows the validity of the PEA-ST. The second one shows the impact on the performance aspect. Both applications have the potential ability of achieving small latency to output the final results when the PEA-ST is applied and the processing flows are modified to pipeline flows with parallel executions of multiple tasks (flow-models).

1. Color image quantization

   The first example is a color image quantization. We will show an realistic example when the PEA-ST is applied to a processing flow graph. Color quantization is a task of reducing the color palette of an image to a fixed number of colors k. The k-means algorithm can easily be used for this task and produces competitive results. Figure 30 shows the processing flow. It consists of four kinds of flow-models. The InitCenterCluster performs the initialization of the clusters' centers which are randomly selected. The SetGroup divides all pixels into k clusters. It calculates the distances from the pixels (RGB) to each center and assigns each pixel to the nearest cluster. The SetNewCenter calculates the new centers. Then it compares the old and the new center. If they are different, it continues iterating the loop of the processing steps with the SetGroup and the SetNewCenter flow-models.

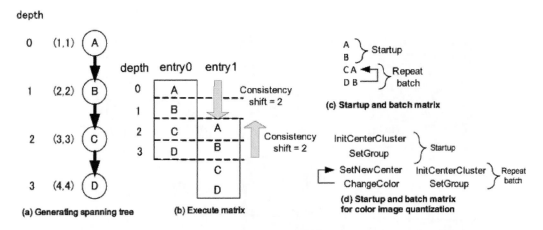

Figure 31. The startup and the repeat batch of the color image quantization application.

Contrarily, if they are the same, it stops the loop and executes the subsequent flow-models. The `ChangeColor` performs a transformation of the color (RGB) of the original image.

Figure 31 shows the pipelined processing flow generated by PEA-ST. Using the figure, let us explain the steps of how to generate pipelined processing flow of k-means example by PEA-ST in detail. Here, we can simplify the structure of the four kinds of flow-models in Figure 30 into the graph of Figure 31(a). Because only the node A can become the root node, only one spanning tree is derived. In other words, the k-means example has just one result of pipeline processing flow according to the PEA-ST. First, the spanning tree generated by the DFST Modified function is shown in Algorithm 3. In the resulting spanning tree, there exists a retreating edge $C \rightarrow B$. Also, we can see that the `max_retreat_offset` of this retreating edge is 2. The `main` function calculates the consistency shift, which is equal to the `max_retreat_offset`. Then the PEA-ST algorithm generates the *execute matrix* with consistency shift. There are four stages and two entries in the execute matrix in Figure 31(b). And at the first iteration of the creation process for the execute matrix, the algorithm assigns the corresponding offset incremented from 0 for the depth to each stage of the nodes from A to D illustrated by *entry0*. In the second iteration, it shifts the depth by the consistency shift of 2, and assigns the nodes of stages again from the shifted depth number as shown in *entry1*. Because the maximum depth is 3 (the original depth of the spanning tree is 3), the nodes is placed in the depth which is larger than the maximum depth. Therefore, the nodes C and D in the *entry1* is canceled. Finally, the startup and the repeat batch are generated from the execute matrix. As shown in Figure 31(c), the repeat batch is the last 2 rows of the matrix because of the consistency shift and it contains all the flow-models of k-means example. And the remaining first two rows are regarded as the startup. The final pipelined result of k-means example is shown in the Figure 31(d). The startup that contains the `SetGroup` and the `SetNewCenter` flow-models is executed once at first. Then the repeat batch is repeated.

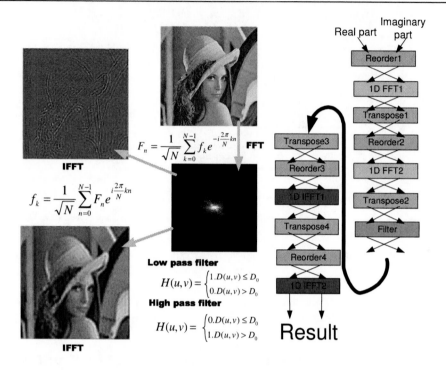

Figure 32. FFT example using PEA-ST.

In this example, the `ChangeColor` outputs the result regarding a single input image. Therefore, if the flow is executed in serial, each flow-model is executed by blocking after the execution because of the I/O data dependencies. Therefore, the total execution time takes the elapsed time of all four flow-models in the execution flow. However, after it is pipelined, the processing flow has been parallelized with two flow-models in a stage. If multiple accelerators are available, the execution time will be improved at most to the one of a single flow-model (`ChangeColor`). Therefore, the PEA-ST approach is effective modification of the processing flow achieving the consistency of the I/O data dependency. Let us see the performance impact on the optimization by the PEA-ST algorithm in the next example.

2. 2D FFT

To evaluate the performance of the PEA-ST, we compare between the serialized and the pipelined processing flows of a common image filtering. Figure 32 shows the processing flow. It consists of four kinds of flow-models. The reorder performs butterfly operation, the FFT and IFFT calculate 1-dimentional FFT and IFFT respectively. The transpose performs a transpose of the 2-dimentional matrix data. The filter is a high-pass or low-pass filter. A CarSh executable of the flow-model is downloaded to accelerator via Caravela runtime. And finally, it is executed by the OpenCL runtime. Figure 33 shows the pipelined processing flow generated by PEA-ST which is packed in two CarSh batches; one is the startup and another is the repeat batch. Totally 13 flow-models are executed in a pipeline manner. The maximum parallelism of the

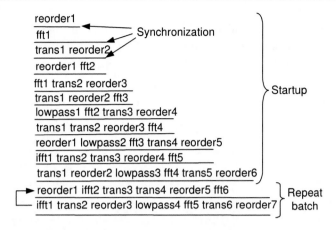

Figure 33. The startup and the repeat batch of the image filtering application resolved by the PEA-ST in the case when the maximum parallelism is seven.

processing flow exploited by the PEA-ST becomes seven as shown in Figure 33.

This application also includes the potential performance improvement function after applying PEA-ST algorithm to the original flow with 13 flow-models. The final IFFT2 output the result of the input single image. Therefore, the original flow graph shows 13 steps to execute all flow-models and it need the latency to execute all the flow-models to calculate a single result. However, after pipelining, the latency to calculate the result from IFFT2 becomes small because IFFT2 is executed at every execution of a stage.

The execution time until the final IFFT is measured with/without parallelization. In the case of the serialized version, the 13 flow-models are executed in serial. On the other hand, the pipelined version generates the final image output after the execution of the stage with IFFT2. Therefore, the actual execution time per final result equals to the elapsed time of the repeat batch. The experimental platform is a PC with a Core i7 2.8GHz with 12 GByte DDR2 memory in which a Tesla C2050 is connected via PCI Express bus. Varying the input image size from 128^2 to 1024^2 using OpenCL runtimes on GPU and CPU. We apply the width of input image to the number of the threads at each kernel program. The execution times until the IFFT2 generates the final image are shown in Table 5. Due to the OpenCL runtime overhead, the speedup (serialized/parallelized) of the GPU case is about 25%. The execution time of each kernel program is small. Therefore, the parallelized version promotes the intensive utilization of GPU resource. On the other hand, in the case of CPU, the parallelized version achieves about 4 times higher performance because the parallel threads for different kernels are working concurrently. Therefore, in any accelerator we have confirmed that the parallelized version generated by PEA-ST achieves better performance than the serialized version.

Table 5. Execution times by resulting IFFT comparison among the serialized and the pipelined versions invoked on CPU and GPU. The startup time shows the elapsed times of the startup part of the batch. The repeat time shows the ones of the repeat batch.

Serialized	128^2	256^2	512^2	1024^2
GPU	1.64 sec	1.67 sec	1.77 sec	2.11 sec
CPU	4.19 sec	4.25 sec	4.38 sec	4.77 sec
Pipelined (startup)	128^2	256^2	512^2	1024^2
GPU	1.79 sec	2.18 sec	2.15 sec	1.85 sec
CPU	2.38 sec	2.40 sec	2.46 sec	2.46 sec
Pipelined (repeat)	128^2	256^2	512^2	1024^2
GPU	1.39 sec	1.40 sec	1.41 sec	1.41 sec
CPU	1.12 sec	1.12 sec	1.13 sec	1.14 sec
Speedup	128^2	256^2	512^2	1024^2
GPU	1.18	1.19	1.26	1.50
CPU	3.74	3.79	3.87	4.18

5.   Exploiting Potential Performance of Manycore Accelerators

5.1.   Swap Execution Method on Manycore Accelerator

5.1.1.   Architecture of GPUs

GPU is the most popular example of the platform for executing the stream-based programs. According to the significant performance growth of the GPU, it is expected for a breakthrough for the recent ceiling Moore's low due to applying the multicore/manycore architecture. For example, the NVIDIA's GPU [32] as depicted in Figure 34 integrates *stream processors* that read/write memories where the data streams are stored. The processor has an individual index that corresponds to the one of the data stream. Therefore, each data unit is assigned to individual stream processor. The data stream will access two kinds of memories; *shared* and *global memories*. The shared memory works as a cache for the data in the global memory. Thus, using the data parallelism in the data stream, the GPU processes data units contained in the data streams by assigning the program to the stream processors.

GPU is equipped in the system connected via a peripheral bus like the PCI Express. This means the CPU needs to download the stream-based program to the GPU side, and also it needs to send/receive the input/output data streams to/from the global memory. This causes overhead during execution of the program because the execution must be setup via the peripheral bus. Especially, the recursive program accumulates the overhead at every iteration. Therefore, it is very important to eliminate or to hide the overhead caused when the CPU accesses the resources in the GPU side.

The memories equipped on the GPU and the host sides are separated. Therefore, the recursive application needs to send/receive the required data for the kernel program via the peripheral bus. This data copies take large overhead and occupy large percentage of the total

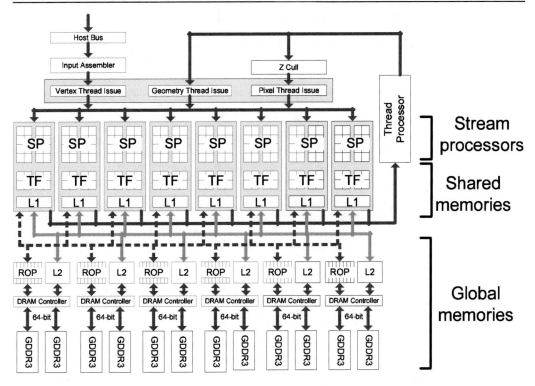

Figure 34. Recent typical architecture of GPU: GeForce Series.

execution time [52] increasing the number of iteration. Thus, this section is focused on this problem and proposes the implementation studies investigating the performance aspects of the recursive applications. The next section will illustrate techniques to eliminate the copy operations.

5.2. Techniques to Eliminate Copy Operations on GPGPU

Let us consider the methods to implement the recursive I/O operations in the stream-based computing on GPU. We can categorize the methods depending on where the copy operation occurs or how the buffer pointers are exchanged as illustrated in Figure 35. We assume that a kernel function receives an input data stream "a" and an output data stream "b", and those are exchanged every execution due to the recursive characteristics. We assume that each side of CPU and GPU owns separated buffer for the "a" or the "b". Let us consider how to exchange the I/O buffers after the first execution of the kernel function.

Figure 35 (a) and (b) include copy operation(s). Figure 35 (a), called *Copy host*, copies eagerly the output data stream (1) from the GPU side to the CPU side, (2) between the buffers and (3) from the CPU side to the GPU side. This case is the default method for the recursive kernel function. We need to address this case to achieve better performance. Figure 35 (b) also performs copy operation. However, the copy operation is performed in the device side. Figure 35 (b), called *Copy device*, is another method with copy operation. It copies data on GPU side. This method achieves better performance than the Copy host

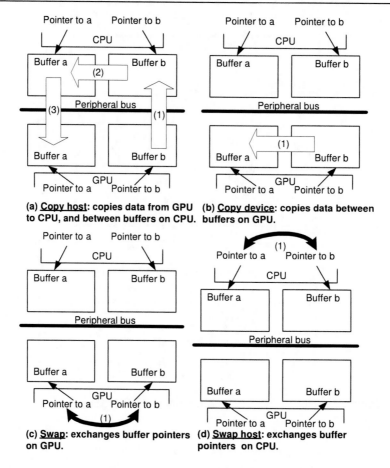

(a) <u>Copy host</u>: copies data from GPU to CPU, and between buffers on CPU.

(b) <u>Copy device</u>: copies data between buffers on GPU.

(c) <u>Swap</u>: exchanges buffer pointers on GPU.

(d) <u>Swap host</u>: exchanges buffer pointers on CPU.

Figure 35. Categorization of methods regarding copy between buffers and pointer exchange.

because it does not need copy operations to/from the CPU side.

To eliminate the copy operation in any part of the system, Figure 35 (c) and (d) exchanges the pointers to the buffers. Figure 35 (c), called *Swap*, exchanges the buffer pointers in the GPU side. This method should achieve perfect performance at every iteration of the recursive kernel because all copy operations are eliminated. This pointer exchange is controlled by the CPU. On the other hand, Figure 35 (d) exchanges the pointers in the CPU side. However, this mechanism needs data transfers from/to GPUs that are performed in Figure 35 (a)-(1) and (3). Therefore, in this section, we do not focus on this method because this method is equivalent to Figure 35 (a).

5.2.1.   Case Studies of Implementations

This section shows how to implement the copy host, the copy device and the swap methods on the CUDA and the OpenCL platforms.

- Case study in CUDA

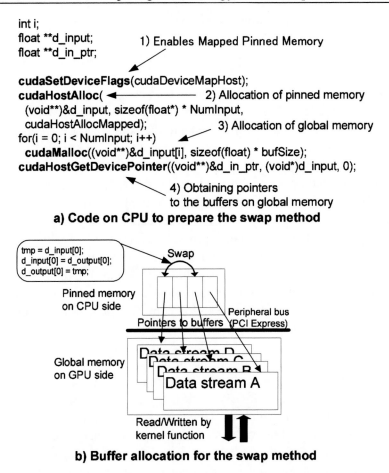

```
int i;
float **d_input;            1) Enables Mapped Pinned Memory
float **d_in_ptr;

cudaSetDeviceFlags(cudaDeviceMapHost);
cudaHostAlloc( ◄─────────── 2) Allocation of pinned memory
  (void**)&d_input, sizeof(float*) * NumInput,
  cudaHostAllocMapped);            3) Allocation of global memory
for(i = 0; i < NumInput; i++)
  cudaMalloc((void**)&d_input[i], sizeof(float) * bufSize);
cudaHostGetDevicePointer((void**)&d_in_ptr, (void*)d_input, 0);
```
4) Obtaining pointers
to the buffers on global memory

a) Code on CPU to prepare the swap method

```
tmp = d_input[0];
d_input[0] = d_output[0];
d_output[0] = tmp;
```
Swap

Pinned memory
on CPU side

Peripheral bus
Pointers to buffers (PCI Express)

Global memory
on GPU side

Data stream D
Data stream C
Data stream B
Data stream A

Read/Written by
kernel function

b) Buffer allocation for the swap method

Figure 36. The Swap method on CUDA environment.

The CUDA prepares the `cudaMemcpy` function that performs data transfer between the CPU and the GPU sides. Using this function, the Copy host method is implemented with additional copy operation between the I/O buffers in the CPU side. The Copy device method is also available on the CUDA environment using the `cudaMemcpy` function with `cudaMemcpyDeviceToDevice` at the fourth argument. The function performs a copy operation between the buffers allocated on the GPU side. Finally, the CUDA environment enables the Swap method applying a tricky mechanism using the *pinned* memory that is allocated on the CPU side, but that is accessed from the GPU via the peripheral bus as depicted in Figure 36. Preparation for the swap method follows the steps as shown in Figure 36a); 1) the `cudaSetDeviceFlags` enables the allocation in the pinned memory, 2) allocation in the pinned memory that obtains the buffer pointers to the data streams placed on GPU side, 3) allocation for the buffers on GPU side and finally 4) registering the pointers to the streams to the buffer of 2). From the 2nd execution of the kernel function, the pointers maintained in the buffer allocated by 2) will be exchanged by CPU side as explained in Figure 36b). This code does not include any copy operation.

Therefore, the optimal performance will be expected.

- Case study in OpenCL

  First, the OpenCL implements the copy method using `clEnqueueWriteBuffer` and `clEnqueueReadBuffer`. Therefore, here explains how to implement the copy device and the swap method. Second, the copy device method is mainly implemented using `clEnqueueCopyBuffer` function that is called by the CPU and performs a copy operation between two buffers in GPU side via the GPU bus. Finally, the swap method is implemented by using `clSetKernelArg` function. This function is used to exchange the parameters to the I/O buffers at each iteration. For example, assume that a kernel has two arguments; `float *inbuf` and `float *outbuf` and two buffers *src* and *dst* are allocated in the GPU side. At the first execution, the `clSetKernelArg` function associates the *src* buffer to the `inbuf` and the *dst* to the `outbuf`. After the execution of the kernel, the function exchanges the `inbuf` and `outbuf` pointers using the function. Thus, the data stored in *dst* buffer is accessed via the `inbuf` without explicit copy operation between buffers.

As explained above, on both the CUDA and the OpenCL environments three methods shown in Figure 35 are available to be implemented. As long as our experintal measurements, comparing to the data transfer performances on a recent personal computer of PCI Express bus where 10 GByte/sec is achieved at most, the one on the GPU achieves higher bandwidth on which the GeForce GTX285 and the Tesla C2050 obtain about 150 GByte/sec. According to the static large performance difference, it is easy to expect that the Copy device method achieves very higher performance than the Copy host one. However, the point is how higher performance the swap method can achieve against the copy device method due to elimination of copy operation. Let us discuss this point in the next section applying dynamic behaviors of kernel functions.

5.2.2. Experimental Performance Evaluations

Let us discuss performance of the three methods explained in the previous sections using dynamic kernel functions: the IIR filter, the Jacobi method and the LU decomposition. Although these applications work recursively, each application has a unique characteristic.

The experimental environment is a PC that consists of an Intel's Core i7 930 processor at 2.80GHz with 12GB DDR3 memory, and an NVIDIA Tesla C2050 with 3GB Memory. The OS in the PC is the Cent OS of the Linux Kernel 2.6.18. The driver version of the GPU is 3.0.

We measure the execution times of each application using the methods when we apply both double precision and single one to the calculation. Regarding the Copy host/device methods, we measure the data transfer time consumed by the copy operation. The time used by the swap operation is also measured. We will show the results on graphs with bars where two parts are included: a gray one shows the time consumed by the copy/the swap operation, and the black one shows the time used for the calculation performed in the kernel.

- IIR filter kernel

The IIR (Infinite Impulse Response) filter is a well-known kernel to be applied to image processing for emphasizing the edges of objects. We use the following equation for the filter with 16 coefficients:

$$y_n = \sum_{i=0}^{15} a_i x_{n-1} - \sum_{j=0}^{15} b_j y_{n-j-1}$$

Here, the y is used in the right side of the equation. Therefore, this is a typical recursive kernel, which exchanges the input data stream of y and the output data stream of y. This exchange is performed by the Copy host/device and the Swap methods. Regarding the parallelization, each y_i calculation is assigned to a stream processor (i.e., a thread in the CUDA and a work item in the OpenCL). The number of total input samples of x and y equivalents to the number of iterations.

Figure 37 and Figure 38 show the execution times among the methods on the CUDA and the OpenCL respectively. During the iteration of the kernel, the size of y does not change. Moreover, the calculation is not heavy. Therefore, the percentage of the copy time in the Copy host method is very large. The copy device and the swap method achieve almost the same time on both environment. Thus, this kernel function has benefit from the elimination mechanism of the swap or the copy device.

- Jacobi Method

The Jacobi method is applied to a system of linear equations where the coefficient matrix is sparse and to be solved approximately with recursive iterations using the following equation:

$$x_i^{(k+1)} = \frac{1}{a_{ii}} \left(b_i - \sum_{j \neq i}^{n} a_{ij} x_j^{(k)} \right)$$

where the $x_i^{(k+1)}$ approximates x_i after kth iteration.

In the kernel function assigned to the thread or the work item, the input data stream for x obtains the approximation after the kth iteration. The output data stream will become the one of the $(k + 1)$th iteration. Therefore, the I/O buffers are exchanged among the recursive iterations.

Figure 39 and Figure 40 show the execution times among the methods on the CUDA and the OpenCL respectively. The number of iterations is normalized to the same as the length of x vector. As the opposite case of the kernel function such as the IIR filter, this kernel function does not treat a large amount of I/O data for the recursive calculation comparing to the amount of calculations. Therefore, three methods achieve almost the same performances without copy/swap overheads.

- LU decomposition

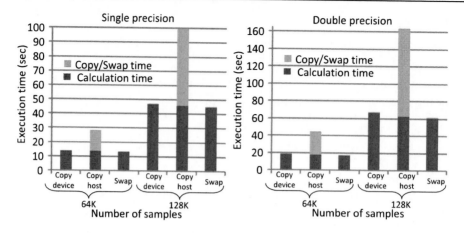

Figure 37. Performance of IIR filter kernel on CUDA.

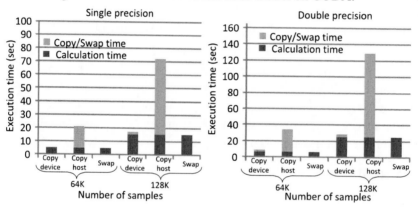

Figure 38. Performance of IIR filter kernel on OpenCL.

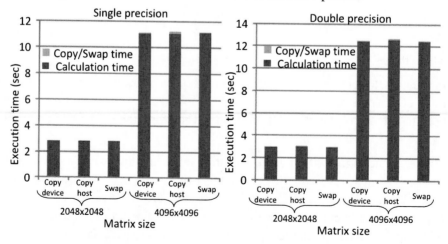

Figure 39. Performance of Jacobi method on CUDA.

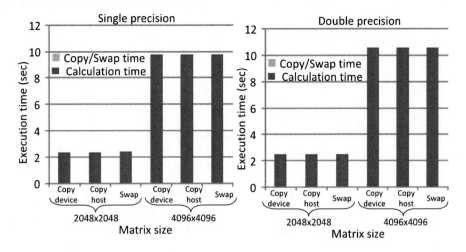

Figure 40. Performance of Jacobi method on OpenCL.

Finally, the LU decomposition is the same objective as the Jacobi method to solve the linear equations. However, it is applied to the case when the coefficient matrix is dense. Figure 41 shows the shape of the matrix after the kth decomposition calculating the equations listed in the left side of the figure. The $L_{22}U_{22}$ is generated as the coefficient matrix for the next iteration. This means that the input data stream is the matrix and also generates the matrix as the output data stream for the next iteration. Thus, the output data streams is recursively used in the input every iteration as the size is decreased.

Figure 42 and Figure 43 show the execution times among the methods on the CUDA and the OpenCL respectively. The sizes of the I/O data streams are controlled by a constant argument to pass the iteration number. Even if the I/O data streams are reduced every iteration, this kernel needs to use $k \times k$ matrix at the kth iteration. Therefore, copy overhead is observed in the cases of the Copy host/device methods. Here we confirmed that the Swap method achieves the best performance again.

Any applications that we have focused in this section achieve the best performance when the swap method is applied. The Copy device method shows also drastically better performances than the ones of the Copy host. However, it also causes some overhead to use the GPU's memory bus during the data copy between the I/O buffers. Thus, we have confirmed that the swap operation should be implemented to avoid the overhead occurred when the recursive data transfer between the I/O buffers is included in the algorithm because it does not have any overhead even if the transferred data size is small as we have observed in the case of Jacobi method. When the data size becomes enormous, it is clear that the Swap method obtain the best performance.

5.3. Scenario-based Execution Method on Manycore Accelerators

The CarSh has addressed the double programming problem on the CPU and the accelerator. It provides an interface to invoke only the accelerator program. This promotes that the pro-

$$k \quad n{-}k$$

$$\begin{array}{c} k \\ n{-}k \end{array} \left(\begin{array}{c|c} U_{11} & U_{12} \\ \hline L_{21} & \begin{array}{c} U_{22} \\ L_{22} \end{array} \end{array} \right)$$

$$U_{11} = A_{11}$$
$$U_{12} = A_{12}$$
$$L_{21} = \frac{1}{A_{11}} A_{21}$$
$$L_{22}U_{22} = A_{22} - \frac{1}{A_{11}} A_{21} A_{12}$$

Figure 41. Algorithm of LU decomposition.

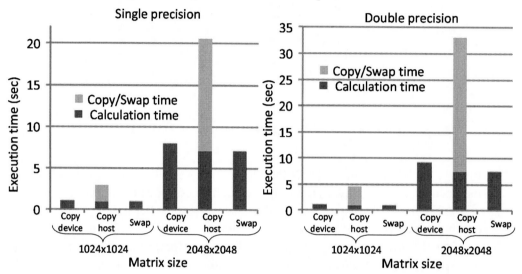

Figure 42. Performance of LU decomposition on CUDA.

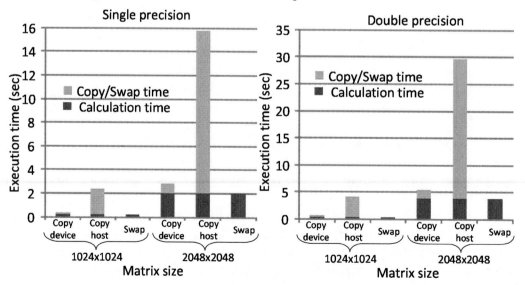

Figure 43. Performance of LU decomposition on OpenCL.

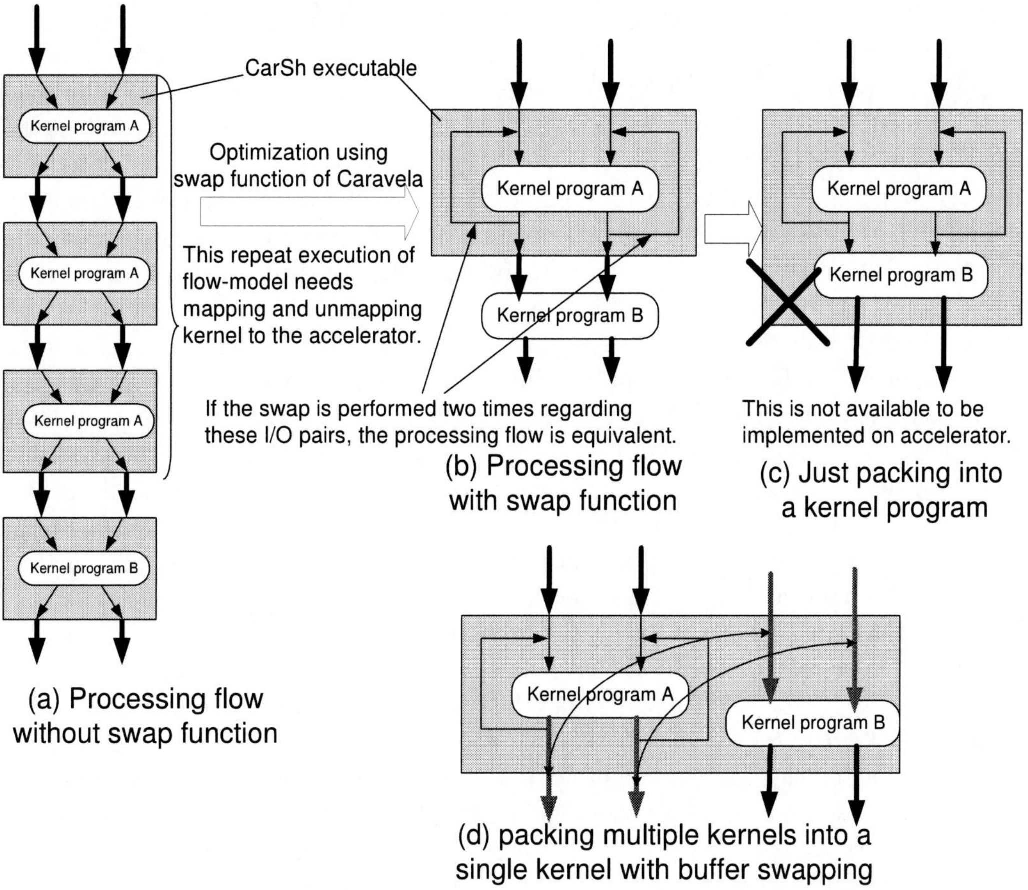

CarSh executable

Kernel program A

Optimization using swap function of Caravela

This repeat execution of flow-model needs mapping and unmapping kernel to the accelerator.

Kernel program A

Kernel program A

Kernel program A

Kernel program B

Kernel program A

Kernel program B

If the swap is performed two times regarding these I/O pairs, the processing flow is equivalent.

(b) Processing flow with swap function

Kernel program A

Kernel program B

This is not available to be implemented on accelerator.

(c) Just packing into a kernel program

(a) Processing flow without swap function

Kernel program A

Kernel program B

(d) packing multiple kernels into a single kernel with buffer swapping

Figure 44. Optimizing repeat execution of a flow-model with the swap function of Caravela.

grammer concentrates to develop the applications only focusing on the stream computing paradigm.

The buffer management has been also addressed by Caravela and CarSh employing the swap function. For example, in the case when a GPU is employed to an accelerator of a processing flow with multiple kernel programs, Figure 44(a) illustrates a processing flow with a repeat execution of a kernel program packed into a CarSh executable. The *Kernel program A* is packed into an executable file of CarSh and executed for three times by passing the data at every execution. The data propagations among the *Kernel program A* can be optimized by the virtual buffer function that the buffers are provided by memory implementation not by files. This achieves the higher performance of the total execution than the conventional one. However, the flow-model execution needs mapping/unmapping the flow-model to/from GPU at every execution. This causes a large overhead because the control performed by the host CPU is returned at every execution of the flow-model. Moreover, the I/O buffers must be configured for the next kernel execution. This causes the data transfer overhead via the peripheral bus.

If we apply the swap function supported by Caravela platform, we can implement the repeat execution on the recursive structure of the flow-model if the I/O buffers are straightly connected as shown in Figure 44(b). This program execution brings an optimization without unmapping the flow-model and keeps the continuous execution on the accelerator without returning the control to the CPU side. However, the *Kernel program B* must be mapped to the accelerator after the swap execution of the *Kernel program A*. This also causes the data transfer overhead via the peripheral bus. The kernel merging techniques such as [17] has been proposed. However, it merges multiple kernels and invokes it at a single mapping to a GPU. It is targeted to utilize the resource on the accelerator without considering the processing flow that conveys the results among multiple kernel programs. Therefore we need to invent a novel technique to eliminate the mapping/unmapping overhead.

To address the overhead problem as discussed above, it is indispensable to develop a new technique that different kernel programs are able to run without unmapping it from the accelerator. For example, Figure 44(c) shows the packing situation of the *Kernel program A* and *B* into a *single kernel program*. The I/O connection in a kernel program is not available in the flow-model because the kernel program is not able to randomly read/write the output data due to the assigned processing unit numbers. In this case, the output data stream from the *Kernel program A* must be transferred to the CPU side once, and then must be unmmaped from the accelerator. Then the *Kernel program B* is mapped to the accelerator. The output data stream is set to the input one again. And finally calculation of the Kernel program B can be started. Therefore, the kernel execution must be reset after the execution of the *Kernel program A* and the output must be swapped with the corresponding input data stream to the *Kernel program B* such as Figure 44(d). This strategy eliminates the overhead for the mapping/unmapping a kernel program and buffer configuration. However, this case implies problems of the execution order and how to select the correct kernel program. To address this, the single kernel must have a special input that receives the execution order of the kernel programs in the desired order specified by the programmer. We call this order a *scenario* of a single kernel program with multiple functions. The main objective of this research is to develop a modeling technique to pack the multiple kernels resolving the I/O swapping timings and the one to insert the additional code that merges multiple kernel programs. From the next section, we propose a novel technique called *scenario-based execution method* that provides how to pack multiple kernel programs. This strategy eliminates the mapping/unmapping a kernel program to/from an accelerator and the buffer configuration overheads.

5.3.1.   Design of Scenario-based Execution Method

In order to implement the scenario-based execution of kernel program, we need to consider two matters; one is the packing technique of multiple kernel programs and another is the I/O buffer definition for the swap function.

First, let us begin to design the I/O buffer definition for the swap function. Assume that we have a processing flow as illustrated in Figure 45(a). The flow consists of three kernel programs named A, B and C. Each kernel program has four input streams named a, b, c and p. It also has four output streams named d, e, f and q. We assume that, of course, the programmer knows the relations among the input and the output streams. The output streams of A are connected to the next kernel program B and the calculated data are propagated to the output of C. Now let us pack the I/Os into swap pairs. Regarding the

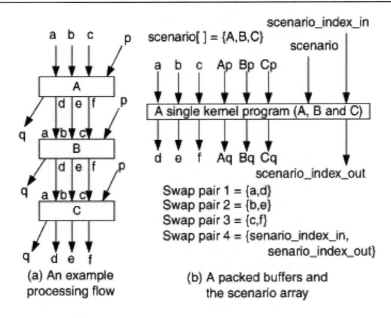

Figure 45. The buffer packing technique for the scenario-based execution.

input stream p, because it is not connected to the previous kernel program, we do not need to care it as the swap pair. The output stream q is also considered as the same. The other I/O streams are connected among the kernel programs one by one. If we define the same length of the I/O buffers of a, b, c, d, e and f, we can pack those into three swap pairs. Therefore, we can define the *swap pair 1* with a and d, the *swap pair 2* with b and e, and the *swap pair 3* with c and f. Thus, we can pack the kernel program A, B and C into a single one with three swap pairs, and also the single kernel program just enumerates the input streams p and the output streams q of A, B and C as illustrated in Figure 45(b). Here, we need to introduce additional input data streams to the single kernel. One is the scenario, which has a set of sequence that implements the processing flow. In the example case, it is an array with three integer elements of A, B and C. Another is the scenario index, which is also an array with one element that represents the index number for the scenario array. The index is incremented at every execution of the single kernel. Therefore, its output stream is indispensable and also those input and output streams must be defined as another swap pair for controlling the behavior of the kernel program.

According to the buffer packing technique explained above, at every execution the I/O buffers defined as the swap pair will be exchanged and also the input data is automatically propagated from one function to another in the processing flow following the scenario. The scenario is also pointed by the scenario index that the redundant output buffer will be exchanged with the input buffer after incrementing the index number. Thus, the buffers can be packed completely to a single kernel program and the single kernel program implements the processing flow.

Next, let us consider the kernel merging into a single program. In order to select a corresponding calculations of each kernel program packed in the single kernel program we can merge all kernel programs using a selection statement of the language used by kernel

```
pid = this processor id;  ◄──────  Getting the own processor id
switch (senario[senario_index_in[0]]){
case A:
        d[pid] = some calculation ...;  ⎫
        e[pid] = some calculation ...;  ⎪
        f[pid] = some calculation ...;  ⎬  Kernel Program A
        Aq[pid] = some calculation ...; ⎪
        break;                          ⎭
case B:
        d[pid] = some calculation ...;  ⎫
        e[pid] = some calculation ...;  ⎪
        f[pid] = some calculation ...;  ⎬ Kernel Program B
        Bq[pid] = some calculation ...; ⎪
        break;                          ⎭
case C:
        d[pid] = some calculation ...;  ⎫
        e[pid] = some calculation ...;  ⎪
        f[pid] = some calculation ...;  ⎬  Kernel Program C
        Cq[pid] = some calculation ...; ⎪
        break;                          ⎭
}
if(pid == 0)  ◄─────────────────  Processor 0 only calclates
        scenario_index_out[0] ++;
```

Figure 46. The kernel merging technique for the scenario-based execution.

program such as *if else* or *switch*. Because it is easy to shape the selection flow we use *switch* statement. The scenario is selected by the index and also will become the selection key for the corresponding function for the kernel program.

Figure 46 shows the perspective of the single kernel program written in a C-like code, which packs the processing flow illustrated into Figure 45(a). The `pid` is the processor ID given by the accelerator's runtime. Each scenario is selected by the scenario index, and jumps to the corresponding calculation. In each case, it performs the calculations of the corresponding `case` statement and generates all output data streams that will be swapped after the kernel execution. Besides, the output data stream not related to the swap pair is generated at the corresponding calculations in the `case` statement. For example, the output stream of Cq is generated at the `case` statement of "C". However, it does not calculate the one of Aq. Because the output data steam is not volatile during swapping the I/O buffers and iterative execution of the single kernel, the output data will be picked up by the host CPU. Finally, the first processor specified by the `pid` increments the `scenario_index_out` that will be used as the next scenario index.

According to the buffer packing and the kernel merging techniques explained above, a processing flow can be packed into a single kernel program with the scenario input. Every execution of the single kernel program, it is not unmapped from the accelerator, and then, the buffers related to the swap pairs are exchanged without copy operation. Because the host CPU just commands to the accelerator the pointer swap operation of the related buffers and re-execution of the same kernel program, the data transfer via the peripheral bus is reduced to the minimal. Thus, the scenario-based execution is expected to exploit the potential

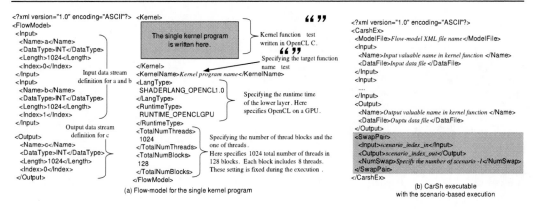

(a) Flow-model for the single kernel program

(b) CarSh executable with the scenario-based execution

Figure 47. Implementation of the scenario-based execution on CarSh framework.

performance of the accelerator eliminating the inevitable overheads conventionally caused in the general execution by mapping/unmapping kernel programs.

5.3.2. Implementation of Scenario-based Execution Method

For the implementation of the scenario-based execution, we employed CarSh environment. As listed in Figure 47(a), first the programmer needs to define a flow-model and packs the single kernel program. In the flow-model, there is no definition of the swap pair. Next, the CarSh executable is defined as listed in (b) of the figure. The CarSh executable includes the relations among the I/O data streams defined in the flow-model and the I/O files that are read/written in order to execute the kernel program. It also includes the swap pair definitions of the data I/Os and the scenario index. The `<SwapPair>` tag includes the number of swaps. It equals to $(N - 1)$ where the N is the number of recursive iterations in the scenario stream. Finally, the programmer needs to setup the input data streams preparing CSV files and also the scenario in the same type of the file.

The CarSh executable invokes the single kernel program embedded in a flow-model reading the swap pair definitions and the number of swap exchanges. It reads the input data streams and the scenario, and thus the execution will be iterated for the specified number of swap exchanges without unmapping the kernel program from the target accelerator.

5.3.3. Restrictions of Scenario-based Execution

The scenario-based execution has the limitations of the freedoms of parallelization and the buffer utilization as explained below:

- Limitation to the freedom of the number of threads
  When the parallelism would change among kernel programs in a processing flow, the scenario-based execution is not able to run those kernel programs equivalently. The parallelism must be the same among all kernel programs because the single kernel program is not able to change the number of threads by itself after the invocation. Therefore, the number of threads of the single kernel program must be defined as equal to the maximum one in the kernel programs. This means that the programmer

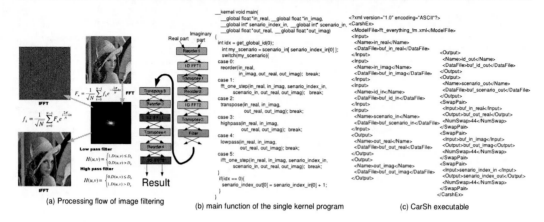

(a) Processing flow of image filtering   (b) main function of the single kernel program   (c) CarSh executable

Figure 48. Image filtering application and the CarSh executable.

needs to program any kernel program in the processing flow with the same number of threads (of course, the kernel program should support any number of threads due to the extensibility).

- Limitation to the I/O buffer size
  The buffer swapping needs the buffers which sizes are the same among the input and the output buffers. If one of the sizes of buffers in a pair does not match to another, the amount of data elements generated by the kernel program will overflow. This means that the buffer sizes of the swap pair must be equal. Therefore, the size of the amount of data outputted from any kernel program in a processing flow is set to the largest number of elements in the I/O buffers of the swap pair.

In some cases such as the application that changes the parallelism at every execution of the kernel like LU decomposition, the programmer would desire to write the kernel program that can change the parallelism and the buffer sizes with the input parameter such as the iteration index. However, in spite of this kind of complex case, the scenario-based execution will achieve the best performance because the copy operations are eliminated during the execution of the single kernel program, and thus it becomes a novel method of the high performance execution to exploit potential performance of any kinds of manycore accelerators.

5.3.4. Experimental Evaluations

Let us evaluate the scenario-based execution using a realistic example. Here we use a typical image filtering with 2D FFT performed often in the image operations. We assume to perform the filtering an $N \times N$ pixel image with a high or a low pass filter. Figure 48(a) shows the processing steps used in the evaluation. An image (*Lena*), which is transformed by the FFT, is passed to a high or low pass filter, and finally transposed by IFFT. This simple process is composed by five flow-models: *reorder* performs butterfly exchanges, *transpose* inverses the rows and the columns, *filter, FFT* and *IFFT*. Totally it executes 13 functional steps in a processing flow as shown in Figure 48(a). The FFT and IFFT needs iteration to

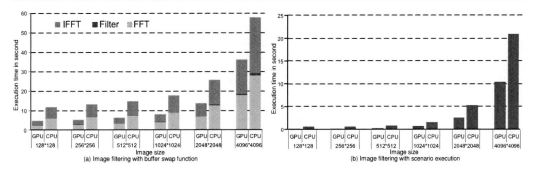

Figure 49. Comparisons of execution times of the image filtering application (a) with and (b) without scenario-based execution.

perform the butterfly operations. The number of iteration is calculated by $log_2 N$ when the input image size is $N \times N$ pixels.

We pack the processing pipeline to a single kernel with the scenario. Figure 48(b) shows the main function of the single kernel program. The scenario changes depending on the input image size because the numbers of iterations of the FFT and the IFTT are varied by the input image size. We have assigned the scenario numbers from 0 to 5 to the *reorder*, the single step of *FFT*, the *transpose*, the *high pass filter*, the *low pass* filter and the single step of $IFFT$ respectively. The scenario input stream obtains the numbers in the processing order specified in Figure 48(a). For example, when the N is 512, the numbers of iteration of FFT and $IFFT$ becomes $log_2 512 = 9$ respectively. Therefore the scenario becomes a sequence of 0, repeating 1 for nine times, 2, 0, repeating 1 for nine times, 2, 3 or 4, 2, 0, repeating 5 for nine times, 2, 0, repeating 5 for nine times. Total number of the swap iterations becomes 45. The `scenario_index_in` is used to point the current scenario and the corresponding *case* statement is selected by the number.

Regarding the buffer packing, the I/Os of the real part and the imaginary part are defined as the swap pairs declared in `<SwapPair>` tag combined with `buf_in_real` and `buf_out_real`, and with `buf_in_imag` and `buf_out_imag` respectively as listed in Figure 48(c). The CarSh maps the single kernel program to the accelerator following the specification of the executable, and performs the buffer swaps. At every execution of the program, the scenario index is incremented and it points the case number from the scenario. Thus, all processing steps of the flow are executed in the accelerator side only.

Let us evaluate the performance using execution times with/without applying the scenario-based execution. Our platform of the performance test is a PC with a Core i7 930 at 2.80GHz with an Nvidia Tesla C2050 GPU. CarSh uses the OpenCL runtime to access both CPU-based and the GPU-based accelerators. We measure the performances on both accelerators.

The first experiment analyzes the baseline performance of the processing flow applying the image filtering. This experiment does not use the swap function in Caravela. Therefore, each flow-model in the processing flow is mapped/unmapped to the accelerator. The execution flow of the multiple kernel programs is given by a CarSh batch using the virtual buffer function passing the real and the imaginary data streams are propagated from the first *reorder* to the final $IFFT$ as shown in Figure 48(a). The performance is shown in the

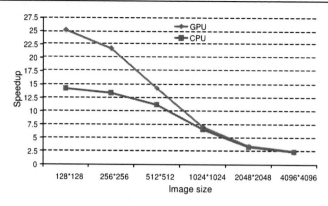

Figure 50. Comparison of speedups between with/without scenario-based execution.

graph of Figure 49(a). Because each kernel program in the flow will be unmapped once and the control will be returned to the host CPU side, it is available to measure the execution time of each kernel program as the graph consists of different colors. As we can see the performance of each part of the flow, we confirm that almost all total execution time is owned by FFT and $IFFT$ due to the copy operations performed by the butterfly operations.

Next, we measured the execution times with applying the scenario-based execution. Figure 49(b) shows the execution times of the performance. During the small sizes of the input image, it drastically achieves the performance than the one without the scenario-based execution. The performance is linearly increasing when the image size becomes double. Moreover, the execution time scales to four times. This means that the accelerator is intensively working to calculate the kernel program. When CPU is used for the accelerator, we also confirmed the performance becomes improved by the swap operation due to the elimination of copy operation because the swap operation on the CPU-based OpenCL accelerator is implemented by just exchanging pointers of buffers.

Figure 50 shows the speedup (with/without scenario). When the input image size for the filter application is small, the speedup shows in both cases very high such as 25 times in the case of GPU and 15 times in the one of CPU. This represents that the overheads are eliminated, which are caused by the mapping/un mapping of the kernel program and the data copy operation from a kernel program to another.

According to the performance evaluation in this section, we have confirmed that the scenario-based execution achieves very reasonably high performance in any processing flow. When we apply two simple techniques discussed in this section, which are the buffer packing and the kernel merging techniques, the processing flow has become an iterative execution of a single kernel program without un mapping it from the accelerator. Therefore, the overhead caused by the data transfer between the host CPU and the accelerator via the peripheral bus is completely eliminated. Thus the scenario-based execution is an indispensable technique to provide the performance goal of the application designer.

6. Remarks

This chapter showed an advanced programming environment of many core accelerators and techniques to exploit the potential performance of these accelerators. The Caravela platform was therefore introduced. It simplifies the programming environment of the accelerators using the flow-model concept. The flow-model was employed to represent algorithms based on the stream computing approach. The Caravela platform is capable of parallelizing the flow automatically and exploiting the potential performance of the accelerators. Even if the flow is concurrently separated into several physical accelerators as in a GPU cluster, the timings of message exchange and kernel execution are automatically adjusted by the Caravela runtime. Moreover, Caravela resolves the overhead of data copy operations among the host CPU and the accelerator using the swap method, after which the execution mechanism is extended to the scenario-based execution using the swap operation. Thus, we can conclude that the Caravela platform completes the fundamental techniques necessary to use the latest many core accelerators.

For the future, we plan to extend the techniques presented in this chapter to the hardware implementation. The hardware is an intelligent many core accelerator that analyzes the processing flow automatically and creates the execution order in a pipeline manner using the PEA-ST algorithm. Then the flow can be optimized by using the scenario-based execution mechanism. In this case, if the CPU side provides an algorithm definition of the pipeline model to the intelligent accelerator, the accelerator will work autonomously without further communicating with the host side.

References

[1] DirectX homepage. http://www.microsoft.com/directx.

[2] Globus alliance. http://www.globus.org/.

[3] Gridlab resource management system http://www.gridlab.org/workpackages/wp-9/.

[4] Barracuda: An OpenCL Library for Ruby. http://gnuu.org/2009/08/30/barracuda-an-opencl-library-for-ruby/.

[5] D. Bernholdt, S. Bharathi, and et al. The Earth System Grid: Supporting the Next Generation of Climate Modeling Research. *Proceedings of the IEEE*, 93:485–495, 2005.

[6] Ian Buck, Tim Foley, Daniel Horn, Jeremy Sugerman, Kayvon Fatahalian, Mike Houston, and Pat Hanrahan. Brook for GPUs: stream computing on graphics hardware. *ACM Trans. Graph.*, 23(3):777–786, 2004.

[7] I. Daubechies. *Ten Lectures on Wavelets*. Number 61 in CBMS/NSF Series in Applied Math. SIAM, 1992.

[8] E. W. Dijkstra. A Note on Two Problems in Connexion with Graphs. *NUMERISCHE MATHEMATIK*, 1(1):269–271, 1959.

[9] Zhe Fan, Feng Qiu, Arie Kaufman, and Suzanne Yoakum-Stover. GPU Cluster for High Performance Computing. In *SC '04: Proceedings of the 2004 ACM/IEEE conference on Supercomputing*, page 47, Washington, DC, USA, 2004. IEEE Computer Society.

[10] Michael L. Fredman and Dan E. Willard. Trans-dichotomous Algorithms for Minimum Spanning Trees and Shortest Paths. *J. Comput. Syst. Sci.*, 48(3):533–551, June 1994.

[11] Alan O. Freier, Philip Karlton, and Paul C. Kocher. *The SSL Protocol Version 3.0*. Netscape communications corporation, 1996.

[12] James Frey, Todd Tannenbaum, Ian Foster, Miron Livny, and Steven Tuecke. Condor-G: A Computation Management Agent for Multi-Institutional Grids. In *Proceedings of the Tenth IEEE Symposium on High Performance Distributed Computing (HPDC10) San Francisco*, 2001.

[13] Al Geist, Adam Beguelin, Jack Dongarra, Weicheng Jiang, Robert Manchek, and Vaidy Sunderam. *PVM: Parallel Virtual Machine A Users' Guide and Tutorial for Networked Parallel Computing*. MIT Press, 1994.

[14] Naga K. Govindaraju, Scott Larsen, Jim Gray, and Dinesh Manocha. A memory model for scientific algorithms on graphics processors. In *SC '06: Proceedings of the 2006 ACM/IEEE conference on Supercomputing*, page 89, New York, NY, USA, 2006. ACM Press.

[15] Hannes Gredler and Walter Goralski. *The Complete IS-IS Routing Protocol*. Springer Verlag, 2004.

[16] William Grosso. *Java RMI*. O'Reilly Media, 2001.

[17] Marisabel Guevara, Chris Gregg, Kim Hazelwood, and Kevin Skadron. Enabling task parallelism in the cuda scheduler. In *Workshop on Programming Models for Emerging Architectures*, PMEA, pages 69–76, Raleigh, NC, September 2009.

[18] Paul Havlak. Nesting of reducible and irreducible loops. *ACM Trans. Program. Lang. Syst.*, 19(4):557–567, 1997.

[19] OpenMP homepage. http://www.openmp.org/.

[20] R. Jacob, C. Schafer, I. Foster, M. Tobis, and J. Anderson. Computational Design and Performance of the Fast Ocean Atmosphere Model, Version One. In *2001 Intl Conference on Computational Science*, 2001.

[21] Vijay Karamcheti and Andrew A. Chien. Software overhead in messaging layers: where does the time go? In *ASPLOS-VI: Proceedings of the sixth international conference on Architectural support for programming languages and operating systems*, pages 51–60, New York, NY, USA, 1994. ACM Press.

[22] N. Karonis, B. Toonen, and I. Foster. MPICH-G2: A Grid-Enabled Implementation of the Message Passing Interface. *Journal of Parallel and Distributed Computing*, 2003.

[23] John Kessenich, Dave Baldwin, and Randi Rost. The OpenGL Shading Language. *3Dlabs, Inc. Ltd.*, 2006.

[24] Polina Kondratieva, Jens Krüger, and Rüdiger Westermann. The Application of GPU Particle Tracing to Diffusion Tensor Field Visualization. In *IEEE Visualization*, page 10, 2005.

[25] Pablo Lamilla, Shinichi Yamagiwa, Masahiro Arai, and Koichi Wada. Elimination Techniques of Redundant Data Transfers among GPUs and CPU on Recursive Stream-Based Applications. In *IPDPS/APDCM11 Anchorage USA*, May 2011.

[26] LAM/MPI Parallel Computing. http://www.lam-mpi.org/.

[27] Sheng Liang. *Java Native Interface: Programmer's Guide and Specification.* Addison-Wesley Professional, first edition, 2001.

[28] Thomas J. Misa and Philip L. Frana. An Interview with Edsger W. Dijkstra. *Commun. ACM*, 53(8):41–47, August 2010.

[29] Kenneth Moreland and Edward Angel. The FFT on a GPU. In *HWWS '03: Proceedings of the ACM SIGGRAPH/EUROGRAPHICS conference on Graphics hardware*, pages 112–119, Aire-la-Ville, Switzerland, Switzerland, 2003. Eurographics Association.

[30] J. Moy. OSPF Version 2. Internet RFC 2328, April 1998.

[31] Aaftab Munshi, Benedict R. Gaster, Timothy G. Mattson, James Fung, and Dan Ginsburg. *OpenCL Programming Guide*. Addison Wesley, 2011.

[32] Hubert Nguyen. *GPU Gems 3*. Addison-Wesley Professional, first edition, 2007.

[33] NVIDIA Corporation. CUDA: Compute Unified Device Architecture programming guide, http://developer.nvidia.com/cuda.

[34] OpenCL. http://www.khronos.org/opencl/.

[35] John D. Owens, David Luebke, Naga Govindaraju, Mark Harris, Jens Kruger, Aaron E. Lefohn, and Timothy J. Purcell. A Survey of General-Purpose Computation on Graphics Hardware. In *Eurographics 2005, State of the Art Reports*, pages 21–51, August 2005.

[36] John D. Owens, David Luebke, Naga Govindaraju, Mark Harris, Jens Kruger, Aaron E. Lefohn, and Timothy J. Purcell. A survey of general-purpose computation on graphics hardware. In *Eurographics 2005, State of the Art Reports*, pages 21–51, August 2005.

[37] Radia Perlman. An Algorithm for Distributed Computation of a SpanningTree in an extended LAN. In *Proceedings of the ninth symposium on Data communications*, SIGCOMM '85, pages 44–53. ACM, 1985.

[38] Radia Perlman. *Interconnections (2nd Ed.): Bridges, Routers, Switches, and Internetworking Protocols*. Addison-Wesley Longman Publishing Co., Inc., Boston, MA, USA, 2000.

[39] R. C. Prim. Shortest Connection Networks and some Generalizations. *The Bell Systems Technical Journal*, 36(6):1389–1401, 1957.

[40] Daniel A Reed, Celso L Mendes, Chang da Lu, Ian Foster, and Carl Kesselman. *The Grid 2: Blueprint for a New Computing Infrastructure - Application Tuning and Adaptation*. Morgan Kaufman, 2003.

[41] Leonel Sousa and Shinichi Yamagiwa. aravela: A Distributed Stream-Based Computing Platform. In *Proceedings of 3rd HiPEAC Industrial Workshop*, 2007.

[42] Tarjan R. E. Testing flow graph reducibility. *J. Comput. Syst. Sci. 9*, pages 355–365, 1974.

[43] William Thies, Michal Karczmarek, and Saman P. Amarasinghe. StreamIt: A Language for Streaming Applications. In *Proceedings of the 11th International Conference on Compiler Construction*, pages 179–196. Springer-Verlag, 2002.

[44] N. Doss William Gropp, E. Lusk and A. Skjellum. A high-performance, portable implementation of the mpi message passing interface standard. In *MPI Developers Conference*, 1995.

[45] Michael Wolfe. *High Performance Compilers for Parallel Computing*. Addison Wesley, 1996.

[46] S. Yamagiwa and Shixun Zhang. Scenario-based execution method for massively parallel accelerators. In *Trust, Security and Privacy in Computing and Communications (TrustCom), 2013 12th IEEE International Conference on*, pages 1039–1048, July 2013.

[47] Shinichi Yamagiwa. Invitation to a Standard Programming Interface for Massively Parallel Computing Environment: OpenCL. *International Journal of Networking and Computing*, 2(2):188–205, 2012.

[48] Shinichi Yamagiwa and Leonel Sousa. Caravela: A novel stream-based distributed computing environment. *Computer*, 40(5):70–77, 2007.

[49] Shinichi Yamagiwa and Leonel Sousa. Design and Implementation of a Stream-based DistributedComputing Platform using Graphics Processing Units. In *ACM International Conference on Computing Frontiers*, May 2007.

[50] Shinichi Yamagiwa and Leonel Sousa. CaravelaMPI: Message passing interface for parallel gpu-based applications. In *In 8th International Symposium on Parallel and Distributed Computing (ISPDC 09)*, 2009.

[51] Shinichi Yamagiwa and Leonel Sousa. Modelling and Programming Stream-based Distributed Computing based on the Meta-pipeline Approach. *Int. J. Parallel Emerg. Distrib. Syst.*, 24(4):311–330, 2009.

[52] Shinichi Yamagiwa, Leonel Sousa, and Diogo Antao. Data buffering optimization methods toward a uniform programming interface for gpu-based applications. In *CF '07: Proceedings of the 4th international conference on Computing frontiers*, pages 205–212, New York, NY, USA, 2007. ACM Press.

[53] Shinichi Yamagiwa and Shixun Zhang. CarSh: A Commandline Execution Support for Stream-based Acceleration Environment. In *Procedia Computer Science, Proceedings of the International Conference on Computational Science, ICCS 2013*. Elsevier, 2013.

In: Horizons in Computer Science Research. Volume 11   ISBN: 978-1-63482-499-6
Editor: Thomas S. Clary, pp. 145-157   © 2015 Nova Science Publishers, Inc.

Chapter 4

H-infinity Recursive Wiener Fixed-Interval Smoother Based on Innovation Approach in Linear Discrete-Time Stochastic Systems

*Seiichi Nakamori**

Department of Technology, Faculty of Education,
Kagoshima University, Kagoshima, Japan

Abstract

This paper designs the H-infinity recursive Wiener fixed-interval smoother and filter, based on the innovation approach, in linear discrete-time stochastic systems. The estimators require the information of the observation matrix, the system matrix for the state variable, related with the signal, the variance of the state variable and the variance of the white observation noise. It is assumed that the signal is observed with additive white noise.

A numerical simulation example is shown to demonstrate the estimation characteristics of the proposed H-infinity fixed-interval smoother and filter.

Keywords: Wiener-Hopf equation, discrete-time stochastic systems, recursive Wiener filter, covariance information, H-infinity fixed-interval smoother

1. Introduction

The estimation problem given the covariance information has been seen as an important research in the area of the detection and estimation problems for communication systems. In [1]-[4], the filter, the predictor, the fixed-point smoother and the fixed-interval smoother are proposed, where it is assumed that the autocovariance function of the signal is expressed in the semi-degenerate kernel form. The semi-degenerate kernel is the function suitable for expressing a general kind of autocovariance function by a finite sum of nonrandom functions.

---

*E-mail address: k6165161@kadai.jp

In [5]-[7], the RLS Wiener filter and fixed-point smoother and fixed-interval smoother are proposed. In [6], the RLS Wiener fixed-interval smoother is designed in linear discrete-time stochastic systems, based on the innovation approach. The recursive Wiener estimators use the following information, i.e.; (1) the observation matrix, (2) the system matrix concerned with the state vector, (3) the variance of the state vector.

The H-infinity recursive Wiener fixed-point smoother and filter are proposed in [8], [9] for linear discrete-time and continuous-time stochastic systems. In [10]-[13], the H-infinity filter is proposed in linear discrete time-invariant systems. In [11], it is pointed out that the H_∞ filter is less sensitive to uncertainty in the exogenious signal statistics and system model dynamics. In [14]-[17], the nonlinear H_∞ filtering problems are considered.

In this paper, the H-infinity recursive Wiener fixed-interval smoother and filter are designed, based on the innovation approach, in linear discrete-time stochastic systems. The estimators require the information of the factorized autocovariance function of the signal. Namely, the estimators use the information of the observation matrix, the system matrix for the state variable, related with the signal, the variance of the state variable and the variance of the white observation noise as in [6]. It is assumed that the signal is observed with additive white noise. The fixed-interval smoothing and filtering algorithms are derived based on the invariant imbedding method [6]. Also, the fixed-interval smoothing error variance function is formulated to verify that the estimation accuracy of the proposed fixed-interval smoother is preferable to the filter.

A numerical simulation example is demonstrated to show the validity of the proposed H-infinity recursive Wiener fixed-interval smoother and the preferable estimation characteristic in comparison with the RLS Wiener fixed-interval smoother and the filter [6].

2.   Fixed-interval Smoothing Problem

2.1.   H-infinity Performance Criterion in Stochastic Systems

Let us consider a linear discrete-time stochastic system

$$x(k+1) = \Phi x(k) + Bu(k), \quad x(0) = x_0,$$
$$y_1(k) = z_1(k) + v_1(k), \quad z_1(k) = Cx(k), \quad k = 0, 1, \cdots . \tag{1}$$

Here, $x(k)$ is an n-dimensional state vector, $y_1(k)$ is an m-dimensional observed value, $u(k)$ is one-dimensional input noise, $v_1(k)$ is observation noise, Φ is an $n \times n$ state-transition matrix and C is an $m \times n$ observation matrix. Furthermore, it is assumed that $u(k)$ and $v_1(k)$ are zero-mean white noise vectors and the covariance matrix is given by

$$E\left[\begin{bmatrix} u(k) \\ v_1(k) \end{bmatrix} \begin{bmatrix} u^*(s) & v_1^*(s) \end{bmatrix} \right] = \begin{bmatrix} \Pi_0 & 0 \\ 0 & R \end{bmatrix} \delta_K(k-s). \tag{2}$$

Here, $\delta_K(k-s)$ represents the Kronecker delta function [14], [15] and the asterisk denotes the complex conjugation. Π_0 and R are $l \times l$ and $m \times m$ positive symmetric matrices respectively. Also, it is assumed that the mean and the variance matrix of the initial value $x(0)(= x_0)$ is expressed as

$$E[x_0] = 0, \quad E[x_0 x_0^*] = Q_0. \tag{3}$$

Q_0 is an $n \times n$ positive symmetric matrix. In general, we consider to estimate some arbitrary linear combination [9] of the state as

$$z_2(k) = Ux(k) \tag{4}$$

using the observed value $y_1(k)$, where U is given $r \times n$ matrix. From (1) and (4), for $U = C$, the problem to estimate $z_2(k)$ is reduced to the estimation of $z_1(k)$.

By the way, in estimating $z_2(j)$, for a given bounded $\gamma^2 > 0$, let us consider a new performance criterion in the stochastic system by taking into accounts of the statistics of (2) and (3) [9].

$$\sup_{\{x_0, u \in h_2, v_1 \in h_2\}} \frac{A(L)}{M(L)} < \gamma^2,$$

$$A(L) = \sum_{j=0}^{k} e_f^*(L)e_f(L), \quad e_f(j) = \check{z}(j) - Ux(j) \tag{5}$$

$$M(L) = (x_0 - \check{x}_0)^* Q_0^{-1}(x_0 - \check{x}_0) + \sum_{j=0}^{L} u^*(j)u(j) + \sum_{j=0}^{L} v_1^* R^{-1} v_1(j)$$

Let $\check{z}(j)$ be a filtering estimate of $z_2(j) = Ux(j)$ and $\check{z}(j)$ is also called a fictitious observed value of $z_2(j)$ [9]. Here, $\check{x}_0$ is the initial guess of x_0.

Along with the same discussion as in [9], let us introduce a scalar quadratic form from the point of the min-max estimation principle.

$$J_f(\check{z}; x_0, u, y_1) = (x - \check{x}_0)^* Q_0^{-1}(x - \check{x}_0) + \sum_{j=0}^{L} u^*(j)\Pi_0^{-1} u(j)$$

$$+ \sum_{j=0}^{L} (y_1(j) - Cx(j))^* R^{-1}(y_1(j) - Cx(j)) \tag{6}$$

$$-\gamma^{-2} \sum_{j=0}^{L} (\check{z}(j) - Ux(j))^* (\check{z}(j) - Ux(j))$$

Here, $\check{z} = (\check{z}(0), \cdots, \check{z}(L))$, $u = (u(0), \cdots, u(L))$ and $y_1 = (y_1(0), \cdots, y_1(L))$. From [9], it might be seen that, for $Q_0 > 0$, $\Pi_0 > 0$ and $R > 0$, the performance criterion (6) is valid if and only if, there exists $\check{z}(j), 0 \le j \le L$, such that for the vector x_0, for all sequences $\{u(j)\}_{j=0}^{L}$ and for all sequences $\{y_1(j)\}_{j=0}^{L}$, the scalar quadratic form satisfies

$$J_f(\check{z}; x_0, u, y_1) > 0. \tag{7}$$

2.2. Krein-space Observation Equation

Let us obtain the Krein-space observation equation in the H-infinity estimation problem.

(6) is rewritten as

$$J_f(\check{z}; x_0, u, y_1) = (x_0 - \check{x}_0)^* Q_0^{-1}(x_0 - \check{x}_0) + \sum_{j=0}^{L} u^*(j)\Pi_0^{-1}$$

$$+ \sum_{j=0}^{L} \tilde{y}^*(j) \begin{bmatrix} R & 0 \\ 0 & -\gamma^2 I \end{bmatrix}^{-1} \tilde{y}(j) > 0, \quad \tilde{y}(j) = \begin{bmatrix} y_1(j) \\ \check{z}(j) \end{bmatrix} - \begin{bmatrix} C \\ U \end{bmatrix} x(j). \tag{8}$$

The min-max problem of $J_f(\check{z}; x_0, u, y_1)$ by $\{y_1(j)\}_{j=0}^L$ results in the observation equation for $z_1(k)$ in (1) with the observation noise variance R from (2) [9]. Similarly, from the min-max problem of $J_f(\check{z}; x_0, u, y_1)$ by $\{\check{z}(j)\}_{j=0}^L$, the observation equation for $z_2(j)(=Ux(j))$ might be obtained as $\check{z}(j) = z_2(j) + v_2(j), [Ev_2(j)v_2^*(s)] = -\gamma^2 I \delta_K(j-s)$. Here, $v_2(j)$ represents the additional observation noise. From [8], [9], the notation $E[v_2(j)v_2^*(s)]$ is replaced with $[Ev_2(j)v_2^*(s)]$ in considering an indefinite space, since $-\gamma^2 I$ is a negative-definite matrix. The Krein space system related with the H_∞ filtering problem is originated in [8], [9] for linear discrete-time estimation problem. By definition, an indefinite inner product is in a real or complex vector space so that the corresponding quadratic form has both positive and negative values [9]. Krein spaces are suitable for treating generalized "random" variables whose covariance matrix is generally indefinite [8], [9]. Henceforth, let a signal vector $z(j)$ consist of components $z_1(j)$ and $z_2(j)$

$$\begin{aligned}
z(j) &= Hx(j) \\
&= \begin{bmatrix} z_1(j) \\ z_2(j) \end{bmatrix}, H = \begin{bmatrix} C \\ U \end{bmatrix}, \\
z_1(j) &= Cx(j), \quad z_2(J) = Ux(j),
\end{aligned} \tag{9}$$

and let an observed value $y(j)$ consist of $y_1(j)$ in (2) and the fictitious observed value $\check{z}(j)$.

$$y(k) = \begin{bmatrix} y_1(j) \\ \check{z}(j) \end{bmatrix} \tag{10}$$

From the above statements and also, by referring to the discussions in [8], [9], it might be seen that the following observation equation for $z(j)$ is obtained.

$$\begin{aligned}
y(j) &= Hx(j) + v(j), \quad z(j) = Hx(j), \\
v(j) &= \begin{bmatrix} v_1(j) \\ v_2(j) \end{bmatrix}, \\
[Ev(j)v^*(s)] &= \Xi \delta_K(j-s), \quad \Xi = \begin{bmatrix} R & 0 \\ 0 & -\gamma^2 I \end{bmatrix}
\end{aligned} \tag{11}$$

Here, $[Ev(j)v^*(s)], 0 \le j, s \le L$, represents the autocovariance function of $v(\cdot)$ in Krein spaces [8], [9]. As in the H_∞ estimation problem in Krein spaces [4], the variance Ξ of the observation noise $v(j)$ is indefinite.

2.3.   Least-squares Estimation Problem of $x(k)$ Based on Krein-space Observation Equation

In [9], using the orthogonality of the innovations and the Krein state-space structure, the Kalman filter in Krein spaces (see, e.g., [12], [13]) is designed. Similarly to this idea, in this section, based on the observation Eq.(11), the estimation problem using the covariance information is proposed. It is a characteristic that the observation equation includes the information of γ^2.

The filtering is to estimate the signal at time k in terms of the innovations process $\{v(i)\}_{i=1}^k, v(i) = y(i) - H\Phi\hat{x}(k-1, k-1)$. The fixed-interval smoothing is to estimate the signal at the time k by using the innovations process $\{v(i)\}_{i=1}^L$.

Let the fixed-interval smoothing estimate $\hat{x}(k, L)$ of the state variable $x(k)$ be given by

$$\hat{x}(k, L) = \sum_{i=1}^{L} g(k, i)v(i) \tag{12}$$

as a linear transformation of the innovation process $\{v(i)\}_{i=1}^{L}$. Here, $g(k, i)$ is an impulse response function. The fixed-interval smoothing estimate of the signal $z(k)$ is expressed by $\hat{z}(k, L) = H\hat{x}(k, L)$. We consider the linear least-squares smoothing problem which minimizes the cost function

$$J = E \|x(k) - \hat{x}(k, L)\|^2 \tag{13}$$

in linear discrete-time stochastic systems. Let $[Ex(k)v^*(s)]$ and $[Ev(i)v^*(s)]$ represent the crosscovariance function of $x(k)$ with $v(s)$ and the autocovariance function of $v(\cdot)$ respectively in Krein spaces [8], [9]. The optimal impulse response function, which minimizes (16), satisfies the Wiener-Hopf equation [18]

$$[Ex(k)v^*(s)] = \sum_{i=1}^{L} g(k, i)[Ev(i)v^*(s)]. \tag{14}$$

Let $[v(i)v * (s)] = \Pi\delta_K(i - s)$ be given, then (14) is written as

$$g(k, s)\Pi(s) = [Ex(k)v * (s)]$$

$$= [Ex(k)(y(s) - H\Phi\hat{x}(s - 1, s - 1))^*]$$

$$= [Ex(k)y^*(s)] - \sum_{j=1}^{s-1} g(k, i)\Pi(i)g^*(s, j)H^*. \tag{15}$$

Let $K(k, s)$ represent the autocovariance function of the state vector $x(k)$. $K(k, s)$ is expressed as

$$K(k, s) = \Phi^{k-s}K(s, s)1(k - s) + K^*(k, k)(\Phi^*)^{s-k}1(s - k), \tag{16}$$

where $1(k - s)$ represents the unit step function.

3. RLS Fixed-interval Smoothing Algorithm [6]

As a step for the derivation of the H-infinity recursive Wiener fixed-interval smoother, the RLS algorithm [6] for the fixed-interval smoothing estimate and the filtering estimate are presented in Theorem 1.

Theorem 1. Let the system matrix Φ, the crossvariance function $K_{xy}(k, k)$ of $x(k)$ with the observed value $y(k)$, the variance $K(k, k)$ of the state variable $x(k)$ and the variance $R(k)$ of the white observation noise be given. Let $L > 0$ represent the fixed interval. Then the recursive Wiener fixed-interval smoothing and filtering equations consist of (17)-(25) in linear discrete-time stochastic systems.

Fixed-interval smoothing estimate of the signal $z(k)$: $\hat{z}(k, L)$

$$\hat{z}(k, L) = H\hat{x}(k, L) \tag{17}$$

Fixed-interval smoothing estimate of the state variable $x(k)$: $\hat{x}(k, L)$

$$\hat{x}(k, k + L) = \hat{x}(k, k) + l_1(k + 1, L) - l_2(k + 1, L) \tag{18}$$

$$\begin{aligned} &l_1(k, L) = K(k - 1, k - 1)\Phi^* K^{-1}(k, k)(I - K(k, k)H^* G^*(k)K^{-1}(k, k)l_1(k + 1, L) + \\ &K(k - 1, k - 1)\Phi^* H^* \Pi^{-1}(k)\upsilon(k), \\ &\upsilon(k) = y(k) - H\Phi\hat{x}(k - 1, k - 1), \\ &l_1(L + 1, L) = 0 \end{aligned} \tag{19}$$

$$l_2(k + 1, L) = S(k)K^{-1}(k, k)l_1(k + 1, L) \tag{20}$$

Filtering estimate of $z(k)$: $\hat{z}(k, k)$

$$\hat{z}(k, k) = H\hat{x}(k, k) \tag{21}$$

Filtering estimate of $x(k)$: $\hat{x}(k, k)$

$$\hat{x}(k, k) = \Phi\hat{x}(k - 1, k - 1) + G(k)(y(k) - H\Phi\hat{x}(k - 1, k - 1)), \quad \hat{x}(0, 0) = 0 \tag{22}$$

Filter gain $G(k)$:

$$G(k) = (K_{xy}(k, k) - \Phi S(k - 1)\Phi^* H^*)\Pi^{-1}(k) \tag{23}$$

$$\Pi(k) = R(k) + HK_{xy}(k, k) - H\Phi S(k - 1)\Phi^* H^* \tag{24}$$

$$S(k) = \Phi S(k - 1)\Phi^* + G(k)\Pi(k)G^*(k), \quad S(0) = 0 \tag{25}$$

4. H-infinity Recursive Wiener Fixed-interval Smoother and Filter

The H-infinity recursive Wiener fixed-interval smoother and filter are obtained in a straightforward manner by formally extending the estimation technique in [6] for the scalar signal to the current signal $z(k)$ of $r + m$ dimension. Theorem 2 proposes the H-infinity recursive algorithms for the fixed-interval smoothing estimates $\hat{z}_1(k, L)$ of $z_1(k)$ and $\hat{z}_2(k, L)$ of $z_2(k)$ and the filtering estimates $\hat{z}_1(k, k)$ of $z_1(k)$ and $\hat{z}_2(k, k)(= \check{z}(k))$ of $z_2(k)$ by use of the covariance information. The algorithm for the filtering estimate $\hat{x}(k, k)$ of $x(k)$ is also presented.

Theorem 2. Let the observation equation be given by (11). Let $\hat{z}_1(k, L)$ and $\hat{z}_2(k, L)$ represent the fixed-interval smoothing estimate at the time k, $1 \leq k < L$, for the signal vector components of $z(k)$, $z_1(k)$ and $z_2(k)$ respectively. Let $\hat{z}_1(k, k)$ and $\hat{z}_2(k, k)(= \check{z}(k))$ represent the filtering estimates of $z_1(k)$ and $z_2(k)$ respectively. Let $y_1(L)(= Cx(L) + v_1(L))$ and $\check{z}(L)(= Ux(L) + v_2(L))$ be the observed values in the observation Eq.(11). Let the system matrix Φ, the observation matrices C and U, the autovariance function $K_x(L, L)$ of the state variable $x(L)$, γ and the observed value $y_1(L)$ be given. Then the recursive Wiener algorithms for the fixed-point smoothing estimates $\hat{z}_1(k, L)$ of the signal

$z_1(k)$ and $\hat{z}_2(k, L)$ of the signal $z_2(k)$ at the time k and the filtering estimates $\hat{z}_1(k, k)$, $\hat{z}_2(k, k)(=\check{z}(k))$ and $\hat{x}(k, k)$ consist of (26)–(37).

Fixed-interval smoothing estimate of the signal $z_1(k)(=Cx(k))$: $\hat{z}_1(k, L)$.

$$\hat{z}_1(k, L) = C\hat{x}(k, L) \tag{26}$$

Fixed-interval smoothing estimate of the signal $z_2(k)(=Ux(k))$: $\hat{z}_2(k, L)$.

$$\hat{z}_2(k, L) = U\hat{x}(k, L) \tag{27}$$

Filtering estimate of the signal $z_1(k)(=Cx(k))$: $\hat{z}_1(k, k)$

$$\hat{z}_1(k, k) = C\hat{x}(k, k) \tag{28}$$

Filtering estimate of the signal $z_2(k)(=Ux(k))$: $\hat{z}_2(k, k)$

$$\hat{z}_2(k, k) = U\hat{x}(k, k) \tag{29}$$

Fictitious observed value: $\check{z}(k)$.
$$\check{z}(k) = \hat{z}_2(k, k) \tag{30}$$

Fixed-interval smoothing estimate of $x(k)$: $\hat{x}(k, L)$

$$\hat{x}(k, L) = \hat{x}(k, k) + l_1(k + 1, L) - l_2(k + 1, L) \tag{31}$$

$$l_1(k, L) = K(k - 1, k - 1)\Phi^* K^{-1}(k, k)(I - K(k, k)H^* G^*(k)K^{-1}(k, k)l_1(k + 1, L) + K(k - 1, k - 1)\Phi^* H^* \Pi^{-1}(k)(y(k) - H\Phi\hat{x}(k - 1, k - 1)), \tag{32}$$
$$l_1(L + 1, L) = 0$$

$$l_2(k + 1, L) = S(k)K^{-1}(k, k)l_1(k + 1, L) \tag{33}$$

$$\Pi(k) = \begin{bmatrix} \Pi_{11}(k) & \Pi_{12}(k) \\ \Pi_{21}(k) & \Pi_{22}(k) \end{bmatrix},$$

$$\begin{aligned} \Pi_{11}(k) &= CK(k, k)C^* + R - C\Phi S(k - 1)\Phi^* C^* \\ \Pi_{12}(k) &= CK(k, k)U^* + R - C\Phi S(k - 1)\Phi^* U^* \\ \Pi_{21}(k) &= UK(k, k)C^* + R - U\Phi S(k - 1)\Phi^* C^* \\ \Pi_{22}(k) &= UK(k, k)U^* - \gamma^2 I - U\Phi S(k - 1)\Phi^* U^* \end{aligned} \tag{34}$$

$\hat{x}(k, k)$: Filtering estimate of the state vector $x(k)$.

$$\hat{x}(k, k) = \Phi\hat{x}(k - 1, k - 1) + (K(k, k)C^* - \Phi S(k - 1)\Phi^* C^*)$$
$$\times(CK(k, k)C^* + R - C\Phi S(k - 1)C^*)^{-1}(y(k) - H\Phi(k - 1, k - 1) \tag{35}$$

$$\begin{aligned} G(k) &= \begin{bmatrix} G_1(k) & G_2(k) \end{bmatrix}, \\ G_1(k) &= (K(k, k)C^* - \Phi S(k - 1)\Phi^* C^*)\Pi^{-1}(k), \\ G_2(k) &= (K(k, k)U^* - \Phi S(k - 1)\Phi^* U^*)\Pi^{-1}(k) \end{aligned} \tag{36}$$

$$S(k) = \Phi S(k - 1)\Phi^* + G(k)\Pi(k)G^*(k) \tag{37}$$

From [9], [12],[13], for $\check{z}(j) = \hat{z}_2(j, j)(= U\hat{x}(j, j)$, it is seen that the proposed filter that achieves the performance criterion (6) for $L = k$ or equivalently the min-max criterion exists if, and only if [9],

$$CK(j, j)C^* + R - C\Phi S(j - 1)\Phi^* C^* > 0,$$

$$UK(j,j)U^* - U\Phi S(j-1)\Phi^* U^* < \gamma^2 I, \quad j = 0, \quad 1, \quad 2,\cdots, \quad k, \quad \cdots, \quad k+L .$$

Proof of Theorem 2 is straightforward from Theorem 1 and section 2.

As $\gamma \to \infty$, the H-infinity recursive Wiener fixed-interval smoother in Theorem 2 is reduced to the RLS Wiener fixed-interval smoother. This suggests that the left hand side of (6) corresponding to the RLS Wiener estimators may be quite large, and that it may have poor robustness properties [9].

5. Fixed-interval Smoothing Error Variance Function of Signal

Let $P(k, L)$ represent the fixed-interval smoothing error variance function of the signal.

$$P(k, L) = E[(z(k) - \hat{z}(k, L))(z(k) - \hat{z}(k, L))^*] \tag{38}$$

Let the second term on the right hand side of (29) in [6] be $f(k, L)$ as follows [6].

$$\hat{x}(k, L) = \hat{x}(k, k) + f(k, L), \tag{39}$$

$$f(k, L) = (B(k) - A(k)r(k))q(k+1, L) \tag{40}$$

From the orthogonal projection lemmas $z(k) - \hat{z}(k, L) \perp \hat{z}(k, L)$ and $x(k) - \hat{x}(k, L) \perp \upsilon(i)$, $i = k+1, k+2, \cdots, L$, (38) is written as, in terms of (12) and (39),

$$
\begin{aligned}
P(k, L) &= HK_{xy}(k, k) - H\sum_{i=1}^{k} g(k, i)E[\upsilon(i)\hat{z}^*(k, L)] - H\sum_{i=k+1}^{L} g(k, i)E[\upsilon(i)\hat{z}^*(k, L)]\\
&= HK_{xy}(k, k) - HE[\hat{x}(k, k)\hat{z}^*(k, L)] - H\sum_{i=k+1}^{L} g(k, i)\Pi(i)g^*(k, i)H^*\\
&= HK_{xy}(k, k) - HE[\hat{x}(k, k)\hat{x}^*(k, L)]H^* - HE[\hat{x}(k, k)f^*(k, L)]H^*\\
&\quad - H\sum_{i=k+1}^{L} g(k, i)\Pi(i)g^*(k, i)H^*.
\end{aligned}
\tag{41}
$$

From (40) with (28) in [6], it is seen that the third term on the right hand side of (41) equals the zero matrix.

The variance function $P(k, k)$ of the filtering error $z(k) - \hat{z}(k, k)$ is expressed as $P(k, k) = HK_{xy}(k, k) - HS(k)H^*, \quad S(k) = E[\hat{x}(k, k)\hat{x}^*(k, k)]$. Hence,

$$0 \le P(k, L) \le P(k, k). \tag{42}$$

This shows that the fixed-interval smoothing estimate might be superior in estimation accuracy to the filter. Also, $HS(k)H^* \le HK_{xy}(k, k)$ means that the variance of the filtering estimate of the signal $z(k)$ is upper bounded by the variance of $z(k)$ and, provided that $HK_{xy}(k, k)$ is bounded, assures the existence of the filtering estimate of $z(k)$. Henceforth, (42) verifies the existence of the fixed-interval smoothing estimate.

6. A Numerical Simulation Example

Let a scalar observation equation be given by

$$y(k) = z(k) + v(k). \tag{43}$$

Let the observation noise $v(k)$ be zero-mean white Gaussian process with the variance R, $N(0, R)$. Let the autocovariance function of the signal $z(k)$ be given by

$$K(0) = \sigma^2,$$
$$K(m) = \sigma^2\{\alpha_1(\alpha_2^2 - 1)\alpha_1^m/[(\alpha_2 - \alpha_1)(\alpha_2\alpha_1 + 1)]$$
$$-\alpha_2(\alpha_1^2 - 1)\alpha_2^m/[(\alpha_2 - \alpha_1)(\alpha_1\alpha_2 + 1)]\}, \quad 0 < m, \tag{44}$$
$$\alpha_1, \alpha_2 = (-a_1 \pm \sqrt{a_1^2 - 4a_2})/2, \quad a_1 = -0.1, \quad a_2 = -0.8, \quad \sigma = 0.5.$$

Based on the method in [5], the observation vector H, the crossvariance $K_{xy}(k, k)$ and the system matrix Φ in the state equation for the state variable $x(k)$ are as follows:

$$H = \begin{bmatrix} 1 & 0 \end{bmatrix}, \quad K_{xz}(k, k) = \begin{bmatrix} K(0) \\ K(1) \end{bmatrix}, \quad \Phi = \begin{bmatrix} 0 & 1 \\ -a_2 & -a_1 \end{bmatrix},$$
$$K(0) = 0.25, \quad K(1) = 0.125. \tag{45}$$

Table 1: MSVs of filtering and fixed-interval smoothing errors

	$a_1 = -0.1,$ $a_2 = -0.8$	$a_1 = -0.1,$ $a_2 = -(-0.8 + 0.05 \cdot p)$
MSV of filtering errors for $N(0, 0.3^2)$ and $\gamma = 0.6$	0.0927	0.0896
MSV of fixed-interval smoothing errors for $N(0, 0.3^2)$ and $\gamma = 0.6$	0.0862	0.0817
MSV of filtering errors for $N(0, 0.5^2)$ and $\gamma = 0.7$	0.1930	0.1785
MSV of fixed-interval smoothing errors for $N(0, 0.5^2)$ and $\gamma = 0.7$	0.1912	0.1751
MSV of filtering errors for $N(0, 0.7^2)$ and $\gamma = 0.9$	0.2962	0.2523
MSV of fixed-interval smoothing errors for $N(0, 0.7^2)$ and $\gamma = 0.9$	0.2951	0.2481
MSV of filtering errors for $N(0, 1)$ and $\gamma = 1.2$	0.4469	0.3586
MSV of fixed-interval smoothing errors for $N(0, 1)$ and $\gamma = 1.2$	0.4474	0.3234

If we substitute (45) into the estimation algorithms of Theorem 1, we can calculate the fixed-interval smoothing estimate $\hat{z}(k, L)$ and the filtering estimate $\hat{z}(k, k)$ of the signal recursively. Fig.1 illustrates the signal $z(k)$, the filtering estimate $\hat{z}(k, k)$ and the fixed-interval smoothing estimate $\hat{z}(k, 200)$ by the proposed H-infinity recursive Wiener fixed-interval smoother and filter vs. k for the white Gaussian observation noise $N(0, 0.5^2)$.

Fig.2 illustrates the mean-square values (MSVs) of the fixed-interval and filtering errors by the proposed H-infinity recursive Wiener fixed-interval smoother and filter vs. γ for the observation noises $N(0, 0.3^2)$, $N(0, 0.5^2)$, $N(0, 0.7^2)$ and $N(0, 1)$. The MSVs of the fixed-interval smoothing and filtering errors are evaluated by $\sum_{k=1}^{200} (z(k) - \hat{z}(k, 200))^2/200$ and $\sum_{k=1}^{200} (z(k) - \hat{z}(k, k))^2/200$. From Fig.1 and Fig.2, the fixed-interval smoothing estimate is superior in estimation accuracy to the H-infinity filtering estimate. Fig.2 shows that the estimation accuracy of the proposed H-infinity recursive Wiener fixed-interval smoother is improved in comparison with the H-infinity recursive Wiener filter. As the noise variance becomes large, the estimation accuracies of the smoothers and the filter are degraded. For $\gamma = 1.5$, the estimation accuracies of the H-infinity recursive Wiener fixed-interval smoother are superior, particularly for the observation noises $N(0, 0.7^2)$ and $N(0, 1)$, to those for $\gamma > 1.5$. Since the value of γ can be selected arbitrarily, for the optimal value of γ, the estimation accuracy of the H-infinity fixed-interval smoother might be the best. Hence, the proposed H-infinity recursive Wiener fixed-interval smoother is suboptimal.

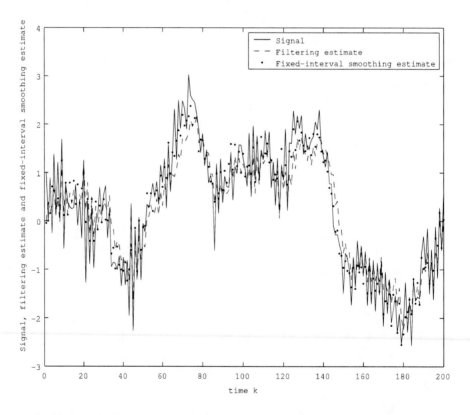

Figure 1: Signal $z(k)$, the filtering estimate $\hat{z}(k, k)$ and the fixed-interval smoothing estimate $\hat{z}(k, 200)$ by the proposed H-infinity recursive Wiener fixed-interval smoother and filter vs. k for the white Gaussian observation noise $N(0, 0.5^2)$.

In Table 1, the MSVs of the filtering and fixed-interval smoothing errors are shown for the observation noise sequences $N(0, 0.3^2)$, $N(0, 0.5^2)$, $N(0, 0.7^2)$ and $N(0, 1)$. p denotes

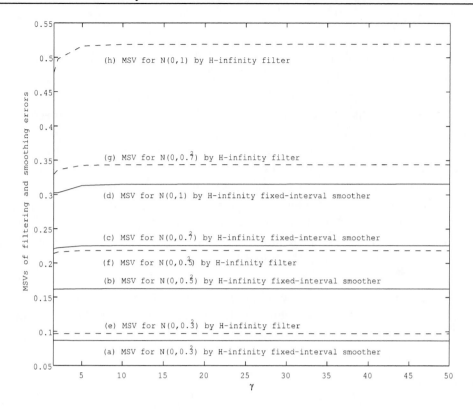

Figure 2: Mean-square values of the fixed-interval smoothing error $z(k) - \hat{z}(k, 200)$ and the filtering error $z(k) - \hat{z}(k, k)$ by the proposed H-infinity recursive Wiener fixed-interval smoother and filter vs. γ for the observation noises $N(0, 0.3^2)$, $N(0, 0.5^2)$, $N(0, 0.7^2)$ and $N(0, 1)$.

the random variable obeying to $N(0, 1)$. Hence, the random variation of the parameter of a_2 is contained as recognized from $a_2 = -(-0.8 + 0.05 \cdot p)$. For the sequences of the observation noise, the values of γ are 0.6, 0.7, 0.9 and 1.2 respectively. From Table 1, compared to the H-infinity filter, the MSV of the fixed-interval smoother is small and the estimation accuracy of the H-infinity fixed-interval smoother is preferable to that of the H-infinity filter for the both cases including and not including variation in a_2. It is interesting that the H-infinity estimation accuracies of the filter and the fixed-interval smoother for the case with the parameter variation is superior to those of the estimators for the case without parameter variation in a_2 respectively.

For references, the autoregressive (AR) model, which generates the signal process, is given by

$$z(k + 1) = -a_1 z(k) - a_2 z(k - 1) + w(k + 1), \quad E[w(k)w(s)] = \sigma^2 \delta_K(t - s). \quad (46)$$

7. Conclusion

In this paper, based on the innovations approach, the H-infinity recursive Wiener fixed-interval smoother and filter have been proposed in linear discrete-time stochastic systems.

From the simulation results, it has been shown that the proposed H-infinity recursive Wiener fixed-interval smoothing algorithm is feasible and its estimation accuracy is superior to the H-infinity recursive Wiener fixed-interval smoother in [6]. For $\gamma = 1.5$, the estimation accuracies of the H-infinity recursive Wiener fixed-interval smoother are superior, particularly for the observation noises $N(0, 0.7^2)$ and $N(0, 1)$, to those for $\gamma > 1.5$. Since the value of γ can be selected arbitrarily, for the optimal value of γ, the estimation accuracy of the H-infinity fixed-interval smoother might be the best. Hence, the proposed H-infinity recursive Wiener fixed-interval smoother is suboptimal.

From Table 1, compared to the H-infinity filter, the MSV of the fixed-interval smoother is small and the estimation accuracy of the H-infinity fixed-interval smoother is preferable to that of the H-infinity filter for the both cases including and not including variation in a_2. It is interesting that the H-infinity estimation accuracies of the filter and the fixed-interval smoother for the case with the parameter variation is superior to those of the estimators for the case without parameter variation in a_2 respectively.

References

[1]   Nakamori, S. (1991). Design of a fixed-point smoother based on an innovations theory for white gaussian plus coloured observation noise. *International Journal of Systems Science*, Vol. 22, No. 12, pp. 2573-2584.

[2]   Nakamori, S. (1998). Design of predictor using covariance information in continuous-time stochastic systems with nonlinear observation mechanism. *Signal Processing*, Vol. 68, No.2, pp. 183-193.

[3]   Nakamori, S. (1999). Design of estimators using covariance information in discrete-time stochastic systems with nonlinear observation mechanism. IEICE Trans. *Fundamentals of Electronics, Communications and Computer Sciences*, Vol. E82-A, No. 7, pp. 1292-1304.

[4]   Nakamori, S. (2003). New design of fixed-interval smoother using covariance information in linear continuous-time systems. *Applied Mathematics and Computation*, Vol. 144, No.2, pp. 557-567.

[5]   Nakamori, S. (1995). Recursive estimation technique of signal from output measurement data in linear discrete-time systems. IEICE Trans. *Fundamentals of Electronics, Communications and Computer Sciences*. Vol. E782-A, No. 5, pp. 600-607.

[6]   Nakamori, S., Hermoso, A. & Linares, J. (2006). Design of a fixed-interval smoother using covariance information based on the innovations approach in linear discrete-time stochastic systems. *Applied Mathematical Modelling*, Vol. 30, pp. 406-417.

[7] Kailath, T. (1976): Lectures on Linear Lest-Squares Estimation, New York, Springer-Verlag.

[8] Nakamori, S. (2001). Design of linear continuous-time stochastic estimators using covariance information in Krein Spaces. IEICE Trans. *Fundamentals of Electronics, Communication and Computer Sciences*, Vol. E84-A, No. 9, pp. 2261-2271.

[9] Nakamori, S. (2002). Design of linear discrete-time stochastic estimators using covariance information in Krein Spaces. IEICE Trans. *Fundamentals of Electronics, Communication and Computer Sciences*, Vol. E85-A, No. 4, pp. 861-871.

[10] Yu, X. & Hsu, C. S. (1997). Reduced order H_∞ filter design for discrete time-variant syatems. *International Journal of Robust and Nonlinear Control*, Vol.7, No. 8, pp.797-809.

[11] Shen, X, Deng, L. & Yasmin, A. (1996). H_∞ filtering for speech enhancement. ICSLP 96, *Fourth International Conference on Spoken Language Processing*, pp.873-876.

[12] Hassibi, B. Sayed, A. H. & Kailath, T. (1996). Linear estimation in Krein spaces—Part I. *IEEE Trans. Autom. Control*, vol. 41, No. 1, pp. 18–33.

[13] Hassibi, B., Sayed, A. H. & Kailath, T. (1996). Linear estimation in Krein spaces—Part II. *IEEE Trans. AutoAutom. Control*, vol. 41, No. 1, pp. 34–49.

[14] Nguang, S. K. & Shi, P. (2000). Nonlinear H_∞ filtering of sampled-data systems. *Automatica*, Vol. 36, No.2, pp. 303-310.

[15] Berman, N. & Shaked, U. (1996). H_∞ Nonlinear filtering. *International Journal of Robust and Nonlinear Control*, Vol. 6, No.4, pp. 281-296.

[16] Fridman, E. & and Shaked, U. (1997). On regional nonlinear H_∞-filtering. *Systems & Letters*, pp. 233-240.

[17] Luan, X. Liu, F., & Shi, P. (2010) . H_∞ filtering for nonlinear systems via neural networks. *Journal of Franklin Institute*, Vol. 347, No. 6, pp. 1035-1046.

[18] Sage, A.P., & Melsa, J. L. (1971): *Estimation Theory with Applications to Communications and Control*, New York, McGraw-Hill.

In: Horizons in Computer Science Research. Volume 11   ISBN: 978-1-63482-499-6
Editor: Thomas S. Clary, pp. 159-198   © 2015 Nova Science Publishers, Inc.

Chapter 5

Virtual Supercomputer as Basis of Scientific Computing

Alexander Bogdanov[1,*], *Alexander Degtyarev*[1,†], *Vladimir Korkhov*[1,‡],
Vladimir Gaiduchok[2,§] *and Ivan Gankevich*[2,¶]
[1]Saint Petersburg State University, Saint Petersburg, Russia
[2]Saint Petersburg Electrotechnical University «LETI»,
Saint Petersburg, Russia

Abstract

Nowadays supercomputer centers strive to provide their computational resources as services, however, present infrastructure is not particularly suited for such a use. First of all, there are standard application programming interfaces to launch computational jobs via command line or a web service, which work well for a program but turn out to be too complex for scientists: they want applications to be delivered to them from a remote server and prefer to interact with them via graphical interface. Second, there are certain applications which are dependent on older versions of operating systems and libraries and it is either non-practical to install those old systems on a cluster or there exists some conflict between these dependencies. Virtualization technologies can solve this problem, but they are not too popular in scientific computing due to overheads introduced by them. Finally, it is difficult to automatically estimate optimal resource pool size for a particular task, thus it often gets done manually by a user. If the large resource pool is requested for a minor task, the efficiency degrades. Moreover, cluster schedulers depend on estimated wall time to execute the jobs and since it cannot be reliably predicted by a human or a machine their efficiency suffers as well.

Applications delivery, efficient operating system virtualization and dynamic application resource pool size defining constitute the two problems of scientific computing: complex application interfaces and inefficient use of resources available — and virtual supercomputer is the way to solve them. The research shows that there are ways to make virtualization technologies efficient for scientific computing: the use of

---

*E-mail address: bogdanov@csa.ru
†E-mail address: deg@csa.ru
‡E-mail address: vladimir@csa.ru
§E-mail address: gajduchok@cc.spbu.ru
¶E-mail address: igankevich@cc.spbu.ru

lightweight application containers and dynamic creation of these containers for a particular job are both fast and transparent for a user. There are universal ways to deliver application output to a front-end using execution of a job on a cluster and presenting its results in a graphical form. Finally, an application framework can be developed to decompose parallel application into small independent parts with easily predictable execution time, to simplify scheduling via existing algorithms.

The aim of this chapter is to promote the key idea of a virtual supercomputer: to harness all available HPC resources and provide users with convenient access to them. Such a challenge can be effectively faced using contemporary virtualization technologies. They can materialize the long-term dream of having a supercomputer at your own desk.

Keywords: virtual supercomputer, virtualization, distributed systems, heterogeneous systems, job scheduling

AMS Subject Classification: 68M14, 68M20

Introduction

A cloud, to wide extent, is an API. It is a certain contract model meeting the principles of the cloud computing. Five principles can be singled out:

- scalability,

- load balancing within the scalability,

- high availability up to being disaster-proof,

- easy access to resources from almost every place of the world and from any device,

- and payment on demand on the rental basis, i. e. on the most favorable terms for the client.

This means that it is necessary to support common standards between the clouds, thus being able to create hybrid clouds, which combine private and public computational resources. What helps to create hybrid clouds? One should be interested in products that both support the standards and provide open source licenses [29]. Eucalyptus and OpenNebula seem to be quite suitable: their API is backward compatible with Amazon [1, 2].

Our researches need the absence of vendor locks and have to be based on the open standards. The components have to be convenient, inexpensive and simple. Resource suppliers have to be interchangeable. Therefore, the result of the work will be universal and test-open for the other teams of scientists (program transferability, repeated use of components etc.). This is the service-oriented approach, when the components interact with the help of an API and the clients get the service that meets the contract guarantees.

So, we propose to use a cloud approach based on open standards and utilizing several up-to-date technologies, that make it very effective for large scale problems. Our main principles are

1. Cloud is determined completely by its API. And it is obvious from the user point of view, but the same must also be true from the point of view of different clouds interaction.

2. Operational environment must be UNIX-like. One of the main problems of computational GRIDs is load balancing and it is very difficult task since user is cut off from the resources. Partly this issue is resolved by problem solution environments, but many standard UNIX tools must be introduced into the API to make it really work.

3. Cloud uses protocols compatible with popular public clouds. Public clouds are not very useful for complex problems and the reason is clear — the more difficult your problem is, the more robust tools you must use. The universal tools cannot be used for complex problems. That is why specialized private clouds must be built for complex problems, but if its resources are not enough, some additional resources can be added from public cloud.

4. Cloud processes the data on the base of distributed file systems. The main problem with public clouds for data processing originates from the fact that for each computer in the cloud its own file system is used. That prevents both processing large data sets and scaling out the problem solution. To overcome this obstacle the distributed file system should be used in a private cloud, the type of which is determined by the nature of problem to be solved. If we add here the three ways of providing data consistency (Brewer's theorem) we can see that there are a lot of possibilities to organize the data processing, but only a few of those are really in use.

5. Consolidation of data is achieved by distributed DB. There are three levels of consolidation — servers, data and resources. It is more or less clear how server consolidation is done. Consolidation of data is more difficult and consolidation of resources is a real challenge to the cloud provider. We assume that most natural way to do this is to use Federal DB tools. Up to now we managed to do this by utilizing IBM's DB2 tools, but we believe that possibilities of latest PostgreSQL release will make it possible to work out freeware tool for such purpose [3].

6. Load balancing is achieved by the use of virtual processors with controlled rate. New high-throughput processors make it possible to organize virtual processors with different speed of computation. This opens natural possibility of making distributed virtual computational system with architecture adapted to computational algorithm and instead of mapping the algorithm onto the computer architecture we will match the architecture with the computational code.

7. Processing of large data sets is done via shared virtual memory. Actually all the previous experience shows that the only way to comfortably process large data sets is to use SMP system. Now we can effectively use shared memory tools (OpenCL) in heterogeneous environment and so make virtual SMP. The same tool is used for parallelization. The possibilities of a single image operational environment are also very effective.

8. Cloud uses complex grid-like security mechanisms. One of the cloud problems is security issues [19] but we feel that proper combination of GRID security tools with Cloud access technologies is possible.

Often virtualization is employed for many components of computing system such as processor, memory, storage subsystem and network interface, however, virtualizing all of them at once is not required in high performance computing where the efficiency of resulting computing system is of utmost importance. First, most of the virtualization comes at a cost of slight performance decrease, which grows with the size of the application. Second, virtualization of some components (i.e. network interfaces, processors) complicates the system's architecture without simplifying problem solution. This led to the scarce use of virtualization technologies in high performance computing; contrary to this, we feel that there is at least one way of using it to simplify architecture of the system and decrease its maintenance effort.

This way consists of storing applications which run on cluster and their dependencies inside lightweight containers. Upon submitting a task, containers are mounted on each host provided by a resource manager and parallel applications are executed inside each of them. The benefit of this approach is that a separate operating system and optimized libraries can be installed for each application without the need to alter host computer configuration. Additionally, it is easy to maintain different versions of applications (due to licensing or compatibility problems) in different containers and to update them in contrast to common shared-folder-for-all-applications configuration where there is a lot of manual work. Finally, since container virtualization does not imply processor virtualization overheads, this approach can be made efficient in terms of application performance.

The ramification of using application containers is that load balancing cannot be done efficiently with container migration, so object migration should be used instead. The main problem of container migration is that copies have too much unneeded data. In contrast to this, object migration which can be implemented in software framework or library is more efficient as the programmer not the system decides what to copy. Such framework was implemented based on event-driven programming approach and system load balancing is done through it.

Load balance is maintained by adjusting distribution of computational tasks among available processors with respect to their performance, and inability to distribute them evenly stem to arise not from technical reasons only, but also from peculiarity of a problem being solved. On one hand, load imbalance can be caused by heterogeneity of the tasks and inability to estimate how much time it takes to execute one particular task compared to some other task. Such difficulties arise in fluid mechanics applications involving solution of a problem with boundary conditions when the formula used to calculate boundary layer differs from the formula used to calculate inner points and takes longer time to calculate; the same problem arises in concurrent algorithms of intelligent systems that have different asymptotic complexities but solve the same problem concurrently hoping to obtain result by the fastest algorithm. On the other hand, load imbalance can be caused by heterogeneity of the processors and their different performance when solving the same problem and it is relevant when tasks are executed on multiple computers in a network or on a single computer equipped with an accelerator. Therefore, load imbalance can be caused by heterogeneity of tasks and heterogeneity of processors and these peculiarities should be both taken into account to maintain load balance of a computer system.

Related Work

One of the first approaches to construct clusters from virtual machines was proposed in [16] and partially realized in In-VIGO [26], VMPlants [24], and Virtual Clusters on the Fly [27] projects. In-VIGO focused on the end-to-end design of a Web service that could employ VMs as part of a cluster computing system, while VMPlants and Virtual Clusters on the Fly focused on rapid construction of virtual clusters. All three systems were particularly concerned with the issue of specifying and adapting to requirements and constraints imposed by the user.

Dynamic Virtual Clustering (DVC) [15] implemented the scheduling of VMs on existing physical cluster nodes within a campus setting. The motivation for this work was to improve the usage of disparate cluster computing systems located within a single entity.

The idea of an adaptive virtual cluster changing its size based on the workload was presented in [10] describing a cluster management software called COD (Cluster On Demand), which dynamically allocates servers from a common pool to multiple virtual clusters.

Grid architecture that allows to dynamically adapt the underlying hardware infrastructure to changing Virtual Organization (VO) demands is presented in [28]. The backend of the system is able to provide on-demand virtual worker nodes to existing clusters and integrate them in any Globus-based Grid.

The goal of current work is to investigate possibilities provided by modern cloud and virtualization technologies to enable personal supercomputing meaning creation of dedicated virtual clusters based on user's and application's requirements. Unlike many of other projects in this area, our intention is to use created clusters of VM as a single resource provided to a single parallel application but not generating sets of worker nodes provided to different applications separately.

Research works on the subject of virtual clusters can be divided into two broad groups: works dealing with provisioning and deploying virtual clusters in high performance environment or GRID and works dealing with overheads of virtualization. Works from the first group typically assume that virtualization overheads are low and acceptable in high performance computing and works from the second group in general assume that virtualization has some benefits for high performance computing, however, the authors are not aware of the work that touches both subjects in aggregate.

In [11] authors evaluate overheads of the system for on-line virtual cluster provisioning (based on QEMU/KVM) and different resource mapping strategies used in this system and show that the main source of deploying overhead is network transfer of virtual machine images. To reduce it they use different caching techniques to reuse already transferred images as well as multicast file transfer to increase network throughput. Simultaneous use of caching and multicasting is concluded to be an efficient way to reduce overhead of virtual machine provisioning.

In [34] authors evaluate general overheads of Xen para-virtualization compared to fully virtualized and physical machines using HPCC benchmarking suite. They conclude that an acceptable level of overheads can be achieved only with para-virtualization due to its efficient inter domain communication (bypassing dom0 kernel) and absence of high L2 cache miss rate when running MPI programs which is common to fully virtualized guest machines.

In contrast to these two works the main principles of our approach can be summarized as follows. Do not use full or para-virtualization of the whole machine but use virtualization of selected components so that overheads occur only when they are unavoidable (i.e. do not virtualize processor). Do not transfer opaque file system images but mount standard file systems over the network so that only minimal transfer overhead can occur. Finally, amend standard task schedulers to work with virtual clusters so that no programming is needed to distribute the load efficiently. These principles are paramount to make virtualization lightweight and fast.

Event-driven architecture have been used extensively to create desktop applications with graphical user interface since MVC paradigm [23] was developed and nowadays it is also used to compose enterprise application components into a unified system with message queues [33, 20], however, it is rarely implemented in scientific applications. One example of such usage is GotoBLAS2 library [17, 18]. Although, it is not clear from the referenced papers, analysis of its source code[1] shows that this library uses specialized server object to schedule matrix and vector operations' kernels and to compute them in parallel. The total number of CPUs is defined at compile time and they are assumed to be homogeneous. There is a notion of a queue implemented as a linked list of objects where each object specifies a routine to be executed and data to be processed and also a number of CPUs to execute it on. Server processes these objects in parallel and each kernel can be executed in synchronous (blocking) and asynchronous (non-blocking) mode. So, compared to event-driven system GotoBLAS2 server uses static task scheduling, its tasks are not differentiated into production and reduction tasks, both the tasks and the underlying system are assumed to be homogeneous. GotoBLAS2 library exhibits competitive performance compared to other BLAS implementations [17, 18] and it is a good example of viability of event-driven approach in scientific applications. Considering this, our event-driven system can be seen as a generalization of this approach to a broader set of applications.

1. Virtual Supercomputer

1.1. Basic Concepts

Virtual supercomputer can be seen as a collection of virtual machines working together to solve a computational problem much like a team of people working together on a single task. There is a known definition of personal supercomputer as a kind of metacomputer which was given in [30], however, in our approach virtual supercomputer is not only a personal supercomputer but it also offers a way of creating virtual clusters that are adapted to problem being solved and to manage processes running on these clusters (Figure 1). This is the case where virtual shared memory cannot be used directly because of high latency and low performance caused by complex data transfer patterns. Migration of processes to data as well as methods of workload balancing [22] can solve this problem and form a basis of load balancing technique for a virtual supercomputer.

---

[1]Source code is available in https://www.tacc.utexas.edu/tacc-projects/gotoblas2/.

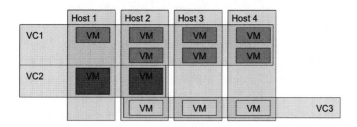

Figure 1. A cloud platform example with three virtual clusters over two physical clusters.

Computers like people need some sort of collective board to share results of their work and advance problem solution one step further. In a distributed computing environment distributed file systems and distributed databases act as such a board, storing intermediate and final results of computation. Apart from a shared desk people in a team need some sort of management to solve a problem in time and computers need a way of combining them into hierarchy helping efficiently distribute tasks among available computing nodes. Finally, from a technical point of view, problem solution should be decoupled from actual execution of tasks by a virtualization layer as not every problem has efficient mapping on physical architecture of a distributed system. So, virtual supercomputer is not only a cluster of machines but also virtualization and middleware layers on top of it.

Although virtual supercomputer can be implemented in many ways and using different combinations of technologies, there are some principles that such implementation is considered to obey. On one hand these principles arise from similarity of different technologies and their implementations, on the other hand the purpose of some principles is to solve problems inherent to existing general-purpose distributed systems. In any case, the principles are useful for solving large-scale problems on virtual supercomputer and some of them can be neglected for problems of small sizes. Explanation of this principles follow.

Virtual supercomputer is completely determined by its application programming interface (API) and this API should be platform-independent. The use of API as the only interface in distributed processing systems is common, but its dependency on operating system or programming language leads to problems in the long run. For example, the first API for portable batch systems (PBS) was implemented in low-level C language and only for UNIX-like platforms which led to inability or inefficiency of its usage in other programming languages and in exposing it as a web service. Moreover, the API does not cover all the functions of underlying PBS [32]. So, using platform-independent API is one of the ways to avoid such integration and connectivity problems. In other words, API is a programming language of a virtual supercomputer and the only way of interacting with it.

Virtual supercomputer API provides functions to connect with other virtual supercomputers and such interaction is seamless. Interaction of different distributed systems is the way of solving large-scale problems [31] and seamless interaction helps compose hybrid distributed systems dynamically: to extend capacity when needed [8]. So it is the way of scaling virtual supercomputer to solve problems that are too complex for one virtual supercomputer.

Virtual supercomputer processes data stored in a single distributed database and this processing is done using virtual shared memory. Efficient data processing is achieved by distributing data among available nodes and by running small programs (queries) on each host where corresponding data resides; this approach helps not only run query concurrently on each host but also minimizes data transfers [25, 12]. However, in existing implementations these programs are not general-purpose: they are parts of algorithm and they are specific to data model this algorithm was developed for. For example, in MapReduce framework programs represent map and reduce functions that are run on each row of table (or line of file) and it is difficult to compose general-purpose program to process any data within this framework [12]. On the other hand, virtual shared memory interface allows processing of data located on any host [6] and does it in efficient way. So, distributed database is a way of storing large data sets and virtual shared memory is a way of writing general-purpose program to process it.

Experiments show that using lightweight virtualization technologies (para-virtualization and application containers) instead of full virtualization is advantageous in terms of performance [7], hence virtual computing nodes should be created using lightweight virtualization technologies only. However, not every operating system supports these technologies and it should be possible to access virtual supercomputer facilities through fully-virtualized hosts. So, lightweight virtualization is inevitable in achieving balance between good performance and ease of system administration in distributed environment and as a consequence operating system should be UNIX-like for it to work.

Load balance is achieved using virtual processors with controlled clock rate and process migration. The first technique allows balancing coarse-granularity tasks and the second is suitable for fine-grained parallelism.

To summarize, virtual supercomputer is an API offering functions to run programs, to work with data stored in a distributed database and to work with virtual shared memory and this API is the only programming language of a virtual supercomputer.

1.2. Virtual Workspace and Small-scale Virtual Clusters

Virtual machine is the main building block of a virtual workspace. In its simplest form a workspace consists of a single virtual machine connected to storage and licensed software repository. If desired, resource capacity can be extended naturally by replicating virtual machine to form a virtual cluster. Cluster can be owned exclusively by a single user or shared by members of a whole research group. Moreover, considering large scale problem one can acquire resources of dedicated high performance machine (SMP or hybrid) or conventional cluster. Resource capacity extension occurs dynamically and acquired resources can be accessed from within single virtual machine.

Intended virtual machine usage is summarized as follows:

- solve scientific problems that fit into single virtual machine resources;

- access to computational resources, both clusters and dedicated machines;

- store experiment's data;

- develop applications (programming using commercial and open source compilers);

Table 1. Crystal09 SrTiO3 test case wall clock time in minutes showing virtual cluster performance degradation. Virtual cluster characteristics: 16 virtual machines on $4\times$BL460c G7, $2\times$Intel X5675 CPUs and 96 GB RAM on one node, 64 cores total.

Total processes	T-Platform cluster	SMP machine	Virtual cluster
32	84	42	35
64	66	36	48

- perform other routine tasks.

Private virtual cluster approach proved to be beneficial when using interactive resource-hungry software like Materials Studio or ADF. In that case computational resources of a single host exposed as a virtual machine are not enough for application to run smoothly, and virtual cluster boosts its performance. However, virtual cluster proved to be inefficient for solving large-scale problems with Crystal09. Running this application on virtual cluster puts heavy burden on network throughput. Careful investigation revealed that virtual cluster interconnect performance is degraded when multiple virtual nodes reside on a single physical host (Table 1). So private virtual cluster can be recommended for interactive small-scale applications used on the daily basis.

To summarize, para- and fully-virtual clusters are efficient at solving small-scale problems and offer rudimentary benefits of virtualization: ease of administration, improved security and resilience to hardware failures. The other use case is private virtual workspace.

1.3. Virtual Clusters for High Performance Computing

Only lightweight virtualization technologies can be used to build virtual clusters for large-scale problems. This stems from the fact that on large scale no service overhead is acceptable if it scales with the number of nodes. In case of virtual clusters scalable overhead comes from processor virtualization which means that no para- and fully-virtualized machines are not suitable for large virtual clusters. This leaves only application container technologies for investigation. The other challenge is to make dynamic creation and deletion of virtual clusters take constant time.

Test system comprises many standard components which are common in high performance computing, these are distributed parallel file system which stores home directories with experiment's input and output data, cluster resource scheduler which allocates resources for jobs and client programs to pre- and post-process data; the non-standard component is network-attached storage exporting container's root files systems as directories. Linux Container technology (LXC) is used to provide containerisation, GlusterFS is used to provide parallel file system and TORQUE to provide task scheduling. The most recent CentOS Linux 7 is chosen to provide stable version of LXC (>1.0) and version of kernel which supports all containers' features. Due to limited number of nodes each of them is chosen to be both compute and storage node and every file in parallel file system is stored on exactly two nodes. Detailed hardware characteristics and software version numbers are listed in Table 2.

Table 2. Hardware and software components of the system.

Component	Details	Component	Details
CPU model	Intel Xeon E5440	Operating system	CentOS 7
CPU clock rate (GHz)	2.83	Kernel version	3.10
No. of cores per CPU	4	LXC version	1.0.5
No. of CPUs per node	2	GlusterFS version	3.5.1
RAM size (GB)	4	TORQUE version	5.0.0
Disk model	ST3250310NS	OpenMPI version	1.6.4
Disk speed (rpm)	7200	IMB version	4.0
No. of nodes	12	OpenFOAM version	2.3.0
Interconnect speed (Gbps)	1		

Creating virtual cluster in such environment requires the following steps. First, a client submits a task requesting particular number of cores. Then according to distribution of these cores among compute nodes a container is started on each node from the list with SSH daemon as the only program running inside it. Here there are two options: either start containers with network virtualization (using *macvlan* or *veth* LXC network type) and generate sufficient number of IP addresses for the cluster or use host network name space (*none* LXC network type) and generate only the port number to run ssh daemon on. The next step is to copy (possibly amended) node file from host into the first container and launch submitted script inside it. When the script finishes its work SSH daemon in every container is killed and all containers are destroyed.

For this algorithm to work as intended client's home directory should be bind-mounted inside the container before launching the script. Additionally since some MPI programs require *scratch* directories on each node to work properly, container's root file system should be mounted in copy-on-write mode, so that all changes in files and all the new files are written to host's temporary directory and all unchanged data is read from read-only network-mounted file system; this can be accomplished via Union or similar file system and that way application containers are left untouched by tasks running on the cluster.

To summarize, only standard Linux tools are used to build the system: there are no opaque virtual machines images, no sophisticated full virtualization appliances and no heavy-weight cloud computing stacks in this configuration.

1.4. Lightweight Virtual Clusters Evaluation

To test the resulting configuration OpenMPI and Intel MPI Benchmarks (IMB) were used to measure network throughput and OpenFOAM was used to measure overall performance on a real-world application.

The first experiment was to create virtual cluster, launch an empty (with */bin/true* as an executable file) MPI program in it and compare execution time to ordinary physical cluster. To set this experiment up in the container the same operating system and version of OpenMPI as in the host machine was installed. No network virtualization was used,

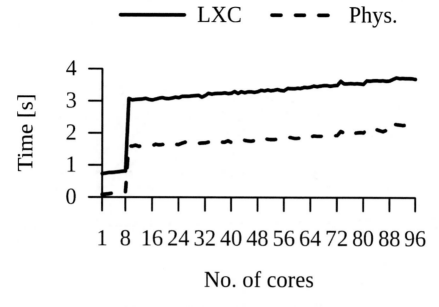

Figure 2. Comparison of LXC and physical cluster performance running empty MPI program.

each run was repeated several times and the average was displayed on the graph (Figure 2). The results show that a constant overhead of 1.5 second is added to every LXC run after the 8th core: one second is attributed to the absence of cache inside container with SSH configuration files, key files and libraries in it and other half of the second is attributed to the creation of containers as shown in Figure 3. The jump after the 8th core marks bounds of a single machine which means using network for communication rather than shared memory. The creation of containers is fully parallel task and takes approximately the same time to complete for different number of nodes. Overhead of destroying containers was found to be negligible and was combined with *mpirun* time. So, usage of Linux containers adds some constant overhead to the launching of parallel task depending on system's configuration which is split between creation of containers and filling the file cache.

The second experiment was to measure performance of different LXC network types using IMB suite and it was found that the choice of network virtualization greatly affects performance. As in the previous test container was set up with the same operating system and the same IMB executables as the host machine. Network throughput was measure with *exchange* benchmark and displayed on the graph (Figure 4). From the graph it is evident that until 214 bytes message size the performance is approximately the same for all network types, however, after this mark there is a dip in performance of virtual ethernet. It is difficult to judge where this overhead comes from: some studies report that under high load performance of bridged networking (*veth* is always connected to the bridge) is decreased [21], but IMB does not have high load on the system. Additionally, the experiment showed that as expected throughput decreases with the number of cores due to synchronization overheads (Figure 5).

The third and the last experiment dealt with real-world application performance and for this role the OpenFOAM was chosen as the complex parallel task involving large amount

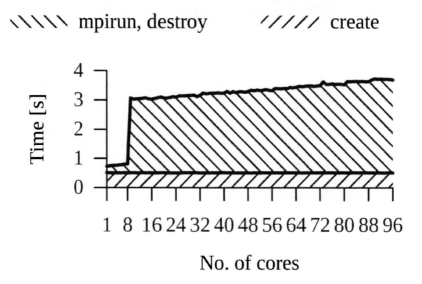

Figure 3. Breakdown of LXC empty MPI program run.

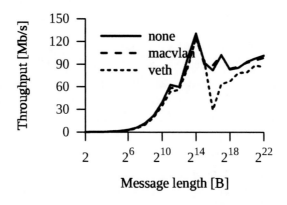

Figure 4. Average throughput of *exchange* MPI benchmark.

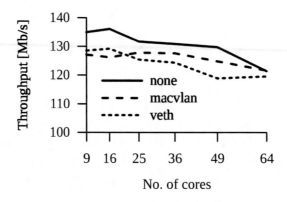

Figure 5. Throughput for 16Kb messages.

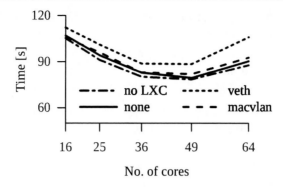

Figure 6. Average performance of OpenFOAM with different LXC network types.

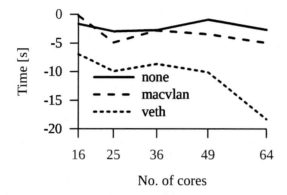

Figure 7. Difference of OpenFOAM performance on physical and virtual clusters. Negative numbers show slowdown of virtual cluster.

of network communication, disk I/O and high CPU load. The dam break RAS case was run with different number of cores (total number of cores is the square of number of cores per node) and different LXC network types and the average of multiple runs was displayed on the graph (Figure 6). Measurements for 4 and 9 cores were discarded because there is a considerable variation of execution time for these numbers on physical machines. From the graph it can be seen that low performance of virtual ethernet decreased final performance of OpenFOAM by approximately 5-10% whereas *macvlan* and *none* performance is close to the performance of physical cluster (Figure 7). So, the choice of network type is the main factor affecting performance of parallel applications running on virtual clusters and its overhead can be eliminated by using *macvlan* network type or by not using network virtualization at all.

To summarize, there are two main types of overheads when using virtual cluster: creation overhead which is constant and small compared to average time of a typical parallel job and network overhead which can be eliminated by not using network virtualization at all.

Presented approach for creating virtual clusters from Linux containers was found to be efficient and its performance comparable to ordinary physical cluster: not only usage of containers does not incur processor virtualization overheads but also network virtualization overheads can be totally removed if host's network name space is used and network bandwidth saved by automatically transferring only those files that are needed through network-mounted file system rather than the whole images. From the point of view of system administrator storing each HPC application in its own container makes versioning and dependencies control easy manageable and their configuration does not interfere with the configuration of host machines and other containers.

2.   Distributed Scheduling

2.1.   Load Balancing

The most general and well-known approach to balancing the load on a multiprocessor system consists of decomposing data (or tasks) into homogeneous parts (or subtasks) and distributing them between available processor cores or computer cluster nodes, however, this approach is far from being the most efficient. Often, the overall number of parts is determined by the constraints of the problem being solved rather than computer architecture or cluster configuration being used. So, there are either too many parts compared to the number of processor cores resulting in process context switching and data copying overheads or there are too few parts to saturate all available processor cores. In addition to this, some problems can have non-homogeneous pattern of data decomposition which creates disbalance among the load on different processor cores. Finally, most of the computer systems in addition to processors consist of many disparate devices such as general purpose accelerators, GPUs and storage disks which play their roles in computation, so the final performance is limited by the performance of the slowest device. So, if the only thing which is taken into account when developing load balancing algorithm is its multi-core processor then the result is the first approximation to the ideal algorithm which can be improved by taking into account other devices of the system.

From mathematical point of view, load balance condition means equality of distribution function F of some task metric (e.g. execution time) to distribution function G of some processor metric (e.g. performance) and the problem of balancing the load is reduced to solving equation

$$F(x) = G(n), \tag{1}$$

where x is task metric (or time taken to execute the task) and n is processor metric (or relative performance of a processor needed to execute this task). Since in general case it is impossible to know in advance neither the time needed to execute the task on a particular processor, nor the performance of a processor executing a particular task, stochastic approach should be employed to estimate those values. Empirical distribution functions can be obtained from execution time samples recorded for each task: task metric is obtained dividing execution time by a number of tasks and processor metric is obtained dividing a number of tasks by their execution time. Also, any other suitable metrics can be used instead of the proposed ones, e.g. the size of data to be processed can be used as a task metric and processor metric can be represented by some fixed number.

It is easy to measure execution time of each task when the whole system acts as an event-driven system and an event is a single task consisting of program code to be executed and data to be processed. In this interpretation, load balancer component is connected to a processor recursively via profiler forming feedback control system. Profiler collects execution time samples and load balancer estimates empirical distribution functions and distributes new tasks among processors solving equation 1.

Static load balancing is also possible in this event-driven system and for that purpose a set of different load balancers can be composed into a hierarchy. In such hierarchy, distribution function is estimated incrementally from bottom to top and hierarchy is used to maintain static load balance. Physical processors are composed or decomposed into virtual ones grouping a set of processors and assigning them to a single load balancer or assigning one physical processor to more than one load balancer at once. So static load balancing is orthogonal to dynamic load balancing and they can be used in conjunction.

To summarize, recursive load balancing approach targets problems exhibiting not only dynamic but also static imbalance and the balance can be achieved solving a single equation.

2.2. Hierarchical Load Balancing

To generalize the algorithm for multiple compute devices load balancing can be decomposed into two stages in order to cope with both heterogeneous problem decomposition pattern and saturation of heterogeneous devices. In the first step parts are distributed to devices according to their nature: computational tasks are assigned to either a processor or an accelerator depending on their implementation. Since storage devices do not have dedicated processors the core which is responsible for writing and reading data should be manually allocated for input/output tasks. The same core can be used for any device which is not capable of performing general purpose computations. In the second step when the device type is chosen the task is distributed to some device of this type by scheduling algorithm. Devices having the same type are almost always homogeneous so only the relative size of parts should be taken into account by the algorithm.

Backfill algorithm with certain modifications can be used as a scheduling algorithm for multi-processor system. This algorithm assumes that task execution time is known beforehand which is not the case for cluster schedulers: this time often manually estimated by people submitting the job to a queue [35]. Since there are many small tasks into which the problem is decomposed it is non-practical to estimate execution time of each task. Instead, task execution time can be reliably predicted by simple statistical means when the task is small. When a program is executed all tasks are assumed to be of the same size. Gradually, when timing is available for some significant number of tasks an average (or linear regression) of all times is computed and taken as prediction for next tasks.

Heterogeneity of devices can be taken into account using the same statistical approach, however, this time prediction should be based on the number of tasks executed by each device during some fixed unit of time.

Statistical approach is valid when the number of tasks is large and tasks are small which is not the case for cluster scheduling systems where tasks can execute for days or even weeks. Even for such systems Backfill algorithm works more efficient for small tasks [35]. There is some difficulty in defining which task is small and which is not so the best choice is to use natural problem decomposition. For example, fluid mechanics problems are often solved on some closed volume, so their natural decomposition is to create a task for each point of volume and then distribute them to processor cores. That way the larger the volume is the more saturated processor cores become and the more balanced the resulting load is. For small problems the load balance is not of a concern.

So, load balancing for multi-processor system is carried in two steps: first the task is sent to a device of appropriate type and then using modified Backfill scheduling algorithm is distributed to some of the devices of this type. Task execution time predictions are based on simple and fast statistical methods.

2.3.   Event-driven System

The whole system was implemented as a collection of C++ classes, and problem-solving classes were separated from utility classes with an event-driven approach. In this approach, problem solution is represented by a set of executable objects or 'employees', each implementing a solution of one particular part of a problem. Each executable object can implement two methods. With the first method employee either solves part of the problem or produces child executable objects (or 'hires' additional employees) to delegate problem solution to them. Since upon completion of this method no object is destroyed, it is called 'production' task or 'upstream' task as it often delegates problem solution to a hierarchy layer located farther from the root than the current layer is. The second method collects execution results from subordinate executable objects and takes such object as an argument. Upon completion of this method the child object is destroyed or 'fired' so that the total number of executable objects is reduced. Hence this task is called 'reduction' task or 'downstream' task since the results are sent to a hierarchy layer located closer to root. Executable objects can send results not only to their parents but also to any number of other executable objects, however, when communication with a parent occurs the child object is destroyed and when the root object tries to send results to its nonexistent parent, the program ends. Execution of a particular object is performed via submitting it to a queue corresponding to a particular processor. Child and parent objects are determined implicitly during submission so that no manual specification is needed. Finally, these objects are never copied and are accessed only via their addresses. In other words, the only thing that is required when constructing an executable object is to implement a specific method to solve a task and object's life time is implicitly controlled by the system and a programmer does not have to manage it manually.

Execution of objects is carried out concurrently and construction of an executable object is separated from its execution with a thread-safe queue. Every message in a queue is an executable object and carries the data and the code needed to process it and since executable objects are completely independent of each other they can be executed in any order. There are real server objects corresponding to each queue in a system which continuously retrieve objects from a queue and execute their production or reduction tasks in a thread associated with the server object. Production tasks can be submitted to any queue, but a queue into which reduction tasks can be submitted is determined by a corresponding parent object so that no race condition can occur. Since each processor works with its own queue only and in its own thread, processing of queues is carried out concurrently. Also, each queue in a system represents a pipeline through which the data flows, however, execution order is completely determined by the objects themselves. So, executable objects and their methods model control flow while queues model data flow and the flows are separated from each other.

Heterogeneity of executable objects can cause load imbalance among different queues and this problem can be solved introducing imaginary (i.e. proxy) servers and profilers to aid in distribution of executable objects. Imaginary server is a server tied to a set of other servers and its only purpose is to choose the right child server to execute an object at.

In the simplest case, a proper distribution can be achieved with round-robin algorithm, i.e. when each arriving object is executed on the next server, however, in general case, some additional information about completed runs is needed to choose the right server and this information can be collected with pluggable profiler objects. When a new object arrives to an imaginary server, actual profiling information is collected from child servers and specified distribution strategy is used to delegate execution of an object to an appropriate server, and some static distribution strategy is also possible. So, imaginary servers together with distribution strategies and profilers can be used to distribute executable objects among real servers taking into account some profiling information of completed object executions.

The class diagram of the whole event-driven system is depicted in the Figure 8 and the system works as follows.

1. When a program execution starts, the hierarchy of imaginary and real servers is composed. All real servers are launched in a separate threads and processing of executable objects starts.

2. The first object is created and submitted to the imaginary server at the top of the hierarchy. The server employs specified distribution strategy to choose an appropriate server from the next layer of the hierarchy to send the object to. The profiler gathers measurements of completed runs from subordinate servers and decides where to send an object.

3. The previous step repeats until the bottom level of the hierarchy is reached and real server which was found with the distribution strategy starts execution of an object.

4. Object is executed and measurements are made by a profiler. If during execution more executable objects are created and submitted to the top imaginary server, the whole algorithm is repeated for each new object; if the root object submits reduction task then all servers in the hierarchy are shut down, and program execution ends.

To sum up, the whole system is composed of the two hierarchies: one hierarchy represents tasks and data and their dependencies employing executable objects, the other hierarchy represents processing system employing imaginary and real server objects. Mapping of the first hierarchy to the second is implicit and is implemented using message queues. Such composition allows easy configuration of dynamic and static load distribution strategies and allows programming with simple executable objects.

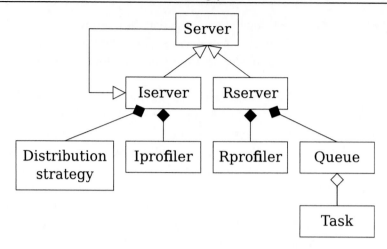

Figure 8. Class diagram for an event-driven system. 'Iserver' denotes imaginary server and 'Rserver' denotes real server.

2.4. Scheduling Algorithm

Recursive load balancing was implemented as a load distribution strategy, however, equation 1 was not solved directly. The first problem occurring when solving this equation directly was that task metric x cannot be computed before actually running the task so it was estimated to be an average metric of a number of previous runs. The second problem was that when the task metric is known, the result of direct solution of equation 1 is not an identifier of a processor to execute the task on but it is number n – relative performance of a processor needed to execute the task and the number n is not particularly useful when determining where to execute the task. Therefore, equation 1 was not solved directly but its main idea was realized in an algorithm similar to round-robin.

The resulting algorithm works as follows.

1. First, algorithm collects samples recorded by profilers of child servers as well as estimates task metric and processor metric using values from previous runs. At this stage, not only averaging but also any other suitable predicting technique can be used.

2. Then, probability of having a task with metric equal to computed task metric is determined by counting samples equal to computed task metric and dividing it by the total number of samples.

3. The cursor pointing at the processor to execute the next task on is incremented by a step equal to a product of computed probability and computed processor metric.

4. Then, by recursively subtracting metric of each processor from the cursor, the needed processor is found and the task is executed on it.

The resulting mathematical formula for each step can be written simply as

$$cursor = cursor + F(\bar{x})\bar{n},$$

where $\bar{x}$ is a task metric and $\bar{n}$ is a processor metric. In case of fully homogeneous system and all tasks having equal metric this algorithm is equivalent to round-robin: all processors have metric equal to 1 and probability is always 1 so that the cursor is always incremented by 1.

Although, the algorithm is simple, in practice it requires certain modifications and a robust profiler to work properly. Since algorithm balances reciprocal values of task metric t (execution time) and processor metric $1/t$ (processor throughput), even a slight oscillation of a task metric can affect the resulting distributions greatly. The solution to this problem is to smooth samples with a logarithm function and it can be done in a straightforward way, because the algorithm does not make assumptions about metrics' dimensions and treat them as numbers. The second problem is that the algorithm should be implemented with integer arithmetic only to minimize overhead of load balancing. This problem can be solved by omitting mantissa after logarithm is applied to a sample and in that case processor metric is equal to task metric but has an opposite sign. The last major problem is that the distribution of task metric may change abruptly during program execution, which renders samples collected by a profiler for previous runs useless. This problem is solved by detecting a sharp change in task execution time (more than three standard deviations) and when an outlier is detected the profiler is reset to its initial state in which distribution is assumed to be uniform. As a result of applying logarithm to each sample the algorithm becomes unsuitable for relatively small tasks and for tasks taking too much time, and although such tasks are executed, the samples are not collected for them as they often represent just control flow tasks. To summarize, the modified algorithm is implemented using integer arithmetic only, is suitable for relatively complex tasks and adapts to a rapid change of a task metric distribution.

One problem of the algorithm that stands aside is that it becomes inefficient in the event of high number of tasks with high metric values. It happens because when task is assigned to a particular processor it is not executed directly but rather gets placed in a queue. If this queue is not empty the task can reside in it for such a long time that its assignment to a particular processor will not match actual distribution function. The solution is simple: these stale tasks can be easily detected by recording their arrival time and comparing it with the current time and when such tasks are encountered by a queue processor, they can be redistributed to match the current distribution function. However, an existence of stale tasks is also an evidence that the computer is not capable of solving a problem fast enough to cope with continuously generated tasks and it is an opportunity to communicate with some other computers to solve the problem together. From a technical point of view, delegation of tasks to other computers is possible because tasks are independent of each other and read/write (serialization) methods are easily implemented for each of them, however, the problem was not addressed herein, and only load redistribution within a single computer was implemented.

Described algorithm is suitable for distributing production tasks, but a different algorithm is needed to distribute reduction tasks. Indeed, when executable objects come in pairs consisting of the child and its parent, all children of the parent must be executed on the same server so that no race condition takes place, so it is not possible to distribute the task on an arbitrary server but a particular server must be chosen for all of the child tasks. One possible way of choosing a server is by applying a simple hashing function to parent's memory address. Some sophistication of this algorithm is possible, e.g. predicting memory allocation and de-allocation pattern to distribute reduction tasks uniformly among servers, however, considering that most of the reduction tasks in tested program were simple (the reason for this is discussed in Section 2.5) the approach seemed to be non viable and was not implemented. So, simple hashing algorithm was used to distribute reduction tasks among servers.

To summarize, recursive load distribution algorithm by default works as round-robin algorithm and when a reasonable change of task execution time is detected it automatically distributes the load in accordance with task metric distribution. Also, if there is a change in processor performance it is taken into account by relating its performance to other processors of computing system. Finally, if a task stays too much time in a queue it is distributed once again to match current distribution function.

2.5. Evaluation for Compute-intensive Problem

Event-driven approach was tested on the example of hydrodynamics simulation program which solves a real-world problem [4, 5, 14, 13]. The problem consists of generating real ocean wavy surface and computing pressure under this surface to measure impact of the external excitations on marine object. The program is well-balanced in terms of processor load and for the evaluation purpose it was implemented using an introduced event-driven approach and the resulting implementation was compared to an existing non event-driven approach in terms of performance and programming effort.

Event-driven architecture makes it easy to write logs which in turn can be used to make visualization of control flow in a program. Each server maintains its own log file and whenever some event occurs, it gets logged in this file accompanied by a time stamp and a server identifier. Having such files available, it gets pretty straight-forward to reconstruct a sequence of events occurring during program execution and to establish connections between these events (to dynamically draw graph of tasks as they are executed). Many of such graphs are used in this section to demonstrate results of experiments.

Generation of a wavy surface is implemented as a transformation of a white noise, autoregressive model is used to generate ocean waves and pressures are computed using analytical formula. The program consists of preprocessing phase, main computer-intensive phase and post-processing phase. The program begins with solving Yule-Walker equations to determine autoregressive coefficients and white noise variance. Then a white noise is generated and gets transformed into a wavy surface. Finally, the surface is trimmed and written to an output stream. Generation of a wavy surface is the most computer-intensive phase which consumes over 80% of program execution time (Figure 18) for moderate wavy surface sizes and this time does not scale with a surface size. So, the program spends most of the time in the main phase generating a wavy surface (this phase is marked with $[G_0, G_1]$ interval in the graphs). The hardware used in the experiments is listed in Table 4. The program was tested in a number of experiments and then compared to other parallel programming techniques.

The first experiment consisted of measuring stale cycles and discovering causes of their occurrence. Program source code was instrumented with profiling directives and every occurrence of stale cycles was written to the log file. Also the total stale time was measured.

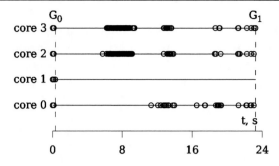

Figure 9. Occurrences of stale cycles in preprocessing and at the end of the main computational phase of a program. Range $[G_0, G_1]$ denotes computationally intensive phase.

Obtained results showed that stale cycles prevail in preprocessing and at the end of main phase but are not present in other parts of the program (Figure 9). The reason for this deals with insufficient amount of tasks available to solve during these phases which in turn is caused by global synchronizations occurring multiple times in preprocessing phase and naturally at the end of a program. Stale cycles in the main phase are caused by computation performing faster than writing results to disk: in the program only one thread writes data and no parallel file system is used. Further experiments showed that stale cycles consume at most 20% of the total execution time for 4 core system (Table 3) and although during this time threads are waiting on a mutex so that this time can be consumed by other operating system processes, there is also an opportunity to speed up the program. Considering file output performance stale cycles can only be reduced with faster storage devices combined with slower processors or with parallel file systems combined with fast network devices and interconnects. In contrast, the main cause of stale cycles in preprocessing phase deals with global synchronization and to minimize its effect it should be replaced by incremental synchronization if possible.

The next experiment consisted of measuring different types of overheads including profiling, load balancing, queuing and other overheads so that real performance of event-driven system can be estimated. In this experiment, the same technique was used to obtain measurements: every function causing overhead was instrumented and also the total time spent executing tasks and total program execution time was measured. As a result, the total overhead was estimated to be less than 0.1% for different number of cores (Table 3). Also the results showed that reduction time is smaller than the total time spent solving production tasks in all cases (Table 3). It is typical of generator programs to spend more time solving data generating production tasks than solving data processing reduction tasks; in a data-centric program specializing in data processing this relation can be different. Finally, it is evident from the results that the more cores are present in the system the more stale time is introduced into the program. This behavior was explained in the previous experiment and is caused by imbalance between processor performance and performance of a storage device for this particular computational problem. To summarize, the experiment showed that event-driven system and recursive load distribution strategy do not incur much overhead even on systems with large number of cores and the program is rather code-centric than data-centric spending most of its execution time solving production tasks.

Table 3. Distribution of wall clock time and its main consumers in event-driven system. Time is shown as a percentage of the total program execution time. Experiments for 4 cores were conducted on the system I and experiments for 24 and 48 cores were conducted on the system II from Table 4.

Classifier	Time consumer	Time spent, %		
		4 cores	**24 cores**	**48 cores**
Problem solution	Production tasks	71	33	19
	Reduction tasks	13	4	2
Stale time	Stale cycles	16	63	79
Overhead	Load distribution overhead	0.01	0.0014	0.0017
	Queuing overhead	0.002	0.0007	0.0005
	Profiling overhead	0.0004	0.0004	0.0003
	Other overheads	0.06	0.03	0.02

In the third experiment, the total number of production tasks solved by the system was measured along with the total number of task resubmissions and it was found that there is high percentage of resubmissions. Each resubmission was recorded as a separate event and then a number of resubmissions for each task was calculated. The experiment showed that on average a total of 35% of tasks are resubmitted and analysis of an event log suggested that resubmissions occur mostly during the main computational phase (Figure 10). In other words 35% of production tasks stayed in a queue for too long time (more than an average time needed to solve a task) so underlying computer was not capable of solving tasks as fast as they are generated by the program. This result leads to a conclusion that if more than one computer is available to solve a problem, then there is a natural way to determine what part of this problem requires multiple computers to be solved. So, high percentage of resubmissions shows that machine solves production tasks slower than they are generated by the program so multiple machines can be used to speed up problem solution.

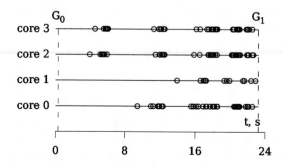

Figure 10. Event plot of resubmission of production tasks staying in a queue for too long time. Range $[G_0, G_1]$ denotes computationally intensive phase.

In the final experiment overall performance of event-driven approach was tested and it was found to be superior when solving problems producing large volumes of data. In the previous research it was found that OpenMP is the best performing technology for the wavy ocean surface generation [4], so the experiment consisted of comparing its performance to the performance of event-driven approach on a set of input data. A range of sizes of a wavy surface was the only parameter that was varied among subsequent program runs. As a result of the experiment, event-driven approach was found to have higher performance than OpenMP technology and the more the size of the problem is the bigger performance gap becomes (Figure 11). Also event plot in Figure 12 of the run with the largest problem size shows that high performance is achieved with overlapping of parallel computation of a wavy surface (interval $[G_0, G_1]$) and output of resulting wavy surface parts to the storage device (interval $[W_0, W_1]$). It can be seen that there is no such overlap in OpenMP implementation and output begins at point W_0 right after the generation of wavy surface ends at point G_1. In contrast, there is a significant overlap in event-driven implementation and in that case wavy surface generation and data output end almost simultaneously at points G_1 and W_1 respectively. So, approach with pipelined execution of parallelized computational steps achieves better performance than sequential execution of the same steps. In other words pipelined execution of sequential phases is an efficient way of exploiting nested (inter- and intra-device) parallelism of a problem.

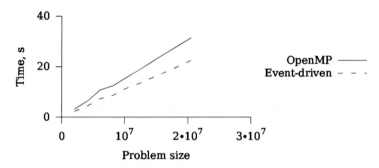

Figure 11. Performance comparison of OpenMP and event-driven implementations.

Although OpenMP technology allows constructing pipelines, it is not easy to combine a pipeline with parallel execution of tasks. In fact such combination is possible if a thread-safe queue is implemented to communicate threads generating ocean surface to a thread writing data to disk. Then using *omp section* work of each thread can be implemented. However, implementation of parallel execution within *omp section* requires support for nesting *omp parallel* directives. So, combining pipeline with parallel execution is complicated in OpenMP implementation requiring the use a thread-safe queue which is not present in OpenMP standard.

To summarize, event-driven programming approach was applied to a real-world high-performance application and it was shown that it incurs low overhead, but results in appearance of stale periods when no problem solving is performed by some threads. The duration of these periods in the main phase can be reduced with faster storage equipment and the duration of stale periods in preprocessing phase can be reduced employing incremental synchronization techniques. Also, event-driven approach offers a natural way of determining whether program execution should scale to multiple machines or not, however, viability

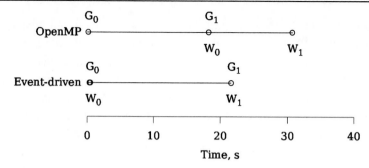

Figure 12. Event plot showing overlap of parallel computation $[G_0, G_1]$ and data output $[W_0, W_1]$ in event-driven implementation. There is no overlap in OpenMP implementation.

of such mode of execution was not tested in the present research. Finally, it was shown that event-driven approach is more efficient than standard OpenMP technology especially for large problem sizes and it was also shown that a pipeline combined with parallel execution works faster than sequential execution of parallelized steps.

Performance of recursive load distribution algorithm was compared to performance of round-robin algorithm and was tested in a number of scenarios with combinations of homogeneous and heterogeneous tasks and homogeneous and heterogeneous processors. In each experiment the total execution time and distributions of task metric and processor metric were measured and compared to uniform distribution case. All tests were performed on the same system (Table 4) and each scenario was run multiple times to ensure accurate results. Also, preliminary validation tests were performed to make sure that the algorithm works as intended. So, the purpose of evaluation was to demonstrate how algorithm works in practice and to measure its efficiency on a real problem.

It has already been shown that the algorithm consumes only a small fraction of total execution time of a program (Table 3), so the purpose of the validation test was to show algorithm's ability to switch between different task metric distributions. The switching is performed when a significant change (more than three standard deviations) of a task execution time occurs. The test have shown that the switching events are present in preprocessing phase and do not occur in the main phase (Figure 18). The cause of the switching is a highly variable task execution time inherent to preprocessing phase. So, profilers' resets occur only when a change of task execution time distribution is encountered and no switching is present when this distribution does not change.

The purpose of the first experiment was to show that the algorithm is capable of balancing homogeneous tasks on homogeneous computer and in that case it works like well-known round-robin algorithm. During the experiment, events of task submissions were recorded as well as additional profiler data and an event plot was created. In Figure 14 relative performance of each processor core is plotted and all the samples lie on a single line in the computational phase. Since this phase consists of executing tasks of equal metric, the straight line represents the uniform distribution of tasks among processor cores constituting round-robin algorithm. So, in the simplest case of homogeneous tasks and processors recursive load balancing algorithm works as round-robin algorithm.

The purpose of the second experiment was to show that recursive load-balancing algo-

Table 4. Testbed setup.

Component	System	
Programming language	C++11	
Threading library	C++11 STL threads	
Atomics library	C++11 STL atomic	
Time measurement routines	`clock_gettime(CLOCK_MONOTONIC, ...)`	
	`/usr/bin/time -f %e`	
Compiler	GCC 4.8.2	
Compiler flags	`-std=c++11 -O2 -march=native`	
	I	**II**
Operating system	Debian 3.2.51-1 x86_64	CentOS 6.5 x86_64
File system	ext4	ext4
Processor	Intel Core 2 Quad Q9650	2×Intel Xeon E5-2695 v2
Cores frequency (GHz)	3.00	2.40
Number of cores	4	24 (48 virtual cores)
RAM capacity (GB)	8	256
RAID device		Dell PERC H710 Mini
RAID configuration		RAID10
Storage device	Seagate ST3250318AS	4×Seagate ST300MM0006
Storage device speed (rpm)	7200	2×10000

rithm is capable of balancing homogeneous tasks on heterogeneous processors and in that case it can distribute the load taking into account performance of a particular processor. Although natural application of such load balancing is hybrid computer systems equipped with graphical or other accelerators, the experiment was conducted by emulating such systems with a hierarchy of servers. It was found that load balancing algorithm can recognize performance of different components and adapt distribution of tasks accordingly (Figure 15): I_1's first and second child servers have relative performance equal to 0.75 and 0.25 respectively whereas all children of I_2 server have relative performance equal to $\frac{1}{3}$. Also, this system setup shows performance similar to performance of the homogeneous computer configuration (Figure 13). So, recursive load balancing algorithm works on heterogeneous computer configurations and the performance is similar to homogeneous system case.

The purpose of the third experiment was to show that the algorithm is capable of balancing heterogeneous tasks on a homogeneous system and the experiment showed that performance gain is small. For the experiment the source code generating a wavy surface was modified so that parts of two different sizes are generated simultaneously. In order to balance such workload on a homogeneous system the step should be equal to $\frac{1}{2i}n, i = 1, 2, ...,$ where n is the processor metric (instead of being equal to 1 when parts have the same size) so that each processor takes two respective parts of the surface. In the Figure 16 showing results of the experiment the step reaches its optimal value of $\frac{1}{2}n$ (0.125 mark), however, it takes almost 8 seconds (or 40% of the total time) to reach this value. The first two cases do not exhibit such behavior and the step does not change during execution. Also, in the course of the experiment it was found that the step oscillates and to fix this it was smoothed

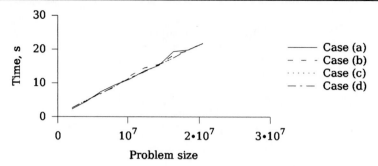

Figure 13. Performance comparison of different server configurations. Configurations are listed in Figure 18.

with five point median filter and the number of samples was doubled. Finally, in subsequent experiments it was found that the more unique parts sizes are present in the main phase, the more samples should be collected to preserve the accuracy of the step evaluation, however, the increase in the number of samples led to slow convergence of the step to its optimal value. In other words, the more heterogeneous the tasks are, the more time is needed to find the optimal step value for them.

The purpose of the fourth and final experiment was to show that the algorithm is capable of balancing heterogeneous tasks on heterogeneous system and results were similar to the previous experiment. System configuration was the same as in the second experiment. Although, in the Figure 17 showing the results metrics and steps of both servers reach nearly optimal values, there are more disturbances in these processes. So, the algorithm works with heterogeneous tasks and system but heterogeneity of a system increases variability of the step. In other words, heterogeneity of a system also increases time needed to find the optimal step value.

To summarize, from the experiments one can conclude, that the algorithm works on any system configuration and with any task combination, but requires tuning for a particular problem. However, experience obtained in the course of the experiments suggests that not only heterogeneity of tasks and computers increases the number of samples and convergence time but also there are certain task size distributions that cannot be handled efficiently by this algorithm and can extend this time indefinitely. One example of such distribution is linearly increasing task size. In this case step is always equal to $1/m$, where m is the number of samples, and there is no way to tune the algorithm to balance such workload. So, the downside of recursive load balancing algorithm is that it is suitable for closed metric distributions with low variability of the metric and more general and simple modified Backfill algorithm can be used in other cases. Also, it is evident from the experiments from the Section 2.5 that in the tested program the dominating performance factor is balance between the speed of wavy surface generation and the speed of writing it to storage device. In that case, load balancing algorithm plays only a second role and any combination of computer and task heterogeneity demonstrates comparable performance as was depicted in Figure 13.

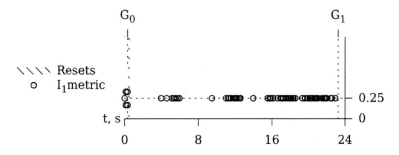

Figure 14. Homogeneous tasks and homogeneous computer case.

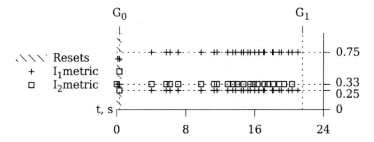

Figure 15. Homogeneous tasks and heterogeneous computer case.

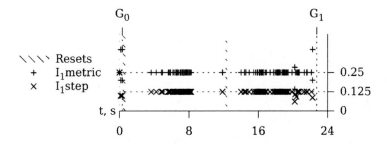

Figure 16. Heterogeneous tasks and homogeneous computer case.

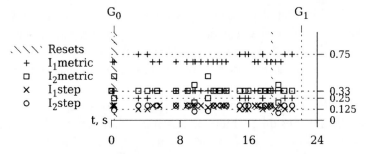

Figure 17. Heterogeneous tasks and heterogeneous computer case.

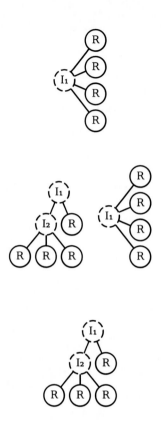

Figure 18. Event plot of task submissions and relative performance of child servers recorded at the time of submissions. I denotes 'Iserver' and R denotes 'Rserver'. Profiled servers are marked with dashed line.

2.6.   Evaluation for Mixed Compute- and Data-intensive Problem

The problem of classification of wave energy spectra is both data- and compute-intensive which makes it on one hand amenable to data-centric programming approaches like Hadoop and on the other hand to parallel programming techniques. In the *mapping* phase spectra should be pre-processed and converted to some convenient format and in the *reduction* phase resulting spectra are classified using genetic optimisation algorithm. These steps represent general algorithm for data processing with Hadoop, however, classification algorithm is itself parallel which makes the problem of classification difficult to program in Java (the language in which Hadoop programs are usually written). Therefore, we feel that Hadoop is not the most efficient way to solve the problem and a distributed program which mimics useful Hadoop behaviour should be used instead.

The NDBC dataset[2] consists of spectra which are sorted by year and station where measurements were acquired. Data for each spectrum is stored in five variables which are

---
[2]http://www.ndbc.noaa.gov/dwa.shtml

Table 5. Dataset properties.

Property	Details
Dataset size	144MB
Dataset size (uncompressed)	770MB
Number of wave stations	24
Time span	3 years (2010–2012)
Total number of spectra	445422

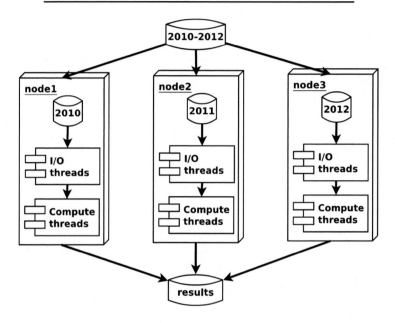

Figure 19. Implementation diagram for distributed pipeline.

used to reconstruct original frequency-directional spectrum with the following formula:

$$S(\omega, \theta) = \frac{1}{\pi} \left[\frac{1}{2} + r_1 \cos\left(\theta - \alpha_1\right) + r_2 \sin\left(2\left(\theta - \alpha_2\right)\right) \right] S_0(\omega, \theta).$$

Here ω denotes frequency, θ is the wave direction, $r_{1,2}$ and $\alpha_{1,2}$ are parameters of spectrum decomposition and S_0 is the measured wave energy spectrum. Detailed properties of the dataset used in evaluation are listed in Table 5.

The algorithm of processing spectra is as follows. First, current directory is recursively scanned for input files. All directories are recursively distributed to processing queues of each machine in the cluster. Processing begins with joining corresponding measurements for each spectrum variables into a single tuple which is subsequently classified by a genetic algorithm (this algorithm is not discussed in the paper and in fact can be replaced by any other suitable classification algorithm). While processing results are gradually copied back to the machine where application was executed and when the processing is complete the programme terminates. The resulting implementation is shown in Figure 19.

Directory structure can be arbitrary and the only thing it serves is to distribute the data,

Table 6. Hardware and software components of the system.

Component	Details	Component	Details
CPU model	Intel Q9650	Operating system	Debian Linux 7.5
CPU clock rate (GHz)	3.0	Hadoop version	2.3.0
No. of cores per CPU	4	GCC version	4.7
No. of CPUs per node	1	Compiler flags	`-std=c++11`
RAM size (GB)	4		
Disk model	ST3250318AS		
Disk speed (rpm)	7200		
No. of nodes	3		
Interconnect speed (Mbps)	100		

however, files containing corresponding measurements should be placed in a single directory so that no joining of variables residing in different machines can happen. In this test spectra were naturally sorted into directories by year and station.

The feature which makes this implementation different from other similar approaches is that both processors and disks work in parallel throughout the programme execution. Such behaviour is achieved with assigning a separate thread (or thread pool) for each device and placing tasks in the queue for the corresponding device in this pool. As tasks that read from the disk complete they produce tasks for CPUs to process the data which was read and place them into a processor task queue. In similar way when tasks processing data complete they place tasks to write the data into disk task queue. In similar vein via a separate task queue network devices transmit the data to a remote node. So, each device has its own thread (or thread pool) and all of them work in parallel by placing tasks in each other's task queues. Since tasks «flow» from one queue to another and queues can reside on different machines this approach is called distributed pipeline.

The system setup which was used to test the implementation consisted of commodity hardware and open-source software (Table 6) and evaluation was divided into two stages. In the first stage Hadoop was installed on each node of the cluster and was configured to use host file system as a source of data so that performance of parallel file system which is used by default in Hadoop can be factored out from the comparison. To make this possible the whole dataset was replicated on each node and placed in the directory with the same name. In the second stage Hadoop was shut down and replaced by newly developed application and dataset directories were statically distributed to different nodes to nullify the impact of parallel file system on the performance.

In the test it was found that Hadoop implementation has low scalability and a performance of approx. 1000 spectra per second and alternative implementation has higher scalability and performance of approx. 7000 spectra per second (Figure 20). The source of such inefficiency was found to be temporary data files which are written to disk by Hadoop on each node. These files represent sorted parts of the key-value array and are part of implementation of merge sort algorithm used to distribute the keys to different nodes. For NDBC dataset the total size of these files exceeds the size of the whole dataset which appears to be the consequence of Hadoop not compressing intermediate data (the initial dataset has compression ratio of 1:5). So, the sorting algorithm and non careful work with compressed data lead to performance degradation and inefficiency of Hadoop for NDBC dataset.

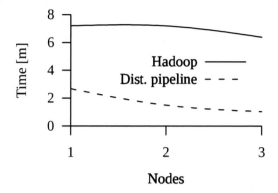

Figure 20. Performance of Hadoop and distributed pipeline implementations.

The sorting is not needed to distribute the keys and in distributed pipeline directory hierarchy is used to determine machine for reduction. For each directory a separate task is created which subsequently creates tasks for each sub-directory and each file. Since each task can interact with its parent when the reduction phase is reached reduction tasks are created on the machines where parents were executed previously.

3.   Scheduling Legacy Applications

The approach discussed in the previous section offers a novel way of parallelization of programs and requires the use of new API. However, rewriting existing well-tested code which uses established standards (e.g. MPI, OpenMP) is not always viable. Developers are resistant to change and tend to use traditional tools even if they are obsolete and show relatively poor performance. As a result, transition to new standards takes time.

Although, there are some established standards in industry and scientific computing, there is no universal one. Each of them has its own application area such as big data processing or parallel and geographically distributed computations, but their convergence continues to make universal standard for distributed computing a reality. For now, standards usually have several implementations that sometimes vary in terms of performance and capabilities. That is why one should consider a multitude of heterogeneous applications that use different approaches and standards when planning scientific computational infrastructure.

The next difference between applications is a software distribution model. There is a good tradition in scientific community to develop and use open source software packages for its own needs. However, sometimes researchers can not find an open source alternative to a proprietary closed source program or such program has capabilities which can not be found in the open source one. A closed source application is a «black box»: developers often do not take time to properly describe algorithms that are implemented in the program or it can be a proprietary secret. For a scheduler it makes difficult to estimate efficiency of such an application.

To summarize, HPC resource in general can be shared by different groups of scientists that use open and closed source software packages, that in turn use various standards which makes efficient resource sharing a challenging problem. One should take into account every scientific application separately. Solving this problem seems to be impossible without intelligent software. Common schedulers and resource allocation systems are limited in their ability to estimate program execution times and their granularity is not fine enough to make sharing of resources possible.

Our approach is to profile application run, analyze the data with simple statistical methods and gradually improve future system utilization with intelligent resource reallocation. This approach makes possible to optimize performance of legacy applications source code of which can not be changed for some reason.

3.1.   Resource Allocation

Distributed resources can be managed in several ways.

- **No management system.** Administrator installs operating system and grants access to nodes to users. It is the simplest approach from infrastructure point of view, but it is really difficult to do resource planning in such system since inexperienced users would probably start their jobs on the first node.

- **Cloud.** Administrator installs a hypervisor on each cluster node and creates a cloud using some cloud platform (e.g. OpenStack). Although, cloud computing simplifies infrastructure management its overhead due to virtualization and virtual machine migration can not be underestimated for efficiency of high-performance applications.

- **Single system image.** Administrator installs MOSIX or ScaleMP on the entire cluster. Such systems are quite convenient for users but this does not come without pitfalls: even though virtual SMP is a simple abstraction the fact that resources are still remote at the physical layer makes it difficult to scale to really large number of nodes. For example, failure of a node in vSMP causes a whole virtual system restart to exclude its processors from the kernel.

- **Classical resource management system.** Administrator installs a portable batch system (TORQUE, PBS Professional) or similar systems (HTCondor or Univa Grid Engine). Despite their age the use of PBS is still common and it is the main reason that evolution of this type of systems forms a basis of a scheduler for legacy applications.

Portable batch systems became somewhat classical in the world of scientific computing. Many universities across the world use one of PBS implementations or similar systems to schedule parallel jobs on their clusters. Why these systems became so popular and widespread in the scientific community? They are simple. PBS implementations can reserve computational resources like CPU cores, memory, GPUs or disk space for job execution. One can view PBS as a generalization of Linux *at* command that uses a scheduler to decide the exact time and the list of nodes to execute a job. If there are not enough free resources then job is put into a queue.

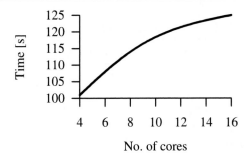

Figure 21. Limited scalability of an OpenFOAM 2.2 test case due to Amdahl's law.

Table 7. Performance of Intel MPI «PingPong» benchmark for TCP/IP, IPoIB and RDMA protocols.

	TCP/IP	IPoIB	RDMA
Network device	2x Ethernet 1G	Infiniband QDR 4x	Infiniband QDR 4x
NIC speed [Gb/s]	2	40	40
PingPong speed [Gbit/s]	1.2	8.9	25.3
MPI library	OpenMPI 1.6.4	OpenMPI 1.6.4	OpenMPI 1.6.4

Such systems usually provide administrators with scarce accounting information and granularity of jobs is not fine: each of them is a long-running parallel application. Common monitoring systems can collect more information but it is mapped to processes not jobs. That is why collecting profiling data from a more «verbose» scheduler can be useful to reallocate resources and minimize their usage for subsequent parallel application runs.

For example, if user submits certain job to a PBS queue several times, performance may vary despite the fact that the same resources are requested each time. Job's execution time depends on mapping of processes to cluster nodes (all processes on one or several nodes), network characteristics in case of several nodes and real processor load. Although, CPU cores are reserved according to user requests, some shared resources like network can be impacted by the number of currently running jobs. There is a possibility that some jobs overload or underload the system, that is, use much more or much less resources than requested or use them inefficiently due to Amdahl's law (Figure 21).

Without knowledge of the underlying levels that a specific application use resource utilization can be inefficient. Table 7 illustrates test run of an MPI application: first time using MPI implementation that works via RDMA and second time corresponds to the another implementation that can work only with IPoIB (IP over Infiniband). Without complex monitoring system it is difficult to track such situations to amend MPI library configuration.

It is easy to understand PBS resource reservations, however, their coarse granularity does not reflect the actual load. For example, 64 cores can be requested for a program that uses only a few of them due to erroneous invocation or insufficient problem size. Additionally, there is no need to specify resources manually when optimal reservation is known beforehand and can be assigned by the system automatically. If a cluster have free resources they can be dynamically reallocated for a job. Continuous resource reallocation and finding optimal reservation is the core ideas of the new scheduler.

Table 8. Test platform characteristics.

Component	Details
CPU	Intel Xeon X5650
No. of nodes	24
No. of CPUs	2
No. of CPU cores	6
CPU freq. [GHz]	2.67
RAM [GB]	96
Network device	InfiniBand QDR 4x
	2x Ethernet 1Gb
Operating system	CentOS 6.4

3.2.   New Scheduler for Legacy Applications

The new scheduler is intended for legacy applications, that is, applications source code of which can not be rewritten for some reason. These programs can be scheduled efficiently without recompilation. The main goal of this scheduler is to improve overall resource utilization and overcome common PBS drawbacks discussed in the previous section while maintaining low overhead of dynamic scheduling.

The main features of the system are listed below.

- **Flexible resource reservation and dynamic resource reallocation.** Instead of fixed resource reservation (the way PBS works) we can make an initial resource allocation for a job but constantly monitor the job and reallocate resources in case of underload or overload. In case of underload we can run another job on the same resources while in case of overload we have three options: keep the job running if there are free resources available and log this information for calculating user rating, suspend this job to run another one (and continue the first job when more resources become free) or completely stop the job and warn the user. This improves resource utilization when the system has some bottlenecks or is being used by inexperienced users.

- **Detailed accounting.** For each process in the job the statistics is gathered and analyzed to find possible bottlenecks and make predictions for optimal resource reservation. Applications can be profiled without necessity to go deeply into the source code and even closed source applications can be profiled.

- **Predictions module.** This module can collect a lot of statistical information from runs of different software packages which in the long term can be used to find optimal resource reservation and improve overall resource utilization. Performance often depends on the specific task so only general statistical information can be gathered. For example, if 10% fraction of a program is sequential, then allocating 128 CPU cores instead of 16 gives up to 1.5 speedup according to Amdahl's law. This fact can be figured out from statistical information to inform users upon submission of a similar job. Another example is two MPI implementations: one uses RDMA protocol and other uses IPoIB. If some application uses the second MPI implementation the good choice is to allocate nodes without Infiniband NICs for that program since

IPoIB is slower than RDMA. Finally, from statistics applications performing many I/O operations can be found to redirect similar jobs to nodes with fast storage in the future. All these can be used to give advises to users or automatically apply additional rules for user jobs (i.e. to adjust the amount of resources). That way user should not care about exact resources that are needed to execute the job and their exact amount. Jobs become «virtual» in a sense that they require no manual resource allocation, all the resource management is automatic and over time becomes optimal for each application.

- **User rating.** This simple feature is rarely used in scientific clusters, but is often used in public clusters and similar areas. Such rating shows how well a user can guess the optimal resource allocation and thus reflects overall efficiency of user jobs. This rating can be used to improve resource utilization: if a job consumes more resources than it was requested or the requested resource pool is much larger than needed, the rating of a user is decreased. There can be different coefficients for underload and overload. So, the rating reflects the overall user experience in running scientific software on clusters and its goal is to implement priority and limitation policies: rating defines job priority and limits resource usage for each user. The rating accelerates finding of optimal resource reservation with help of the most experienced users.

- **The possibility to use profiling modules with existing PBS installation.** Accounting module can be seamlessly used in existing PBS cluster. In this case, administrator should rewrite *prologue* to pass user script as an argument to profiling module.

- **Use of low-level native API.** There are two APIs that are used in the profiler: *ptrace* operating system call and Pthreads library. Jobs are monitored, suspended and started using *ptrace*. Accounting module uses fork: the main process forks a profiler that monitors child processes and collects data and then the main process calls *ptrace* with *PTRACE_TRACEME* option and executes a user program with *execve* function. The profiler is notified when the main process creates or terminates child processes to collect profiling information from proc virtual file system. This approach is native for Linux but not for UNIX distributions.

The work flow of such system can be described as follows (Figure 22). A job is started under the control of the profiling program. Profiling is triggered by a timer and information is gathered for all nodes. When a new job is submitted, the server program looks for suitable nodes for this job and invokes prediction module to optimize resource reservation. If there are no free resources the server checks resource utilization of running jobs. If it finds that some job uses fewer resources than requested the server can reallocate these resources for a new job. However, if the resource utilization is increased the new job will be suspended.

So, in addition to the classical queue and nodes with running jobs there are some suspended jobs that can be resumed immediately. The mechanism is akin to kernel process management at a scale of the whole cluster. The behavior can be adjusted by different policies and changed by administrator in real time (for example, unimportant jobs can be suspended manually to start some mission critical one).

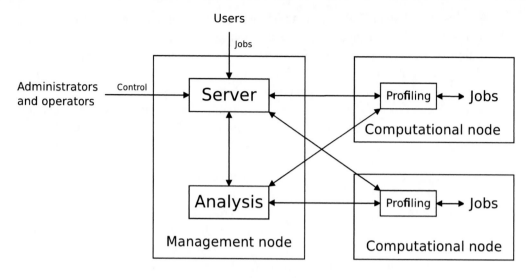

Figure 22. Profiling scheduler work flow.

Table 9. Time spent running well-balanced and non-optimal jobs (with overused resources) with PBS and profiling system.

	PBS	Profiling scheduler
Well-balanced	100%	102%
Overload	100%	85%

Since the profiler is an intermediate program that forks a real one, there is no need to run background services on each node. On a remote node profiler is invoked by amending SSH command that MPI uses to launch remote parallel processes.

Profiling applications involves only a small overhead which is lesser or equal to 2% of the total wall clock time of a job (Table 9). Jobs that repeatedly start many short-living processes give more overhead, however, these types of jobs are rare. Profiling scheduler efficiently handles non-optimal jobs without losing overall resource utilization (Table 9).

Although, the system is developed mainly for Linux operating system there are possibilities to develop analogous systems for other UNIX platforms. All tests in this section were performed on a hybrid cluster (Table 8).

Conclusion

It is known that virtualization improves security, resilience to failures and eases administration substantially due to dynamic load balancing [9] without introducing substantial overheads. Moreover, a proper choice of virtualization package can improve CPU utilization.

The use of standard cloud technologies combined with process migration techniques can improve overall throughput of a distributed system and adapt it to problems being solved. In that way a virtual supercomputer can help people efficiently run applications and focus on domain-specific problems rather than on underlying computer architecture and placement of parallel tasks. Moreover, described approach can be beneficial in utilizing stream processors and GPU accelerators dynamically assigning them to virtual machines.

Virtual workspace hides intricacies of distributed computing behind a virtual machine to streamline and boost scientific research workflow. It provides a convenient way of accessing hardware and software resources using unified tools, consolidates experiment's data and offers options to dynamically extend available resources using either private virtual cluster or high performance dedicated machines and public university cluster. Resources are accessed universally and in a unified way.

The key idea of a virtual supercomputer is to harness all available HPC resources and to provide a user with convenient access to them. Such a challenge can be effectively faced only using contemporary virtualization technologies. They can materialize the long-term dream of having virtual supercomputer at your desk.

Event-driven approach biggest advantage is the ease of parallel and distributed programming. First of all, what is needed from a programmer is to develop a class to describe each independent task, create objects of that class and submit them to a queue. Programming in such a way does not involve thread and lock management and the system is flexible enough to have even the tiniest tasks executed in parallel. Second, relieving programmer from thread management makes it easy to debug this system. Each thread maintains its own log and any of both system and user events can be written to it so the sequence of events can be restored after the execution ends. Finally, with event-driven approach it is easy to write load distribution algorithm for your specific problem (or use an existing one). The only thing which is not done automatically is decomposition and composition of tasks, however, this problem requires higher layer of abstraction to solve.

Proposed load balancing approach increases efficiency when using heterogeneous devices: it adds nested level of parallelism by pipelining execution of problem parts on different devices. In other words, it separates different kinds of workload and processes them concurrently. This feature lets it outperform OpenMP and Hadoop on computation- and data-intensive problems.

Finally, scheduling legacy applications can be done using similar approach but with somewhat coarser granularity. Each job submitted to portable batch system is profiled and its optimal resource reservation is determined. For subsequent submissions, this reservation is used by default. In contrast to event-driven approach this one does not use pipelining but rather uses traditional parallel programming libraries and does not require rewriting or even recompiling application source code.

Acknowledgments

The research presented in the chapter was carried out using computational resources of Resource Center Computer Center of Saint-Petersburg State University within frameworks of grants of Russian Foundation for Basic Research (project No. 13-07-00747) and Saint Petersburg State University (projects No. 9.38.674.2013, 0.37.155.2014).

References

[1] AWS-Compatible Private Cloud. Available online: https://www.eucalyptus.com/aws-compatibility. Retrieved: 2015-01-21.

[2] Extend private cloud into Amazon Web Services with OpenNebula. Available online: https://cloudbestpractices.wordpress.com/2011/11/07/extend-private-cloud-into-amazon-web-services-with-opennebula-2/. Retrieved: 2015-01-21.

[3] Foreign data wrappers — PostgreSQL wiki. https://wiki.postgresql.org/wiki/Foreign_data_wrappers. Retrieved: 2015-01-21.

[4] Degtyarev A. and Gankevich I. Wave surface generation using OpenCL, OpenMP and MPI. In *Proceedings of 8th International Conference «Computer Science & Information Technologies»*, pages 248–251, 2011.

[5] Degtyarev A.B. and Reed A.M. Modelling of incident waves near the ship's hull (application of autoregressive approach in problems of simulation of rough seas). In *Proceedings of the 12th International Ship Stability Workshop*, 2011.

[6] Ping An, Alin Jula, Silvius Rus, Steven Saunders, Tim Smith, Gabriel Tanase, Nathan Thomas, Nancy Amato, and Lawrence Rauchwerger. STAPL: An adaptive, generic parallel C++ library. In *Languages and Compilers for Parallel Computing*, pages 193–208. Springer, 2003.

[7] Paul Barham, Boris Dragovic, Keir Fraser, Steven Hand, Tim Harris, Alex Ho, Rolf Neugebauer, Ian Pratt, and Andrew Warfield. Xen and the art of virtualization. *ACM SIGOPS Operating Systems Review*, 37(5):164–177, 2003.

[8] Alexander Bogdanov and Mikhail Dmitriev. Creation of hybrid clouds. In *Proc. of 8th International Conference «Computer Science & Information Technologies»*, pages 235–237, 2011.

[9] A.V. Bogdanov, A.B. Degtyarev, I.G. Gankevich, V.Yu. Gayduchok, and V. I. Zolotarev. Virtual workspace as a basis of supercomputer center. In *Proceedings of 5th International Conference on Distributed Computing and Grid-Technologies in Science and Education*, pages 60–66, 2012.

[10] Jeffrey S Chase, David E Irwin, Laura E Grit, Justin D Moore, and Sara E Sprenkle. Dynamic virtual clusters in a grid site manager. In *Proc. of the 12th International Symposium on High Performance Distributed Computing*, pages 90–100. IEEE, 2003.

[11] Yang Chen, Tianyu Wo, and Jianxin Li. An efficient resource management system for on-line virtual cluster provision. In *Proc. of International Conference on Cloud Computing (CLOUD)*, pages 72–79. IEEE, 2009.

[12] Jeffrey Dean and Sanjay Ghemawat. MapReduce: simplified data processing on large clusters. *Communications of the ACM*, 51(1):107–113, 2008.

[13] A. Degtyarev and I. Gankevich. Evaluation of hydrodynamic pressures for autoregression model of irregular waves. In *Proceedings of 11th International Conference on Stability of Ships and Ocean Vehicles, Athens*, pages 841–852, 2012.

[14] Alexander B Degtyarev and Arthur M Reed. Synoptic and short-term modeling of ocean waves. *International Shipbuilding Progress*, 60(1):523–553, 2013.

[15] Wesley Emeneker and Dan Stanzione. Dynamic virtual clustering. In *Proc. of International Conference on Cluster Computing*, pages 84–90. IEEE, 2007.

[16] Renato J Figueiredo, Peter A Dinda, and José AB Fortes. A case for grid computing on virtual machines. In *Proc. of the 23rd International Conference on Distributed Computing Systems*, pages 550–559. IEEE, 2003.

[17] Kazushige Goto and Robert Van De Geijn. Anatomy of high-performance matrix multiplication. *ACM Transactions on Mathematical Software (TOMS)*, 34(3):12, 2008.

[18] Kazushige Goto and Robert Van De Geijn. High-performance implementation of the level-3 BLAS. *ACM Transactions on Mathematical Software (TOMS)*, 35(1):4, 2008.

[19] Kevin Hamlen, Murat Kantarcioglu, Latifur Khan, and Bhavani Thuraisingham. Security issues for cloud computing. *International Journal of Information Security and Privacy (IJISP)*, 4(2):36–48, 2010.

[20] Mark Hapner, Rich Burridge, Rahul Sharma, Joseph Fialli, and Kate Stout. Java message service. *Sun Microsystems Inc., Santa Clara, CA*, 2002.

[21] T Yu James. Performance evaluation of Linux Bridge. In *Telecommunications System Management Conference*, 2004.

[22] Vladimir V Korkhov, Jakub T Moscicki, and Valeria V Krzhizhanovskaya. The user-level scheduling of divisible load parallel applications with resource selection and adaptive workload balancing on the Grid. *Systems Journal*, 3(1):121–130, 2009.

[23] Glenn E Krasner, Stephen T Pope, et al. A description of the model-view-controller user interface paradigm in the smalltalk-80 system. *Journal of object oriented programming*, 1(3):26–49, 1988.

[24] Ivan Krsul, Arijit Ganguly, Jian Zhang, Jose AB Fortes, and Renato J Figueiredo. Vmplants: Providing and managing virtual machine execution environments for grid computing. In *Proc. of the ACM/IEEE Supercomputing Conference*, page 7. IEEE, 2004.

[25] Grzegorz Malewicz, Matthew H Austern, Aart JC Bik, James C Dehnert, Ilan Horn, Naty Leiser, and Grzegorz Czajkowski. Pregel: a system for large-scale graph processing. In *Proceedings of ACM SIGMOD International Conference on Management of data*, pages 135–146. ACM, 2010.

[26] Andréa M Matsunaga, Maurício O Tsugawa, Sumalatha Adabala, Renato J Figueiredo, Herman Lam, and José AB Fortes. Science gateways made easy: the In-VIGO approach. *Concurrency and Computation: Practice and Experience*, 19(6):905–919, 2007.

[27] Hideo Nishimura, Naoya Maruyama, and Satoshi Matsuoka. Virtual clusters on the fly-fast, scalable, and flexible installation. In *Proc. of the 7th International Symposium on Cluster Computing and the Grid (CGRID)*, pages 549–556. IEEE, 2007.

[28] Manuel Rodríguez, Daniel Tapiador, Javier Fontán, Eduardo Huedo, Rubén S Montero, and Ignacio M Llorente. Dynamic provisioning of virtual clusters for grid computing. In *Euro-Par 2008 Workshops-Parallel Processing*, pages 23–32. Springer, 2009.

[29] Peter Sempolinski and Douglas Thain. A comparison and critique of Eucalyptus, OpenNebula and Nimbus. In *Proc. of the 2nd International Conference on Cloud Computing Technology and Science (CloudCom)*, pages 417–426. IEEE, 2010.

[30] Larry Smarr and Charles E Catlett. Metacomputing. *Communications of the ACM*, 35(6):44–52, 1992.

[31] Douglas Thain, Todd Tannenbaum, and Miron Livny. Distributed computing in practice: The condor experience. *Concurrency and Computation: Practice and Experience*, 17(2-4):323–356, 2005.

[32] Peter Troger, Hrabri Rajic, Andreas Haas, and Piotr Domagalski. Standardization of an API for distributed resource management systems. In *Proc. of the 7th International Symposium on on Cluster Computing and the Grid (CCGRID)*, pages 619–626. IEEE, 2007.

[33] Steve Vinoski. Advanced message queuing protocol. *Internet Computing*, 10(6):87–89, 2006.

[34] Kejiang Ye, Xiaohong Jiang, Siding Chen, Dawei Huang, and Bei Wang. Analyzing and modeling the performance in Xen-based virtual cluster environment. In *Proc. of the 12th International Conference on High Performance Computing and Communications (HPCC)*, pages 273–280. IEEE, 2010.

[35] Dmitry Zotkin and Peter J Keleher. Job-length estimation and performance in back-filling schedulers. In *Proc. of the 8th International Symposium on High Performance Distributed Computing*, pages 236–243. IEEE, 1999.

INDEX